Mountain Witches

Mountain Witches

Yamauba

Noriko Tsunoda Reider

Utah State University Press
Logan

© 2021 by University Press of Colorado

Published by Utah State University Press
An imprint of University Press of Colorado
245 Century Circle, Suite 202
Louisville, Colorado 80027

 The University Press of Colorado is a proud member of
the Association of University Presses.

The University Press of Colorado is a cooperative publishing enterprise supported, in part, by
Adams State University, Colorado State University, Fort Lewis College, Metropolitan State University of Denver, Regis University, University of Colorado, University of Northern Colorado,
University of Wyoming, Utah State University, and Western Colorado University.

∞ This paper meets the requirements of the ANSI/NISO Z39.48–1992 (Permanence of Paper).

ISBN: 978-1-64642-054-4 (paperback)
ISBN: 978-1-64642-055-1 (ebook)
https://doi.org/10.7330/9781646420551

Library of Congress Cataloging-in-Publication Data

Names: Reider, Noriko T., author.
Title: Mountain witches : yamauba / by Noriko Reider.
Description: Logan : Utah State University Press, [2020] | Includes bibliographical references
    and index.
Identifiers: LCCN 2021003990 (print) | LCCN 2021003991 (ebook) | ISBN 9781646420544
    (paperback) | ISBN 9781646420551 (ebook)
Subjects: LCSH: Yōkai (Japanese folklore) | Crones—Japan—Folklore. | Witches in literature. |
    Supernatural in literature. | Folklore—Japan.
Classification: LCC GR340 .R355 2020 (print) | LCC GR340 (ebook) | DDC 398.20952—dc23
LC record available at https://lccn.loc.gov/2021003990
LC ebook record available at https://lccn.loc.gov/2021003991

Cover illustration: Yamauba in *Kokkei sharekyōgaen* (Cornucopia of humorous pictures) by Maki
Bokusen (1775–1824), courtesy of International Research Center for Japanese Studies

To Brent, MaryEllen, and Warwick Reider

My family, my love

Contents

Figures

Acknowledgments

Yamauba and Oni are among the cornerstones in my life that have made it so fascinating. In the score and more years I've been writing about the supernatural in literature I've benefited from the guidance of many exceptional people. I owe special thanks to Peter Knecht, Shelley Fenno Quinn, Richard Torrance, and Mark Bender, whose intellectual guidance has been wonderful. Komatsu Kazuhiko, Yamada Shōji, John Breen, Yasui Manami, Kiba Takatoshi, Araki Hiroshi, Inaga Shigemi, Kusunoki Ayako, Shiraishi Eri, Goza Yūichi, and Saka Chihiro of the International Research Center for Japanese Studies (Nichibunken) have been gracious in their assistance and encouragement. I am also very grateful to a great many scholars and intellectuals, including Tokuda Kazuo, Asakura Yoshiyuki, Kagawa Masanobu, Sasaki Takahiro, Tokunaga Seiko, Nagahara Junko, Matsumura Kaoruko, Michael Dylan Foster, Rebecca Copeland, Ann Sherif, Keller Kimbrough, Cody Poulton, Mauricio Martinez, Yuriko Suzuki, Felicia Katz-Harris, and Ben Dorman. The two anonymous reviewers of the manuscript were immensely generous and kind, giving valuable comments. Likewise, comments, friendship, and encouragement from the members of the Midwest Japan Seminar (MJS), especially Ethan Segal, Michael Bathgate, Louis Perez, Laura Miller, Elizabeth Lublin, Roy Hanashiro, and Thomas Rogers, are much appreciated. Discussions at meetings of the Midwest Japan Seminar have been invaluable for my publications. The students in my course Japanese Tales of the Supernatural at Miami Universiy have always been an inspiration, giving me new ideas and perspectives.

Utah State University Press acquistions editor Rachael Levay, director Darrin Pratt, assistant director and managing editor Laura Furney, and production manager Daniel Pratt have been so helpful and encouraging. Anne Morris Hooke, my neighbor and friend, Suzy Cincone and Robin DuBlanc, professional copyeditors, were professional and patient in proofreading my English. Appreciation is also extended to the staff at museums and historical sites in Japan and the United States. The staff at the Interlibrary Loan

Office of Miami University Libraries and at the International Research Center for Japanese Studies have been invaluable in helping me obtain the many books and articles I requested for research. Many thanks go to the International Research Center for Japanese Studies, the Iwase Bunko Library of Nishio City, Ritsumeikan University Art Research Center, Hiroshima University Library, Japanese National Diet Digital Library, Itsukushima Shrine, Museum of Fine Arts, Boston, and Dayton Art Museum for supplying the illustrations for the book.

My colleagues in the Department of German, Russian, Asian, and Middle Eastern Languages and Cultures (GRAMELAC) at Miami University, especially Margaret Ziolkowski, John Jeep, Shi Liang, and Kazue Harada, as well as the director of the Interactive Language Resource Center, Daniel Meyers, and Stan Toops and Ann Wicks of the East Asian Studies Program, are exemplars of collegiality—supportive always.

The research in this book was made possible by financial support from Miami University (through a Faculty Improvement Leave in the academic year of 2018–2019), the Committee of Faculty Research, the Japan–United States Friendship Commission, the Northeast Asia Council of the Association for Asian Studies, and the International Research Center for Japanese Studies in Kyoto. The environment—faculty, staff, resource, facilities, location—of the International Research Center for Japanese Studies, where I stayed from January to July 2019, was superb and provided marvelous access to sources indispensable to completing this manuscript.

Chapter 1 is a revised and expanded version of the article that appeared as "Yamauba versus Oni-Women: Devouring and Helping Yamauba Are Two Sides of One Coin," *Asian Ethnology* 78 (2) (2019). I am grateful to the journal editor, Ben Dorman, for permission to use the article in its revised form. Chapter 4 is an expanded version of an article I submitted to *Japan Reivew* in 2018. John Breen, the editor of *Japan Review*, and the two anonymous reviewers provided valuable comments that enabled me to enhance reader comprehension. When the publication date of this manuscript was advanced, the article was withdrawn, but their guidance specific to the work remains.

Finally, but not least, the love and encouragement of my family—my husband Brent, daughter MaryEllen, and son Warwick—are as precious as they are inspirational. As Brent was diagnosed with cancer in the winter of 2020 over 2021, my family have fought the illness with him together in unison under the COVID-19 environment. This book is thus dedicated to my family.

Mountain Witches

Introduction

Yamauba's Topos, Archetype, History, and Gender

IN MANY CULTURES, WHEN HUMAN BEINGS ENCOUNTER SOME inexplicable phenomena—especially if it's mysterious and inspires fear—they endeavor to make sense of them by invoking supernatural creatures. This is true of Japanese culture and society. As Michael Dylan Foster writes in *The Book of Yōkai*, *yōkai* (weird or mysterious creatures) have often been called upon in Japan to explain incomprehensible phenomena (Foster 2015, 5).[1] A *yamauba* (sometimes *yamanba* or *yamamba*), often translated as a mountain witch or mountain crone, is one such being. To many contemporary Japanese, the word *yamauba* conjures up images of an unsightly old woman who lives in the mountains and devours humans. The witch in the Grimm Brothers' "Hansel and Gretel" and Baba Yaga of Russian folklore can be considered Western/Eurasian counterparts of the yamauba figure. A yamauba is commonly described as tall, with long hair, piercing eyes, and a large mouth that opens from ear to ear (Komatsu 2000, 428). As Monica Bethe and Karen Brazell write, a yamauba appears in various Japanese texts as "a god, a demon, an entertainer, a mother; enlightened, tormented, helpful, and harmful" (Bethe and Brazell 1978, 8). She is an enigmatic woman living in the mountains.

In recent years, the figure of the yamauba has attracted much attention among scholars of women's literature as a woman not constrained by conformative gender norms or social expectations (Kobayashi Fukuko 2016, 2). Thus a yamauba connotes not only a mysterious female in the mountains but also the ambivalent status of Japanese women past and present, as well as the Japanese psyche that creates and re-creates prototypes. Broadly speaking, the old women who appear in the 156th episode of *Yamato monogatari* (*Tales of Yamato*, ca. mid-tenth century) and in "The Old Woman on the Mountain" and "How the Hunters' Mother Became an Oni and Tried to Devour Her Children," tales from the *Konjaku monogatarishū* (*Tales of Times Now Past*, ca. 1120), may be considered yamauba, and their portrayal has relevance to contemporary daughter-in-law and mother-in-law relationships, elder issues, and dementia.[2]

DOI: 10.7330/9781646420551.c000

Situating the yamauba within the construct of yōkai and archetypes, this study investigates the attributes of yamauba, and offers an interpretation through the examination of yamauba narratives including folktales, literary works, legends, modern fiction, manga, and anime. I believe a holistic image of yamauba will emerge through an examination of both yamauba's well-known and lesser-known traits. Investigating how and why these attributes have appeared in various texts over time sheds light on the process of adaptation and re-creation of a prototype. Hence, this study also involves the creation, dissemination, and transformation of narratives and imagery.

YAMAUBA AS YŌKAI

According to Ema Tsutomu (1884–1979), historian and the author of *Nihon yōkai henge-shi* (History of Japanese yōkai shape-shifters, 1923), the majority of yōkai shape-shifters in narratives created before the Muromachi period (1336–1573) took male form when they appeared in front of humans. However, in narratives created after the Ōnin War (1467–1477), and especially in the early modern period, the number of yōkai shape-shifters in female form increased dramatically, appearing two and a half times more often than male figures (Ema 1923, 131). The reasons for this were, Ema writes, because in tales of the early modern period ghosts and apparitions were motivated by passion or grudges, traits associated with women because they form stronger attachments than men. Yōkai that originally appeared as animals, plants, or tools were also probably transformed into women because, Ema states, being female made it easier for them to trick and cajole men (Ema 1923, 131).

Folklorist Miyata Noboru's (1936–2000) explanation for the large number of female yōkai is more sympathetic to women. He contends that in narratives young women often played the role of messengers between this world and the world beyond, and in doing so they had a tendency to become yōkai. Miyata noted that a young woman's spiritual power, a kind of spirit possession, was at work, particularly among young maids of the lowest social strata. Fundamentally this is because of the spiritual power that women possess. Women are said to be more attuned to the spiritual realm than men; Yanagita Kunio (1875–1962), the founder of Japanese folklore studies, called this power *imo no chikara* (women's power) (Miyata 1987, 117, 248–49).[3] But the question remains whether men were considered to be more attuned to the spiritual realm than women before the Ōnin War. I speculate that a key to the answer lies in societal changes surrounding women in Japan. The period of increasing numbers of female yōkai in narratives coincides with a decline in the status of women.

The early modern period is often referred to as a dark age for Japanese women (Hayashi R. 1982, 325), a time when women's social activities were extremely limited (Fukuda M. 1995, 257). Even before the early modern period, attitudes toward women had steadily declined. "Conventionally, the fourteenth century is known as the period when virolocal institutions (*yomeiri kon*) became common, as evident in the delivery of dowries and a new term for divorce (*oidasu*, 'to chase out [the wife]'). Moreover, the wife increasingly came to be viewed as the husband's possession" (Farris 2006, 156). Probably women, increasingly confined and suppressed by societal and cultural norms and constraints, found their emotional outlet in ghostly, monstrous figures. In the same vein, men's feelings of guilt or sympathy toward such women may have helped create and increase the number of female yōkai.[4]

THE TERM *YAMAUBA* (*YAMANBA* OR *YAMAMBA*)

The terms *yamauba*, *yamanba*, and *yamamba* are presently all written in the same kanji, or sino-characters, 山姥, and many Japanese use these terms interchangeably. Some dictionaries, however, make the distinction that the pronunciation *yamauba* often seems to be used for legendary or folkloric figures, whereas the nasalized forms, *yamanba* or *yamamba*, are used in texts for the performing arts such as noh and kabuki.[5] In this study, I have chosen to primarily use *yamauba* because of my heavy reliance on folktales and legends.

Whereas the characters 山姥 are used in contemporary Japan, various other characters were used in premodern times. For example, the characters 山優婆 (literally, gentle crone in the mountains) are used to describe the noh play *Yamanba* (early fifteenth century), generally attributed to Zeami (1363–1443), and in an *otogizōshi* tale titled *Tōshōji nezumi monogatari* (Tales of mice at Tōshōji temple, 1537).[6] The edition of the Japanese dictionary *Setsuyōshū* from the second year of Kōji (1556) defines the term *uba*, 優婆, as an "ordinary old woman" (Sasaki R. 2008, 203). Isshiki Tadatomo (d. 1597), a military lord and poet, also used the characters meaning gentle crone in the mountains in his *Getsuan suiseiki* (Getsuan's collection of tales) (Isshiki 2008, 84). But the yamanba of the noh play had also been written as 山祖母 (grandmother in the mountains), 山婆 (old woman in the mountains), and 山伯母 (elder aunt in the mountains) (Sasaki R. 2008, 203).

The first appearance of the term *yamauba* in literary materials occurred in the Muromachi period (Komatsu K. 2000, 428; Orikuchi 2000, 300). As attested by early works that describe yamauba, including the aforementioned noh play *Yamanba* and the entry on the sixth month of 1460 in *Gaun nik-kenroku*, a diary of Zen priest Zuikei Shūhō (1391–1473), the term predates the Ōnin War. It does not appear in the *Wamyō ruijushō* (Japanese names for things classified and annotated, ca. 930s), the first Japanese-language dictionary, or in an encyclopedia complied during the Muromachi period titled *Ainōshō* (ca. 1446). However, the *Nippo jisho* (*Japanese-Portuguese dictionary*), compiled by a Jesuit missionary and published around 1603–1604, has an entry for yamauba that reads: "The face of the yamauba is not known. They are believed to live in the mountains" (Doi et al. 1980, 809). Several years later a yamauba is mentioned in the entry for the fourth month of 1609 in *Tōdaiki* (Records of the present age), a historical record possibly written by Matsudaira Tadaaki (1583–1644), a maternal grandson of the founder of the Tokugawa shogunate, Tokugawa Ieyasu (1543–1616). In this entry, a yamauba appears in a show in the area of the Tōfukuji temple of Higashiyama in Kyoto: "Her hair is white and she is red around the eyes. She swallows her food in a gulp. The high and low see her. If one listens carefully, she is a crazy albino, so I hear" (Zoku Gunsho Ruijū Kanseikai 1995, 149).

Interestingly, the *Wakan sansaizue* (Japanese-Chinese collected illustrations of the three realms, ca. 1713), an encyclopedia, explains the yamauba as an animal, native to the regions of Guangdong and Guangxi in China, that has only one leg, three toes and three fingers on each hand, and begs for food from people at night. The author, Terajima Ryōan (b. 1654), mentions nothing about Japanese yamauba. I should note, however, that the presence of three toes and three fingers is typical in portrayals of *oni* (demons, ogres, monsters). Yamauba have a very strong relationship with oni.

Yamaoka Genrin (1631–1672), a widely recognized intellectual of seventeenth-century Japan, states that the *uba*, 姥, of yamauba is more in line with the *hime*, 姫, of Tatsutahime (goddess of autumn) and Yamahime (princess of the mountains), interpreting it more broadly than meaning simply an old woman (Yamaoka 1993, 46). This is the same as Yanagita Kunio's observation that yamauba and yamahime were originally euphemisms (used by villagers) for a mysterious woman living deep in the mountains (Yanagita 1978–1979, 1:255). In the same vein, folklorist Konno Ensuke (1914–1982) explains that yōkai-like creatures that are believed to live in the mountains are usually considered the yamahime type; and if they are old, they are called yamauba or *yamahaha* (literally, mountain mother). As there are a number of people who believe that *hime* refers to young women and *uba* to old women, they came to be thought of as two distinct types: young and old, yama-hime and yamauba. But originally there was probably only one type: strange women in the mountains.

Figure 0.1. Yamauba in *Bakemono zukushi emaki* (Picture scroll of monsters, Edo period), by Hokusai Suechika. (Courtesy of International Research Center for Japanese Studies.)

Konno categorizes female yōkai into three types: yamauba, spirits of snow (*yuki no sei*), and strange creatures of the ocean (*umi no kai*) (Konno 1981, 221; 223–66).[7] Ōba Minako (1930–2007) writes in her short story "Yamanba no bishō" ("The Smile of a Mountain Witch," 1976): "Surely these old witches [yamauba] cannot have been wrinkled old hags from birth . . . For one reason or another, however, we never hear about young witches living up in the mountains" (Ōba M. 1991, 195).

YAMAUBA'S TOPOS: MOUNTAINS WHERE EERIE THINGS HAPPEN

"Perhaps no image signifies the danger of the uncontainable, ravenous female as readily as the *yamamba*," writes Rebecca Copeland, scholar of Japanese literature (Copeland 2005, 21). As she says, the voracious appetite of the yamauba, especially her man-eating trait, is her most well-known characteristic. Indeed, a survey conducted by Komatsuzaki Susumu and

Komatsuzaki Tatsuko reveals that "the image children have of yamanba is fixed regardless of their age or gender"; children say that "a yamauba eats people and changes her appearance. She knows everything about mountains. She lives in the mountains and eats people who are lost. She eats oxen and horses. A creepy old woman" (Komatsuzaki and Komatsuzaki 1967, n.p.).[8] The survey notes that yamauba's fixed image could be due to well-circulated folktales, but the influence of illustrated children's books and manga is believed to be significant, too.

As Mizuta Noriko (1937–), scholar of comparative literature, emphasizes, "Yamauba's identity is the topos of mountains" (Mizuta 2002, 13). Mountains are considered to be sacred places in many cultures, and this is true in Japan as well. Miyake Hitoshi (1933–), scholar of religious studies, gives several reasons for this, but two are especially pertinent to this study: "Mountains are viewed as the dwelling place of spirits of the dead and ancestor spirits. Tombs are built on mountains," and "Mountains are regarded as liminal space between this world and the otherworld. The mountain is an avenue to heaven; a mountain cave is an entrance to the otherworld" (Miyake 2001, 78–79).

The idea that mountains are "the dwelling place of spirits of the dead and ancestor spirits" reminds one of the *mukashibanashi* (old tales, folktales) called "Obasute-yama"—stories of abandoning old people, especially old women, in the mountains. While there is no evidence of abandoning old people in agricultural societies, such tales are still popularly narrated in various media. Ōshima Tatehiko (1932–), folklore scholar, notes that mukashibanashi and legends of Obasute are deeply related to Japanese funeral customs such as aerial sepulture (*fūsō*) and the double-grave system (*ryōbosei*). In the double-grave system, a single deceased person has two graves, one for burying the body and one a tombstone erected by the family to visit and pray for the deceased. The place where old women are abandoned in Obasute stories would correspond to the burial site or aerial sepulture, where the actual dead body is buried (or abandoned). The word *obasute* is considered to have come from the term *ohatsuse*, originally meaning a burial site. That is, Obasute was a name for a graveyard called Ohase or Ohatsuse. Hase temple and Hatsuse in Kyoto are located on the borderline between the *sato* (settlement, village) and the mountains, indicating there was once a cemetery there (Ōshima 2001a, 4–5; Miyata 1997, 20).

There are many cases in real life where a mountain is designated as a place for burial. The purpose was to appease deceased spirits through the spiritual power of the mountain (Saitō 2010, 274). Indeed, in the noh play *Yamanba*, Yamanba projects a mountain landscape of the dead in her song:

"Awesome, the deep ravines. In graveyards, beating their own bones, fiendish wraiths groan, bemoaning their deeds from former lives. In cemeteries, offering flowers, angelic spirits rejoice in the good rewards of enlightened acts" (Bethe and Brazell 1978, 217; *SNKBZ* 1994–2002, 59:575).

Wakamori Tarō (1915–1977), historian and folklorist, assumes that the "Obasute-yama" stories focus on a belief in the existence of some eerie beings deep in the mountains or at the bottom of nearby mountain valleys. Wakamori suspects this belief arose because of the strange or disorienting experiences villagers had when they went into the mountains, including having hallucinations or visions of human-like beings. Perhaps long ago, villagers surmised, people were pushed into deep valleys or mountains to put an end to their lives, and their angry spirits, forced to die untimely deaths and unable to go on to the other world, appeared in the mountains to harass villagers (Wakamori 1958, 215). Although Wakamori is writing about the Obasute stories, these eerie beings can be easily interpreted as old women, yamauba. The basis for the belief that something eerie existed in the mountains was already there, and the groundwork for yamauba to emerge in the medieval period (1185–1600) already existed in ancient times.[9]

Baba Akiko (1928–), poet and critic, asserts that "it is important to acknowledge these *setsuwa* (tale literature or narrative; myths, legends, folktales, anecdotes, and the like) have been handed down as reality.[10] That is, people had strong beliefs of and fear about the existence of strange, aged woman in the mountains—like a mountain mother who could be a counterpart of a mountain father . . . these women never wanted to live a life outside the mountains" (Baba Akiko 1988, 279). Baba finds a clue to an origin of yamauba in a description of three entertainers met by Lady Sarashina (the daughter of Sugawara no Takasue, b. 1008) at Mt. Ashigara. Lady Sarashina left a memoir known to us as *Sarashina nikki* (*As I Cross a Bridge of Dreams*, ca. eleventh century). In the memoir of her experience traveling to Mt. Ashigara as an impressionable twelve-year-old girl, Lady Sarashina writes: "We lodged at the foot of the mountain, and I felt fearfully lost in the depth of the moonless night. From somewhere in the dark three women singers emerged, the eldest being about fifty, the others about twenty and fourteen . . . Our party was charmed by their appearance and even more impressed when they started singing, for they had fine, clear voices that rose to the heavens . . . We were all so sad to see them disappear into those fearful mountains" (Sugawara no Takasue no musume 1971, 47; *SNKBZ* 1994–2002, 26:287–88). Baba believes that these entertainers made their based on being near the mountains, and she conjectures that as these women became old, they become yamauba. The text of the noh play

Yamanba, Baba continues, reveals the existence of such mysterious women (Baba Akiko 1988, 276–77).

Yanagita Kunio provides some suppositions as the basis for the origin of mountain woman traditions: yamauba were believed to exist in the deep mountains both in the past and in the present (in his case, 1925, when his article was first written); and there were women who went into the mountains of their own volition (Yanagita 1968, 378–80). Certainly the women whom Lady Sarashina encountered were willing residents of the mountains.

<h2 style="text-align:center">APPEARANCE OF YAMAUBA IN THE MUROMACHI PERIOD</h2>

Why did the term *yamauba* appear during the Muromachi period? In the ancient and medieval periods of Japan, fear of the unknown or of something strange and eerie often manifested in narratives in the form of oni, as seen in the stories in *Konjaku monogatarishū*. One tale, "Sanseru onna minami Yamashina ni yuki oni ni aite niguru koto" ("How a Woman with Child Went to South Yamashina, Encountered an Oni, and Escaped"), describes an old woman who eats babies.[11] A young pregnant woman secretly gives birth in the mountain hut of a seemingly kind old woman, only to discover that she is actually an oni who plans to eat the newborn baby. As the appellation *yamauba* was not yet coined at this time, any anthropophagous being, regardless of sex, was simply called an oni. If the term *yamauba* had existed in the twelfth century, surely this woman would have been called that.[12]

I suppose the term or signifier *yamauba* came into being during the Muromachi period because such women in the mountains, true or imagined, became more visible and noticeable to villagers and travelers, including religious practitioners. These mountain women could not be identified simply by the term *oni*—perhaps because they possessed helpful, supportive elements (from humans' viewpoint), the positive side of their duality. As travelers or villagers started to meet or imagine good and kind mountain women, a new term was required to separate these mysterious females from oni.

According to William Farris, between the period 1280 to 1450, the population of Japan expanded from around 6 million to about 10 million: this was a 67 percent increase from the early medieval era to 1450 (Farris 2006, 128). The fourteenth century has been considered a turning point in Japan in several aspects: industry, agriculture, shipping technology, commerce, family structure, and demographic expansion. "In particular, for the half century from the cessation of widespread hostilities in 1368 until the famine of 1420, residents entered an age appropriately termed 'the Muromachi

Optimum,' when the new shogunate was at its height and social and economic expansion most vigorous" (Farris 2006, 94–95). Commerce grew
during the period of the northern and southern courts, "when even military
encampments served as markets . . . Mt. Kōya oversaw eight markets in one
of Japan's most advanced areas, Kii Province . . . Monks and local peasants
also bought and sold at these centers" (Farris 2006, 143).

Farris notes, "With the massive expansion of the old capital's population and religious and government building during Yoshimitsu's era
[1358–1408], it is not surprising to find merchants going farther and farther
afield to locate adequate supplies. Hida, Mino, and Shikoku were especially
popular" (Farris 2006, 149). As more people went into the mountainous
areas hitherto relatively unknown—to cut trees or hunt, to travel to a newly
created marketplace, to transport goods, for religious pilgrimages, or simply
to live in the mountains—people would encounter various strange creatures, and may well have wondered who those strange creatures were.

Moreover, Shirane Haruo writes that the area known as *satoyama*, which
included both *sato* (human settlement) and *yama* (surrounding hills), came
to the fore around the twelfth century and that the satoyama landscape was
saturated with deities (*kami*) of different types, many of them related to
farming, hunting, and fishing. The mountains (and sometimes large trees
and rocks) surrounding the satoyama were believed to be the homes of
gods (Shirane 2012, 114–16). The satoyama landscape expanded with economic and technological advancement. "The gods of the mountains (*yama
no kami*) were often believed by rice farmers to come down in the early
spring to become the gods of the rice fields (*ta no kami*) and then return to
the mountains in the autumn. Shrines were built at the foot of the mountains" (Shirane 2012, 116). Farm villagers might have wondered if a mysterious woman from the surrounding mountains could be related to the god
of the mountains, or could herself be a mountain deity.

APPEARANCE OF YAMAUBA AND THE ROLE OF YAMABUSHI

As people from all walks of life wandered, wondered, and talked about
their strange experiences in and around the foot of the mountains, I speculate that the *yamabushi*'s role was particularly significant. The timing of the
appearance of yamauba coincides with the secularization of yamabushi
(mountain ascetics, practitioners of Shugendō). Yamabushi were most
active and influential during the medieval period. They went through rigorous training and wandered through the mountains with bases in Yoshino,
Kumano, Mt. Hakusan, Mt. Haguro, Mt. Hiko, and others, performing

incantations, prayers, and exorcisms. During times of war, they traveled all over Japan, sometimes employed as exorcists and healers for a certain clan, and sometimes as spies (Miyake 1978, 5; 44–47; Murayama 1970, 18). The activities of yamabushi saw the most development involving politics and the military during the sixty-year period of civil war, from Emperor GoDaigo's (1228–1339) plot against the Kamakura government through the unification of the northern and southern courts in 1392 (Murayama 1970, 224). Tokunaga Seiko reports that the establishment of the term *Shugendō* in terms of the medieval concept (with the components of exoteric and esoteric Buddhism) dates from the late thirteenth to early fourteenth century; she writes that the word *shugen* with the specific meaning of training by traveling through mountains to acquire miraculous powers didn't appear until after the twelfth century, and the emergence of the use of the word *Shugendō* was in the late thirteenth century (Tokunaga 2015, 86).

Sendatsu (leaders of yamabushi or *shugenja*) brought their *danna* (patrons), including priests and nuns of regional shrines and temples, family members or servants of warriors, and common people such as farmers and merchants, from all over the country to Kumano. The danna's religious needs and arrangements for lodging were taken care of by escorts known as *oshi*. During their long journeys through the mountains, or even in the course of short errands, I would imagine, people saw some mysterious dwellers. They may have been explained as the manifestation of mountain spirits, dead spirits, or evil spirits that act against religious practitioners and others. As mentioned above, as the frequency of travel through the mountains increased, the number of encounters with strange creatures inevitably increased as well, and it is possible that people recounted the strange events of their journeys back in their villages. While the associations of sendatsu were founded in the fifteenth century, the first appearance of oshi in writing predates this era, seen in the 1109 account of Fujiwara no Munetada's pilgrimage to Kumano (Miyake 2001, 14; 18–23). It is also conceivable that yamabushi who had settled in villages during the Muromachi period told some interesting and/or miraculous stories, including those about yamauba, to villagers for entertainment (see Murayama 1970, 304).

YAMABUSHI SUBJUGATING YAMAUBA

Tokuda Kazuo, scholar of Japanese literature, writes that the folktale known as "Yamauba to ishimochi" ("Yamauba and Stone Rice Cakes") is recorded in medieval documents that tell of miracles at sacred grounds in the mountains. In "Yamauba to ishimochi" a yamauba meets her demise by eating burning-hot stones.[13] Tokuda argues that a story framework in which a religious practitioner subjugates an evil creature had already existed and taken root in the sacred mountains of various provinces.[14] An example of this story type appears in *Daisenji engimaki* (Legends of Daisenji temple, ca. early 1320s) of Hōki province (present-day Tottori Prefecture) (Tokuda 2016c, 43). Mt. Daisen of Hōki province has been known from the olden days as an important place for Shugendō.

According to *Daisenji engimaki*, there was a great sendatsu and renowned ascetic named Shuchi Kongōbō in Nankōin on Mt. Daisen. While he was leading many yamabushi for training, sometimes a frightening-looking *ubai*, 優婆夷 (transliteration of Sanskrit *upāsikā*, devoted lay female follower of Buddhism) would appear around the Batō cavern and harass the yamabushi. Late one night, this *uba*, 優婆 (the name changed from earlier ubai) secretly came and warmed her breast at the sacred fire. Kongōbō, surprised and thinking she must be the one causing trouble, mentally uttered magic words of the fire realm. He then asked who she was and told her to leave immediately. The "oni-woman" responded that she was warming her chest because it hurt and asked for medicine. He threw a round, burning-hot stone to her, saying it was medicine. She immediately ate it. After this was repeated two or three times, the sendatsu gave her a bowl of oil, saying that candy (the oil looked like candy) went well with rice cakes. When the oni-woman drank the bowl of oil, she immediately breathed fire from her mouth. As Kongōbō continued his incantation, her pain became unbearable; she ran to a valley and was incinerated. After this, the yamabushi could practice their ascetic training without any hindrance (Kondō and Miyachi 1971, 198–99).[15] The story ends with praise for the miraculous power of Shingon Buddhist magic words and for the unparalleled virtue of the practitioner who uses this power. Interestingly, the frightening-looking ubai is described as an uba and later as an oni-woman.

An ubai is a woman who approaches monks and listens to their sermons, makes offerings to monks, and helps with their daily lives. *Ubai* also means "attend to" or "wait on" (Hirakawa 1972, 244). In the aforementioned yamabushi tale, the ubai or uba is cast in an evil role, which seems to fit the general Buddhist view of women. While the yamabushi's enemy appears here as an ubai or uba and is identified as an oni-woman in *Daisenji engimaki* from the early fourteenth century, almost seventy years later, at the beginning of the Muromachi period, this oni-woman is literally named yamauba in *Hōki no kuni Daisenji engi* (Legends of Daisenji temple in Hōki province, 1398). The sino-characters used to describe this yamauba are 山優婆, which is *yama* 山 (mountains) plus *ubai* 優婆夷 (devoted female follower of Buddhism) minus *i* 夷 (foreign, barbarian). If one interprets each character of yamauba, 山優婆, independently and then puts them together, it means "gentle old woman in the mountains."[16] The plot of the story in *Hōki no kuni Daisenji engi* is the same as the earlier version: a great miracle-working ascetic named Shuchi Kongōbō in Nankōin on Mt. Daisen is training around Batō cavern on Mt. Daisen when a yamauba comes and asks for chest medicine. He gives her a burning-hot stone, calling it medicine. As soon as she eats the stone, fire comes out of her mouth and she burns up completely. After this, yamabushi could train themselves on the mountain without worries (Hanawa 1959, 213; Tokuda 2016c, 42).[17]

One may speculate from these stories that the term *yamauba* was used (or even coined) in the late fourteenth century in religious settings to promote their institutions. The demonic being that harassed Shugendō practitioners was first symbolically described as an oni-woman and ubai. Then the evil existence became a yamauba. As will be explained in more detail in chapter 1, in the noh play *Yamanba*, the protagonist laments that she is considered an oni-woman, although the entertainer traveling through the mountains for religious purposes sees her as one; this mixing of the images of oni and yamauba fits the above narrative.

YAMAUBA AS ARCHETYPE

Gorai Shigeru explains that the original or fundamental nature (*genshitsu*) of mountain deities served by yamabushi can be understood from the viewpoint of Shugendō as souls of the deceased who used to live at the foot of a mountain. These souls go into a different realm of the mountain after death and stay there. These souls also become ancestral spirits who may protect and love their descendants or punish them: they have dichotomous aspects (Gorai 1984, 13; 30; 43).

As a mountain deity, yamauba is also portrayed as symbol of fertility. An often-cited example of yamauba's fertility is a legend in Shimoinagun, Nagano Prefecture, which tells of a yamauba giving birth to 7,800 children at one time. Yoshida Atsuhiko (1934–), scholar of mythology, recounts that this yamauba was having difficulty giving birth and asked for water from Ōyamazu no mikoto, who happened to be hunting in the mountains. Because Ōyamazu no mikoto helped the yamauba deliver the 7,800 babies and name them, he was rewarded by an abundance of game. Yanagita theorized that yōkai were deities who had become degraded—that is, had fallen from their status as deities, and following Yanagita's thoughts, Yoshida asserts that yamauba used to be worshipped as goddesses and that the remnants of their worship and rites are visible all over Japan (Yoshida 1992, 31–41).[18]

Hori Ichirō (1910–1974), scholar of religion, writes: "In the popular belief of rural areas, the mountain deity is believed to be a goddess who gives birth to twelve children every year. She is therefore called Mrs. Twelve (*Jūni-sama*), and her twelve children symbolize the twelve months of the year" (Hori I. 1968, 167). The aforementioned fifteenth-century diary entitled *Gaun nikkenroku* notes that "the reason why the summer of that year had lots of rain was because the yamauba gave birth to four children, namely, Haruyoshi (Good spring), Natsusame (Summer rain), Akiyoshi (Good autumn), and Fuyusame (Winter rain)" (Tokyo Daigaku Shiryō Hensanjo 1961, 125). The year's abundant rainfall, the priest suggests, is the result of the yamauba's multiple childbirth. The children's names seem to reflect an expression of reverence to a higher power and hope for good seasonal weather to come. An archetype is "a symbol, usually an image, which recurs often enough in literature to be recognizable as an element of one's literary experience as a whole" (Frye 2006, 331).[19] A yamauba may be understood as a goddess or as an archetype that represents four seasons: "In the divine world the central process or movement is that of the death and rebirth . . . This divine activity is usually identified or associated with one or more of the cyclical processes of nature" (Frye 2006, 147).

Orikuchi Shinobu (1887–1953), Japanese literature scholar and folklorist, writes that yamauba was originally a maiden who waited on a mountain deity; although one tends to associate the term *uba*, うば, with the kanji 姥 (old woman), it has a commonality with *oba*, 小母, a term used to address any unrelated adult woman. First the maiden nursed the deity to health and later she became his wife. Orikuchi speculates that these maidens tended to live long, so people started to think of uba as old women (Orikuchi 1995, 363). As to why the notion of mountain deities in female form spread among the populace, folklorist Yamagami Izumo (1923–) argues that in folklore studies it is thought that because the masters of religious ceremonies for mountain deities were women, the genders of these male deities and female masters of ceremonies were mixed up. However, Yamagami notes that a prototype of yamauba was the divine wife of a mountain dragon or thunder deity and that one has to seek the emergence of the concept of yamauba in mythological worlds (Yamagami 2000, 374–75).

Baba Akiko (1988) considers yamauba legends as representative of the downfall of *kunitsukami* (deities of the land), who were relegated to lower positions by the imperial authority in the lineage of heavenly deities. It seems that Baba follows Yanagita's theory of degradation (1968). Further,

Yoshida Atsuhiko writes, roots of the yamauba can be found in various female deities in Japanese myths such as Ōgetsuhime in the *Kojiki* (Ancient matters, compiled 712), the oldest imperially sponsored chronicle of the mytho-history of Japan, and Ukemochinokami in *Nihon shoki* or *Nihongi* (Chronicles of Japan, 720), the second oldest chronicle in Japan; these deities produce food from different parts of their bodies. He goes further and asserts that the real identity of yamauba is the mother goddess (*boshin*) that Japanese had been worshipping since the very ancient times of the Jōmon period (14,000 BCE–300 BCE) (Yoshida 1992, iii; 108–12).

Komatsu Kazuhiko (1947–), anthropologist and authority on yōkai culture, observes that conventionally in folklore studies yamauba's older forms or origins have been sought in mountain deities or goddesses, and that yamauba is thought of as a ruined form of these originals; that is to say, the yamauba's horrifying attributes are a result of their downfall from their earlier status as mountain deities or goddesses. Komatsu warns, however, that this downfall theory is only a supposition, and that the yamauba described in literature and folklore materials have always possessed a duality of good and evil. Yamauba are characterized by this very duality, and which aspect is emphasized depends on the relation between yamauba and individuals or the interests of the time period (Komatsu K. 2000, 429–30). Unlike Yanagita Kunio, who considers that yōkai are deities fallen from grace, Komatsu grasps that worshipped supernatural beings are deities and unworshipped ones are yōkai (Komatsu K. 1994, 283). One half of yamauba's genealogy goes back to goddesses, and the other half to oni (Komatsu K. 2000, 432; 1994, 297–304). Indeed, while there are many legends of yamauba as mountain deities, they are simultaneously inseparable from oni, as we will see throughout this book. It is not that yamauba fell from the high position she held in ancient Japan and was relegated to the negative side as time passed. She was perceived by contemporary people, at least people in the capital, to be oni-like from the beginning of her appearance in the medieval period.

According to Yamaguchi Motoko (1954–), a Jungian psychologist, the image of yamauba is an archetype that is deeply rooted in the collective unconsciousness of the Japanese; it could be considered a distinctive Japanese manifestation of the "Great Goddess"—an archetype that exists widely in the human imagination (Yamaguchi 2009, 44). The Great Mother brings fertility and wealth as well as death and destruction, similar to mythico-religious figures such as Isis and Kali. In medieval Europe, the pagan archetype of the Great Mother who always possessed two aspects did not become less complicated as it fell under the influence of Christian civilization; the light side was represented by the officially worshipped Virgin Mary, and the dark side, excluded from the image of Mary and maintaining much of its pagan influence, degenerated into a witch (Franz 1974, 105, 195).[20] Kawai Hayao (1928–2007), a Jungian psychologist, regards Kannon as the positive image of the Great Mother in Japan, and the yamauba, who appears in fairy tales as an all-devouring mountain witch, as the negative image (Kawai 1996, 27–66).

Yamauba encompass good and evil sides. While yamauba's roots are found in ancient goddesses, I believe yamauba are the products of the medieval zeitgeist. For people who were awed and frightened by mountains, strange women in the mountains symbolized manifestations of mountain spirits and seasons. The name and characteristics of the yamauba were creations of the medieval period, amalgamating various elements—both positives and negatives—into an archetype.

YAMAUBA'S GENDER

As mysterious and contradictory as yamauba can be, her overarching qualities are connected to mountains and her female sex. As we will see in the following chapters, yamauba is often mixed up with an oni-woman—a female oni. However, the gender of an oni-woman can actually be male because an oni can freely transform itself. The sex of a yamauba, a mother of many children, is always female. Here, I use *sex* to refer to a set of biological attributes and *gender* to refer to the socially constructed roles, behaviors, and expressions.

A brief explanation of oni's gender may be required here. In ancient times, oni were invisible. In early Onmyōdō (the Way of yin-yang), the word *oni* referred specifically to invisible evil spirits that caused human infirmity (Komatsu K. 1999, 3).[21] Takahashi Masaaki identifies an oni as a deity that causes epidemics (Takahashi Masaaki 1992, 4), while Kumasegawa Kyōko interprets an oni as an individual and/or societal shadow (Kumasegawa 1989, 204). The character to express *oni* in Chinese, 鬼, means invisible soul or spirit of the dead, both ancestral and evil. According to the aforementioned *Wamyō ruijushō* (ca. 930s), the word *oni* is explained as a corruption of the reading of the character *on* (hiding), "hiding behind things, not wishing to appear . . . a soul or spirit of the dead" (Takahashi Masaaki 1992, 41).[22] Peter Knecht notes that the expression *kokoro no oni* (oni in one's heart), used in Heian (794–1185) court literature, shows one aspect of the multifaceted oni: "In this case the oni serves to give concrete form to an otherwise hard to express and invisible disposition in one's mind, namely the dark and evil side of one's heart, such as evil or mischievous thoughts and feelings toward fellow humans. This kind of oni is said to hide in a dark corner of the heart and to be difficult to control. However, in consequence of an impetus from outside it may be thrown into consciousness and its noxious nature may show itself" (Knecht 2010, xv). Thus, invisible oni were not related to either gender, and I assume the Japanese associated the negative qualities they attributed to oni—rage, murderous thoughts and actions, cold-bloodedness, and the like—as separate from any specific gender, until they were manifested in a character.

But now oni are popularly portrayed as masculine. I believe that this assumption regarding gender comes primarily from the pictorial representation of oni's appearance. According to Kosugi Kazuo, scholar of Japanese art history, the Japanese oni received its appearance from Chinese *guishen* (ghosts and spirits) around the twelfth century at latest (Kosugi 1986, 205). More often than not, oni are depicted with muscular bodies and are scantily clad, wearing a loincloth of tiger skin. Oni are hairy and customarily portrayed with one or more horns. They sometimes have a third eye in the center of their forehead, and they vary in skin color but most commonly they are black, red, blue, or yellow. They often have large mouths with conspicuous canine teeth.[23]

According to Hayashi Shizuyo, who has studied the sex of oni in the tales collated as *Yomigatari* (Reading aloud [old tales], 2004–2005), the majority of oni are male, and when female oni appear in these stories they do so with an age signifier such as *oni-baba*, *oni-banba*, or *oni-basa*, all meaning old oni-woman or oni-hag (Hayashi S. 2012, 78).[24] No such signifiers are attached to male oni. Hayashi surmises that all the oni-women in *Yomigatari* are described as old because their aged appearance might resemble a frightening male oni (Hayashi S. 2012, 79). Further, when a male oni is implied, the word *oni* stands by itself, without any suffix. In other words, in order to depict the creature as female, a female suffix must be added. In the aforementioned story titled "Sanseru onna minami Yamashina ni yuki oni ni aite niguru koto" from the *Konjaku monogatarishū*, the old woman is described simply as an oni—not an oni-woman. A female oni could be a male oni transformed—as often appears in literary sources.

For that matter, in the medieval period the label *oni* was applied to the specters of ordinary household objects such as tools and containers after they reached a hundred years of age. These abandoned man-made objects, *tsukumogami*, bear grudges against people.[25] Household objects do not have gender in Japanese. He, she, or it, *oni* is invariably situational, and may arguably be considered gender-defiant.

Compared with the ambiguous gender of oni, yamauba are and have always been female. The term *female* may invoke a symbolic outside or the Other.[26] Claire R. Farrer quotes Simone de Beauvoir's in *The Second Sex*: woman "is defined and differentiated with reference to man . . . she is the incidental, the inessential as opposed to the essential. He is Subject, he is Absolute—she is the Other" (Farrer 1975, xiii). As Farrer states, the image of women as Other has had a constraining influence (Farrer 1975, xiii), especially in a patriarchal society like premodern Japan. Yamauba, however, are much less constrained by the traditions, customs, and social norms expected of women. And that is the major reason why yamauba have attracted much attention recently among scholars of women's literature.

From the viewpoint of gender studies, Mizuta Noriko says yamauba is gender transcendent. She contrasts yamauba with the women of the sato. The sato is considered a safe place where people are protected and insulated from the dangers of the mountains. According to Mizuta, the women of the sato are idealized and standardized—they are good mothers, good wives, chaste, humble, and obedient to their fathers and husbands (Mizuta 2002, 10–12). Conversely, a yamauba is someone who falls distinctly outside of the norm. Although she often has excessive fertility, she lacks the feminine traits ascribed to the women of the sato, namely, chastity, obedience, and compassion. Mizuta notes that the norm for the sato's women cannot be applied to yamauba, for her essential qualities are so nebulous and polysemous that she nullifies it. In other words, the yamauba exists outside the sato's gender system (Mizuta 2002, 12–15). She refuses to be assigned a household role such as mother or daughter and will not be confined. Mizuta emphasizes that while the women of the sato stay in one place, yamauba are comparatively nomadic, moving constantly through the mountains, appearing in an array of locales, often outside or away from a town's territorial boundary (Mizuta 2002, 10). A yamauba moves about as she wishes. The common thread of the mysterious, enigmatic creatures called yamauba living in the mountains is that they are female beings.

YAMAUBA'S FEATURES

What are the specific features of yamauba as they appear in oral and literary tradition? Yamauba's well-known attributes are that she is an anthropophagous woman living in the mountains, she possesses the duality of good and evil, and she has the transformational power to manifest herself as an ugly crone or a young beauty. Invisible yamauba also exist. Some yamauba are mothers of divine children. Lesser-known attributes of yamauba include flying and bloodsucking. Miyata Noboru writes that the image of childbirth lurked in the shadows of mountain women (Miyata 2000, 189). Yamauba in some tales can foretell the future and read people's minds. Yamauba's relationship to spiders and spinning are often pointed out. Just as yamauba are fertile, spiders are fecund. As recounted in narratives, an attack by yōkai *tsuchigumo* (earth spiders) on warriors leads to the spiders' demise; likewise, yamauba's assaults on men backfire. How and why did these traits or features come into being? Are there any modern interpretations of some of yamauba's behaviors? A yamauba is often considered a type of oni-woman; the terms are frequently used interchangeably. What, then, makes a yamauba distinct from an oni-woman? It is said that "the yamamba is one of the best known yōkai in Japan" (Foster 2015, 144). What is the appeal of yamauba and what do yamauba have to say to us in present Japanese society? These are the points I address in this book.

ORGANIZATION OF THE BOOK

Chapter 1, "Man-Eating, Helping, Shape-Shifting Yamauba: Yamauba's Duality," examines yamauba's familiar features, in particular duality, in relation to oni or oni-women. Although malevolent yamauba in such folktales as "Kuwazu nyōbō" ("The Wife Who Does Not Eat"), "Ushikata to yamauba" ("The Ox-Leader and the Yamauba"), and "Sanmai no ofuda" ("Three Charms") are contrasted with the benevolent yamauba that appear in "Ubakawa" ("The Old Woman Skin") and "Komebuku Awabuku" ("Komebuku and Awabuku"), and the otogizōshi *Hanayo no hime* (*Blossom Princess*, ca. late sixteenth or early seventeenth century), there is a complementary relationship between the good and evil yamauba. Their stories possess a complementary narrative format as well. The chapter further addresses how and why yamauba's traits came into being. While the noh play *Yamanba* is an indispensable text in understanding medieval yamauba and beyond, I also consider the noh play *Kurozuka* (Black mound, mid-fifteenth century) with its "taboo of looking" theme, a critical text in the formation of yamauba's image.

Chapter 2, "Mother Yamauba and Weaving: Childbirth and Bloodsucking, Spinning and Spiders," discusses yamauba as a mother of divine children or children with superhuman power. I believe yamauba's motherly aspects became well known during the early modern period through legends, folktales, literary works, woodblock prints, and performing arts. As mentioned above, Miyata Noboru writes that the image of childbirth follows yamauba. I surmise that yamauba's bloodsucking attribute is a vestige of oni.

The chapter also examines yamauba's association with strings, spinning, and weaving. In many stories of "Kuwazu nyōbō," a representative yamauba story, the real identity of the protagonist wife is a spider, known for spinning. I speculate that the connection between yamauba and spiders is also deeply related to their commonalities with oni.

Chapter 3, "Reading Minds and Telling Futures: 'Yamauba and the Cooper,' 'The Smile of a Mountain Witch,' and *Throne of Blood*," studies yamauba's mind-reading ability through an examination of the folktale "Yamauba and the Cooper" and its predecessors, as well as Ōba Minako's modern short story, "The Smile of a Mountain Witch." I speculate on the origin of yamauba's mind-reading attribute and how the idea or inspiration for the yamauba protagonist came to Ōba Minako. Further, the chapter discusses yamauba's ability to tell one's fortune. A foretelling yamauba appears in such tales as "Naranashi tori" ("Picking Wild Pears") and Akira Kurosawa's film *Kumonosu-jō* (*The Castle of the Spider's Web*, 1957), known in the West as *Throne of Blood*. The evil spirit of *Throne of Blood* corresponds to the three weird sisters of Shakespeare's *Macbeth*, upon which Kurosawa's film was based. Kurosawa's witch spins out the thread of fate of two ambitious generals.

Chapter 4, "Yamauba, Yasaburō Basa, Datsueba: Images of Premodern Crones, Yamauba's Flying Ability, and Re-creation of a Prototype," examines a prototypical image of premodern crones and yamauba's flying power. In some folktales and legends, yamauba are described running fast through the mountains in pursuit of their victims. Recently I encountered a description based on the legends of Yasaburō Basa (Yasaburō's old mother), who lived on Mt. Yahiko in Niigata Prefecture, in which a yamauba is able to fly. Can a yamauba really fly like a witch? What is Yasaburō Basa and how does Yasaburō Basa relate to yamauba? The narrative of Yasaburō Basa legends and the statue of Myōtara Ten'nyo—Yasaburō Basa's deified name—remind one of Datsueba (literally, stripping-clothes old woman), who sits at the Sanzu River and mercilessly strips the clothes off the dead. Is there a relationship between yamauba, Yasaburō Basa, and Datsueba? This chapter addresses these questions and further studies classical and folkloric oni stories in relation to Yasaburō Basa.

In premodern times, an extraordinarily long-lived creature, or even object, was believed to become an oni. The yamauba of *Hanayo no hime* who has outlived her descendants and lives in the mountains forever becomes an oni's companion, and although she does not eat humans, she is seen as an oni herself. There is a certain connection between long-lived beings and yamauba or oni. Chapter 5, "Aging, Dementia, and Abandoned Women: An

Interpretation of Yamauba," considers a modern interpretation of yamauba and examines issues of aging and family conflict through the stories of Obasute-yama (abandoned women in the mountains), narratives still popular in contemporary aging Japanese society.

Chapter 6, "Yamamba Mumbo Jumbo: Yamauba in Contemporary Society," studies current depictions of yamauba and yamauba-like figures such as *yamanba-gyaru* (yamauba gals) whose unique fashion took major cities, particularly Shibuya in Tokyo, by storm from 1998 through 2000. Kuraishi Tadahiko, a folklorist, observes that the appearance of the yamanba-gyaru in Shibuya is fitting, considering yamauba's proclivity to appear in village marketplaces (quoted in Shibuya Keizai Shinbun Henshūbu, 2002). This chapter also looks into contemporary depictions of yamauba in various types of literature and media, including film and manga.

Japanese names that appear in this work are written according to Japanese custom, with the family name appearing first. For example, the family name of Komatsu Kazuhiko, a folklorist and scholar of anthropology, is Komatsu. The exception to this rule occurs when names are well known outside of Japan. For example, the name of film director and animator Hayao Miyazaki appears in this order, even though Miyazaki is his family name.

1

Man-Eating, Helping,
Shape-Shifting Yamauba
Yamauba's Duality

THE DISTINCTIVE FEATURES OF THE YAMAUBA ARE THAT she is often said
to be an anthropophagous woman living in the mountains; to possess
the duality of good and evil, bringing death and destruction as well as
wealth and fertility; and to have the power of transformation, manifesting herself alternately as an ugly crone or a young beauty (see Takashima
2014, 116; Murakami 2000, 345). Yanagita Kunio writes that the yamauba described in setsuwa are atrocious and cannibalistic like oni-women
(female demons/ogres/monsters), and they are cruelly punished, but that
when yamauba are talked about as local beings in legends—for instance,
when a villager references "a yamauba living in a certain mountain a long
time ago"—they are thought of fondly (Yanagita 1978–1979, 1:248; 2014,
167). That yamauba possess a good side, such as when they are portrayed as mountain deities helping human beings, and an evil side, such as
when they resemble oni-women, is especially evident in mukashibanashi
(*SNKBZ* 1994–2002, 58:565).

When one looks at the above characteristics, however, one notices that
it is actually the yamauba's most conspicuous trait, anthropophagy, that is
the evil part of her duality. This chapter discusses the yamauba's familiar
traits and how her opposing characteristics can be reconciled. Special attention is paid to the yamauba and oni/oni-women paradigm, because I believe
the man-eating destructive yamauba and the helping, gift-giving yamauba
are two sides of the same coin, and that the complementary nature of
good and evil exists through the intermediary of oni. Further, the chapter addresses how and why the yamauba's traits came into being and what
makes the yamauba distinct from oni-women.

DOI: 10.7330/9781646420551.c001

The noh plays *Yamanba* and *Kurozuka* are the crucial texts for understanding the medieval yamauba and the formation of the yamauba's image. In addition, the "do not look" taboo that appears in both mukashibanashi and *Kurozuka* will be investigated as one of the contiguous threads between the yamauba and the oni-woman.

YAMAUBA VERSUS ONI/ONI-WOMEN

As written in the introduction, the first appearance of the term *yamauba* in literary materials occurred in the Muromachi period (Komatsu K. 2000, 428; Orikuchi 2000, 300). In earlier literature, the enigmatic witch-like female one encountered in the mountains was often described as an oni or oni-woman (Foster 2015, 147).[1] Komatsu Kazuhiko explains that supernatural deities worshipped by Japanese are known as *kami*, while those that are not worshipped are called *yōkai*, and those yōkai with a strong negative association are known as *oni* (Komatsu K. 1979, 337). Likewise, Michael Dylan Foster writes that when malicious emotions, intentions, or actions are "antisociety and antimoral," they are associated with oni (Foster 2015, 118).

It is no surprise, then, that such an abhorrent antisocial act as cannibalism is considered a major trait of oni (see Reider 2010, 14–29). An oni can eat a person in a single gulp, as the phrase "oni hitokuchi" (oni in one gulp) suggests (see Gorai 1984). The sixth episode of *Ise monogatari* (*Tales of Ise*, ca. 945) tells of a man who falls hopelessly in love with a woman well above his social status. The man decides to elope with her. On the night they run away, a severe thunderstorm forces them to shelter in a ruined storehouse. The man stands on guard at the entrance of the shelter, but the lady is eaten by an oni in one gulp (*SNKBZ* 1994–2002, 12:117–18; McCullough 1968, 72–73). Stories of oni's cannibalism are frequently recorded in Japan's official history, too. According to *Nihon sandai jitsuroku* (True records of three generations in Japan, 901), on the seventeenth of the eighth month of 887 three beautiful women walking near Butokuden, one of the buildings in the imperial palace compound, see a good-looking man under a pine tree. The man approaches one of the women and begins talking with her. When the other two women look back in the direction of the pine tree, they are horrified to see the woman has been dismembered, her limbs strewn on the ground, her head missing. At the time, people believed that an oni had transformed into a handsome man in order to eat the woman (for a text of the episode, see Fujiwara T. et al. 1941, 464). I believe that yamauba inherited this anthropophagous nature of oni when the term *yamauba* emerged.

While showing the oni's cannibalistic side, this episode in *Nihon sandai jitsuroku* also illustrates the oni's exceptional metamorphic abilities. Changing from its grotesque form to a handsome man allows the cunning oni to gain the trust and interest of his victim so that he can easily devour her. Oni are capable of transforming into both male and female forms at will. Yamauba perhaps acquired the transformation ability from oni as well, though as far as I know, a yamauba does not change her appearance to a man to lure her victim—who is usually male. As described later, she shape-shifts to a young woman to attract a man.

Although there are many overlapping qualities between yamauba and oni-women, they are not exactly the same. Michael Dylan Foster explains: "It is important not to conflate all female demon figures. The female oni is often characterized by her jealous rage—in fact, this rage is sometimes the very thing that turns a regular woman into a demon in the first place. This is, for example, one characteristic of the demonic female *hannya* mask used in many a noh play. Akin to male oni, the female oni is distinguished by horns sprouting from her head. In contrast, most descriptions of yamamba do not include horns; nor generally is her monstrousness attributed to jealousy or sexual passion" (Foster 2015, 147; see also Li 2012, 173–96; Tanaka T. 1992, 256.).

The distinction is true, although there are exceptions. In a number of folktales oni-women do not express jealousy or anger. The yamauba portrayed in *Hanayo no hime* (*Blossom Princess*) has horns on her head, as do yamauba in some other literary works.[2] I would add that the major differences are, as described in the introduction, that yamauba's topos is the mountains, whereas a female oni does not require a mountainous setting: a field, village, city, or palace are as good. Further, yamauba remain female, whereas an oni-woman can transform into a male oni, because oni's gender is equivocally ambiguous or situational.

CANNIBALISM, THE DESTRUCTIVE SIDE OF YAMAUBA'S DUALITY, AND THE POWER OF TRANSFORMATION

Cannibalism shows the demonic side of yamauba's dual nature. Cannibalism is probably the strongest element connecting yamauba to oni, or I should say *continuing* from oni to yamauba. Indeed, in mukashibanashi when the yamauba is perceived as a man-eater, the appellations oni-baba or oni are used interchangeably with yamauba for the main character. Since the cannibalistic yamauba character is almost always found in mukashibanashi, I describe below the three major folktale story types in which cannibalistic yamauba appear and examine which name—yamauba, oni-baba, or oni—is most often used. I have used Seki Keigo's *Nihon mukashibanashi taisei* (Complete works of Japanese folktales; hereafter *NMT* 1978–1980).

"Kuwazu nyōbō" ("The Wife Who Does Not Eat")

The folktale "Kuwazu nyōbō," which is known all over Japan, is often used as an exemplar of the human-eating yamauba.[3] The story opens with a man muttering to himself (in some versions he mutters to a friend) about how he wants a wife who does not eat. Soon afterward a beautiful young woman appears at his house and declares that since she does not eat, she would like to be his wife.[4] The man marries her. But this seemingly ideal wife turns out to be a monstrous woman who has a second mouth at the back of her head. While she does not eat anything when the man is at home, as soon as he goes out she prepares food and eats ravenously with this mouth.[5] When the man finds out the truth, she reveals her true yamauba appearance. She throws him into a tub, which she carries on her head as she runs toward the mountains. The man narrowly escapes, hiding himself in mugwort and iris. The yamauba finds the man but cannot reach him—mugwort and iris are poisonous to her. The man kills her by throwing mugwort and iris at her. This story was widely known by the early modern period. In *Kokon hyakumonogatari hyōban* (An evaluation of one hundred strange and weird tales of past and present, 1686), written by Yamaoka Genrin (1631–1672), a well-known intellectual of his day, his student asks, "People say, 'a yamauba takes human life, and there are stories about a yamauba transforming herself into a wife.' Is she a real woman?" (Yamaoka 1993, 46).[6] The story must have roused the curiosity of seventeenth-century urban folks. Significantly, Yamaoka Genrin's student's question, like the story itself, reveals yamauba's other distinctive feature, the power of transformation, for she first appears as a young woman. Equally important, while the yamauba does not tell her husband not to watch, the story has the theme of "taboo of looking," which I will discuss in detail later.[7]

   Although "Kuwazu nyōbō" is the representative story depicting yamauba, oni appear as main characters more frequently than yamauba. Oni appear in twenty-eight stories of this type, while yamauba appear in eighteen. Nine stories feature an oni-baba as the protagonist. In one story the character is written as an oni-wife. Oni-wife could mean she is an oni but not old enough to be called oni-baba, or she could be a human being who became an oni's wife. Therefore, even if this oni-wife is excluded because of her ambiguous status, there are thirty-seven stories in which the

Figure 1.1. "Futakuchi onna" (The woman with two mouths) from *Tōsanjin yawa*. (Courtesy of the Iwase Bunko Library of Nishio City.)

anthropophagous character is an oni (either oni or oni-baba), in contrast to eighteen where the character is yamauba. Interestingly, the spider appears most frequently as the main character, in forty-three stories.[8] Kawai Hayao, Jungian psychologist, notes that a yamauba transforms herself into a spider in many versions of "Kuwazu nyōbō," either when her clandestine eating is revealed or during her chase after the man (Kawai 1996, 30).[9] While the issue as to why a yamauba changes to a spider or vice versa will be studied in chapter 2, this changeability brings the shape-shifting ability of yamauba to the fore.[10]

"Kuwazu nyōbō" is fascinating in that the seemingly ideal wife becomes demonic after her husband sees her secret—that is, her unsightly appearance—reminding one of the story of Izanagi encountering Izanami in the nether land. In Japan's creation myth in the *Kojiki*, after the death of Izanami, the female creator of Japan, Izanagi, her husband and male counterpart, misses her so much that he goes to the underworld to retrieve her. But Izanami says that she has already eaten the food of that realm and so cannot return. It was believed that eating food cooked at the nether land's hearth would turn one into a full-fledged being of that world, preventing one from returning to the living world (*NKBT* 1957–1967, 1:64n2).[11] She tells him to wait, but not to look. The taboo against looking is a familiar folkloric motif—unable to resist temptation, a protagonist often breaks that taboo. Sure enough, Izanagi breaks his promise not to look at Izanami—just as Orpheus does on his journey to bring Eurydice back to the world of the living in the Greek myth. When Orpheus looks to see if she is following, beautiful Eurydice slips forever into the world of the dead. When Izanagi looks at Izanami, she is ugly, with maggots squirming and eight thunder deities growing around her entire body. Izanami, furious because he broke the promise/taboo, attacks Izanagi, saying he has caused her "undying shame." Terrified, Izanagi quickly makes his way back to this world, whereupon Izanami dispatches Yomotsu-shikome (literally, ugly woman in the underworld) from the underworld to avenge her shame.[12]

Interestingly, Kawai Hayao considers that the shame Izanami feels reveals the formative experience (*gentaiken*) of the shame of the Japanese race, and further, he notes that the remarkable feature of Japanese stories about the "don't look" taboo is their emphasis upon the shame of being seen, not the guilt of breaking the taboo (Kawai 1975, 683; 1996, 23). Citing eighteenth-century Japanese Nativist scholar Motoori Norinaga (1730–1801), Ishibashi Gaha considers Yomotsu-shikome as an origin of the Japanese oni (Ishibashi 1998, 4). This precursor of Japanese oni was a female born from a goddess who felt shame when her unsightly appearance was revealed and who attacked her husband without concern for her own appearance (i.e., shamelessly). Although it is not described in the mukashibanashi, the wife who does not eat may have felt undying shame because her husband saw her unsightly form. If so, this wife-yamauba shares the same ancestor as the oni. After all, a major root of yamauba is oni. Indeed, Yamagami Izumo asserts that from the mythological point of view, Izanami is the prototype of yamauba duality, and the yamauba was developed and dramatized from this prototype (Yamagami 2000, 383; see also Hulvey 2000).

Although the folktale "Kuwazu nyōbō" clearly teaches moral lessons such as "be careful what you wish for" and "appearances can be deceptive," Fujishiro Yumiko connects the protagonist of "Kuwazu nyōbō," who is an ideal wife in front of her husband but who turns out to have a hidden enormous appetite, with eating disorders, especially bulimia nervosa (Fujishiro 2015, 55–63). Bulimia nervosa is characterized by a cycle of binge eating and compensatory self-induced vomiting. At any given point in time, 1 percent of young women have bulimia nervosa (National Eating Disorders Association 2017). Similarly, Yamaguchi Motoko finds a connection with young female patients of anorexia nervosa, an eating disorder characterized by weight loss, fear of gaining weight, and food restriction (Yamaguchi 2009, 85–88). This mukashibanashi encompasses the underlying desire of women to look beautiful in the public eye—to look pleasant and agreeable to men more than to women, perhaps—and to be accepted by the public—both men and women, but again perhaps men in particular. Pressure on the female to make her appearance acceptable to the male seems to be reflected in the tale.

"Ushikata to yamauba" ("The Ox-Leader and the Yamauba")

Another famous folktale that underscores the cannibalistic aspect of yamauba is "Ushikata to yamauba." Unlike the protagonist of "Kuwazu nyōbō," who tries to hide her large appetite from her husband, from the very beginning of the story the yamauba in "Ushikata to yamauba" openly devours anything she can obtain. The yamauba first approaches a young man carrying fish in his ox cart back to his village. She demands the fish and then the ox—then sets her sights on eating the man. Fleeing, he comes upon a lone house in the woods that turns out to be the yamauba's dwelling. But with the help of a young woman who lives there, he vanquishes the yamauba.[13]

According to *Nihon mukashibanashi taisei*, forty-seven stories of this type feature the yamauba as a devouring character, compared to twenty with oni-baba. The oni accounts for twelve stories.[14] Here again, the terms *yamauba* and *oni-baba* or *oni* are used interchangeably. The young woman character who lives in the yamauba's house and helps the young man does not necessarily appear in every story. Sometimes the young man kills the yamauba all by himself. But this young woman is interesting and mysterious. Why is she in the yamauba's dwelling? Perhaps she was kidnapped from a village, like characters who appear in the story "Oni no ko Kozuna" ("Kozuna, Ogre's Child"), which will be discussed later.

The yamauba in both "Kuwazu nyōbō" and "Ushikata to yamauba" has an enormous appetite. Meera Viswanathan writes, "The figure of a man-eating female demon is peculiar neither to Japan nor to premodern narratives . . . The delineation of these ravenous figures suggests an overarching preoccupation with the danger posed by female consumption as well as the need to defuse the threat, leading us to question whether the provenance of such man-eaters, ironically, is rather in the realm of male anxieties about castration than simply in female notions of resistance" (Viswanathan 1996, 242–43). This appetite could also imply memories of famine in villages. In one "Kuwazu nyōbō" story from Okayama Prefecture, a peasant wants a wife but, because of the ongoing famine, he wishes for a wife who eats nothing (*NMT* 1978–1980, 6:197). The enormous appetite could also suggest a suppressed female desire for food. Appetite is a fundamental biological desire, but in Japan, too great an appetite—especially for women—is frowned upon in public or private, in villages or cities. The yamauba who chases after her prey without shame or concern with appearances spurns standard societal expectations.

"Sanmai no ofuda" ("Three Charms")

Another famous story about a human-eating character is "Sanmai no ofuda," which also possesses the theme of the "taboo of looking." The old *bonze* (Buddhist monk) in a mountain temple drives his mischievous novice away from the temple to teach him a lesson (or, in some versions, the novice insists on going chestnut picking). Before the boy leaves, the bonze gives him three charms to protect him in case of dire need. As the novice picks nuts on the mountain, an old woman appears and invites him to her house. During the night, the novice peeks into a room to see the woman has transformed into a monstrous shape, and she tries to eat him. He escapes using the magic charms; each charm delays the yamauba in her chase, but nonetheless she eventually reaches the temple. As she is about to enter, the bonze shuts the gate, crushing and killing the yamauba. In some stories, when the yamauba reaches the temple, she demands that the bonze hand over the novice, and the bonze challenges the yamauba to a disguise contest. She scoffs at the challenge and turns into a bean, whereupon the master eats the bean-yamauba.[15] This story again reveals yamauba's power of transformation. She can transform herself into anything from a giant to a bean.

Unfortunately for the yamauba, showing off her power of transformation can lead to her demise. The story also suggests that she is simple-minded.

Among the stories of this type, thirty-six stories have an oni-baba as the anthropophagous character, compared to yamauba in fourteen, old woman in thirteen, and oni in eleven.[16] I should note that in the story printed in Yanagita's *Nippon no mukashibanashi kaiteiban*, the cannibalistic being is called yamauba until the very end, when it suddenly changes to oni-baba (Yanagita 1960, 67). In this particular tale, collected from Akita Prefecture, the yamauba pretends to be the novice's aunt and invites him to her house. In spite of the old bonze's warning, the novice goes to the woman's house. The aunt tells the novice to sleep in bed while she fixes a feast for him. He follows her instructions at first, but after a while he peeks into her room, where he finds his aunt has turned into a yamauba, who sharpens her butcher's knife beside a big boiling kettle. He barely escapes, using the charms to delay her chase. She follows him to the mountain temple, where the bonze challenges her to a shape-shifting contest. The yamauba changes into a bean, whereupon the bonze eats her. But the yamauba inside the bonze's stomach hurts him so badly he breaks wind, and out comes the yamauba. She then goes back to the mountain (Yanagita 1960, 65–67; English translation in Yanagita 1966, 58–60). The part where the yamauba is eaten by the bonze and then violently attacks his stomach reminds one of the famous folktale "Issun bōshi" ("Little One-Inch"), in which Little One-Inch hurts the oni's stomach with his sword.[17] In any case, the interchangeability between yamauba and oni is remarkable.

This pattern of the novice throwing his charms one by one to delay the yamauba's chase, allowing him just barely to reach the safe zone, parallels Izanagi's escape from the underworld. Izanagi throws his personal belongings to delay his pursuers, Yomotsu-shikome and the thunder gods. First, he unties the black vine securing his hair and throws it down, whereupon it immediately bears grapes. While Yomotsu-shikome eats the grapes, Izanagi continues his run. When Yomotsu-shikome is catching up with him, Izanagi throws his comb, which turns into bamboo shoots. While Yomotsu-shikome eats the bamboo shoots, he runs. Again, the roots of yamauba can be found in Yomotsu-shikome or Izanami, who is also a root of the oni.

HELPER AND FORTUNE GIVER:
THE POSITIVE SIDE OF YAMAUBA'S DUALITY

While the terrifying aspect of the yamauba is highlighted in the stories just discussed, she can also be a helper and can bring good fortune, like Frau

Holle in the Brothers Grimm. This is the positive side of yamauba duality, which I believe was the major reason that the term *yamauba* came into being in the Muromachi period; as written in the introduction, the positive side of her helping humans was not readily identified with the image of an anti-human oni.[18] The yamauba's positive side probably comes from her archetypal nature as a goddess, as discussed in the introduction. When she helps human beings or brings them good fortune, none of the oni-related appellations—oni-baba, oni-woman, or oni—are used to describe her. Even so, yamauba are not entirely disconnected with oni; they often live in an oni's house. The following two stories, "Komebuku Awabuku" and "Ubakawa," are frequently cited as exemplars foregrounding the positive side of yamauba.

"KOMEBUKU AWABUKU" ("KOMEBUKU AND AWABUKU")

"Komebuku Awabuku" ("Komebuku and Awabuku") is a stepdaughter story. Komebuku's stepmother gives her a bag with holes and a good bag to her real daughter, Awabuku, and sends the girls to the mountains to fill their bags with chestnuts. The sun sets, and the two lose their way. They find a house in the mountains that turns out to be a yamauba's house. The yamauba reluctantly lets them in. She tells them to hide because it is an oni's residence, thereby saving their lives.[19] She also asks them to take huge lice off her head. Komebuku helps her with the lice, but Awabuku does not. When they leave the house, the yamauba gives Komebuku a treasure box and Awabuku some roasted beans. Later the mother takes Awabuku to a theatrical play but makes the stepdaughter stay at home to perform tasks such as carrying water. With the help of a traveling priest and a sparrow, Komebuku finishes the tasks and goes to the play, wearing beautiful clothes she found in the treasure box the yamauba gave her. A young man at the play falls in love with Komebuku and proposes marriage to her. Her stepmother tries to procure him for her real daughter, but the young man marries the stepdaughter. Awabuku wants to be married, so her mother goes to seek a suitor, carrying her daughter in a mortar. They fall into a stream and turn into mud snails (*NMT* 1978–1980, 5:86–111; Seki 1966, 111; Mayer 1986, 44–46).

Among stories of the "Komebuku Awabuku" type printed in *NMT*, seventeen designate a yamauba as the character who gives treasures and clothes to the good child. Seven of the stories state that the helper is an old woman; in four of these seven, the old woman lives in an oni house and hides the sisters from the oni.[20] The terms *oni-baba* or *oni* are not used to describe this helper. It should be noted that in giving good fortune, the yamauba is not indiscriminate. She judges people. If one is a good character, the yamauba rewards him or her accordingly. This selective behavior on the part of the yamauba satisfies the audience's sense of justice.

"U<small>BAKAWA</small>" ("T<small>HE</small> O<small>LD</small> W<small>OMAN</small> S<small>KIN</small>")

The "Ubakawa"-type stories are also stepdaughter stories. A stepmother hates her stepdaughter and drives her away. The heroine, who is to be married to a serpent bridegroom, flees from him. The girl finds a solitary house in the mountains in which an old woman lives. The old woman says it is an oni's house and hides the heroine from the oni. This old woman, a yamauba, takes pity on the girl and gives her an *ubakawa* (literally, an old woman's skin), which makes the wearer appear dirty or old. Wearing the ubakawa, the girl is employed in a rich man's house as an old kitchen maid. After the rich man's son catches a glimpse of her in her natural form when she is in her room alone, he becomes sick. A fortune-teller tells the rich man that his son's illness is caused by his love for a certain woman in his house. One by one all the women in the house are taken before the son to offer him tea or medicine. He refuses all until he sees the heroine in the ubakawa; he smiles at her and takes a drink from the cup she offers him. She takes off the ubakawa and becomes the son's wife (Mayer 1986, 48–49; *NMT* 1978–1980, 5:173–87; Seki 1966, 114–15).

Among the stories of "Ubakawa" type, the old woman turns out to be a frog saved by the heroine's father in eighteen stories. Only two stories designate the helper as a yamauba.[21] Again, the terms *oni-baba* or *oni* are not used for the helper. In many stories, as in "Komubuku Awabuku," the helper lives in an oni's house, but she is not herself considered an oni. Who is this old woman living in an oni's house and helping the main character in mukashibanashi?

FEMALE COHABITANT IN ONI'S HOUSE

The relationship between the mysterious old woman who lives in an oni's house and the oni she resides with is not described, nor is there any explanation of how the yamauba has come to live with him. She could have originally been a human who turned into a yamauba, as in the story *Hanayo no hime* (discussed later). Or she may have been abducted by the yamauba and forced to live in her house. A series of mukashibanashi stories entitled "Oni no ko Kozuna" provides some insights that help us understand how a female human could become the companion of an oni and bear an oni-child. In "Oni no ko Kozuna," a girl is kidnaped by an oni and becomes his wife. The girl's father, brother, or husband goes in search of her. He meets the girl's child, named Kozuna, who guides him to the oni's house. The oni's wife hides her father (brother or husband). The oni comes home and says he smells a human being.[22] The girl tells him that it is probably because she is pregnant with the oni's child. Pleased with this information, the oni celebrates, drinking himself to sleep. While he is sleeping, the oni's wife, her father (brother or husband), and the child escape from the house. Although the oni soon wakes up and chases after them, they arrive home safely (Seki 1966, 47; for Japanese text, see *NMT* 1978–1980, 6:253–67).

This mukashibanashi has commonality with one of Yanagita's stories about a farmer's daughter who goes to a mountain to gather chestnuts and never returns. The parents think she is dead and hold a funeral, but two or three years later, a hunter from the same village encounters the girl when he goes to the mountain. The two are surprised to see each other. According to the hunter who hears her story, she was kidnapped by a frightful man in the mountain and was too scared to escape. She had several children with him but the man either abandoned or killed them all, saying they did not resemble him (Yanagita 1978–1979, 1:230–31). Yanagita observed that in addition to grown women who leave their parents' house and became yamauba, there are other women who were born in the mountains (Yanagita 1978–1979, 1:255). Yamauba-related mukashibanashi reveal fragments of a holistic yamauba—and perhaps women living in the mountains; the "Oni no ko Kozuna" mukashibanashi and Yanagita's story indicate how a woman could stay in the mountains and became an oni's companion and mother of oni children.

DEVOURING AND HELPING YAMAUBA: TWO SIDES OF THE SAME COIN

While terrifying yamauba in such mukashibanashi as "Kuwazu nyōbō" are often contrasted with the helping yamauba that appear in "Ubakawa" and "Komebuku Awabuku," they are actually two sides of the same coin, not only through their connection with oni but also through their complementary narrative format. In all of the three frightening tales, it is the yamauba who seeks out and approaches her prey in the open—somewhere outside her house—and thus she is proactive. In "Kuwazu nyōbō," the yamauba appears in front of the man, outside his house, saying specifically that she wants to be his wife because she does not eat. The yamauba in "Ushikata to yamauba" first talks to the ox-cart puller who is on his way back to his village. In "Sanmai no ofuda" the yamauba shows up before the acolyte on the mountain, introducing herself as his aunt.

On the other hand, in both "Komebuku Awabuku" and "Ubakawa," it is the daughter (or daughters) who approaches the yamauba, who is in her own private space—her own house in the mountains. The girl who loses her way seeks a night's lodging at a lone house, a yamauba's residence. Inside the house, the yamauba responds to the girl's request; thus, the yamauba is reactive. While the anthropophagous yamauba tries to eat humans, the helping yamauba saves the main character from the devouring cohabitant oni. The cannibalistic yamauba is one side of the coin and the helping yamauba is the other.

One interpretation of this finding is that the yamauba is benevolent as long as she stays in her house in the mountains, but she becomes an evil oni when she is proactive and ventures out to seek more food or to take food away from men. One of the major reasons for the mixture of yamauba, oni, and oni-woman lies in the yamauba's oni roots, but the influence of patriarchy, in particular the Confucian-style patriarchy imported from China, is certainly perceptible. The appearance of the term *yamauba* in the Muromachi period corresponds to the time of the spreading patriarchal household system and the declining status of women.

The helping side of yamauba seems more prevalent in other areas of literature such as otogizōshi (companion tales), the performing arts, and many legends. It is important to note that even when yamauba is helpful, her association with oni is still strong, and she is often visually portrayed as oni-like, as explained below.

HANAYO NO HIME (BLOSSOM PRINCESS) OF OTOGIZŌSHI

Hanayo no hime, an otogizōshi tale, is known for its strong folkloric elements and is associated with "Komebuku Awabuku," "Ubakawa," and other folktales (see Reider 2016, chap. 6). The yamauba character is a helper, like the yamauba in "Komebuku Awabuku" and "Ubakawa," and the narrative pattern is the same: the yamauba of *Hanayo no hime* lives in a cave deep in the mountains and the good heroine Blossom Princess, who is treated cruelly by her stepmother, comes to the yamauba's dwelling at night. The yamauba's cave is also an oni's residence, and she tells the heroine that her husband is an oni. She hides Blossom Princess from her oni husband so that the princess does not get eaten. The yamauba gives Blossom Princess directions about where to go, and bestows on her treasures that save her at a critical moment.

Figure 1.2. Blossom Princess encounters the yamauba. (Courtesy of Hiroshima University Library.)

The yamauba never calls herself an oni, and the narrator does not call her one either, but she is treated like an oni by the main characters (and by the author[s] and readers). A popular belief dictates that a religious service should be held for the departed souls of one's ancestors so that these ancestors will protect their descendants. Unattended souls are thought to roam in this world doing harm to people as oni. Takahashi Mariko notes that the yamauba in *Hanayo no hime* is considered an oni because she does not have anyone to pray for her—she can finally rest in peace only after a memorial service is held for her by the family of Blossom Princess (Takahashi Mariko 1975, 30; see also Yanagita 1988).

It is significant that the yamauba's physical features resemble an oni; the yamauba is "fearful-looking." Blossom Princess reacts tearfully when she first meets the yamauba precisely because of the yamauba's terrifying appearance. The yamauba had "a square face. Her eyes were sunk deep into her head but still her eyeballs protruded. She had a big mouth, and the fangs from her lower jaw almost touched the edges of her nose. That nose resembled a bird's beak and her forehead was wrinkled up; her hair looked as though she had recently worn a bowl on her head . . . On her skull were fourteen or fifteen small horn-like bumps" (*MJMT* 1987–1988, 10:530–31; Reider 2016, 181, 183). The illustration accompanying the text shows the yamauba with two distinct horns on her head. Blossom Princess believes from her appearance that the yamauba is an oni. The yamauba's oni-like appearance and the cannibalism associated with oni make the princess feel hopeless despairing. One may conclude that the narrator or the persona of the author(s)—and by extension the readers of that time—equated yamauba with oni or with an oni-like appearance.

THE NOH PLAY *YAMANBA*, A STARTING POINT

The reaction of Blossom Princess when she first sees the yamauba—fear and despair—is exactly the same as that of the entertainer Hyakuma Yamanba in the noh play *Yamanba* (*SNKBZ* 1994–2002, 59:564–82; Bethe and Brazell 1998, 207–25), one of the earliest texts to use the term *yamauba* (*yamanba*). The text reveals a helping (and self-reflective) yamauba in spite of her scary looks, and shows how deeply the image of yamauba is interwoven with that of oni. Indeed, I believe this noh play, whose authorship is generally attributed to Zeami (1363–1443), is a fundamental and extremely influential literary text in creating the image of yamauba.

In the first act, Hyakuma Yamanba, an entertainer who became famous in the capital by performing a yamanba song and dance, is traveling to Zenkōji temple with her attendants. As they pass through the mountains, the sky suddenly becomes as dark as night and Yamanba (the *mae-shite*, or protagonist of the first act; I use Yamanba with a capital "Y" when referring to this protagonist) appears disguised as an old woman. Yamanba in the first

Figure 1.3. Yamanba in the noh play *Nōgaku zu e: Yamanba*. (Courtesy of Ritsumeikan University Art Research Center, *Nōgaku zu e: Yamanba*, arcUP0939.)

act is proactive, approaching Hyakuma's troupe in an open space. She offers them lodging for the night and requests that Hyakuma sing her yamanba song and perform her dance. Yamanba thinks that Hyakuma should pay tribute to her, as the source of the entertainer's fame, and she hopes the performance will act as a prayer for Yamanba's salvation.[23] Revealing that she is Yamanba, she disappears, marking the end of the first act. During the interlude, daylight returns. Hyakuma's attendant asks a villager of the place what a yamanba is, but he has no clue. In the second act, Yamanba (the *nochi-shite*, or protagonist of the second act, wearing a yamanba mask) appears at night in her true form. Yamanba dances, describing her mountain rounds in every season, explaining how she invisibly helps humans, and then she disappears.

YAMANBA'S ONI IMAGE

When Yamanba reveals her true form, Hyakuma sees "a thicket of snowy brambles for hair, with eyes that sparkle like stars, and a face that's painted red—a demon gargoyle crouching at the eaves" (Bethe and Brazell 1998, 218; *SNKBZ* 1994–2002, 59:576). Hyakuma is petrified that she will be devoured like the lady in the *Ise monogatari* (*Tales of Ise*); she moans, "The demon of the ancient tale, who devoured a maiden in a single gulp one rainy night / A thunder clapped with a fearsome roar / That night, after the maiden had asked 'What are these? Peals?' / Should that be my fate?" (Bethe and Brazell 1998, 218–19; *SNKBZ* 1994–2002, 59:576). The terrifying appearance of Yamanba causes Hyakuma to view Yamanba as an oni who devours humans, as in this old story. The noh yamanba mask and wig worn by the lead actor correspond to this description. Her changing shape, from an ordinary-looking woman in the first act to Yamanba in the second act, is a clear transformation or shape-shifting, one of yamauba's distinctive traits. *Yamanba* was the fourth most frequently performed piece during the period between 1429 and 1600 (Nose 1938, 1314). Its popularity suggests that the visual image of the yamauba it portrays could very well have influenced the general image of the yamauba in the medieval period.

From the villager's nonsensical talk about the origins of yamanba it is apparent that no one knew exactly what a yamauba looked like at this time. When Yamanba asks Hyakuma's attendant if he has any idea what a true yamanba is like, he speculates, based on Hyakuma's dance, that yamanba is "a demoness [*kijo*] dwelling in the mountains." This is perhaps how Hyakuma, the narrator, and people at the time thought of yamauba—as in the case of the yamauba in *Hanayo no hime*. In response, Yamanba asks, "Isn't a demoness a female demon [*onna no oni*]? Well, whether demon or human, if you're talking about a woman who lives in the mountains, doesn't that fit my situation?" The chorus sings, "Bound to fate, clouds of delusion, like bits of dust, mount up to become Yamamba," who is "a demoness in form [*kijo ga arisama*]" (Bethe and Brazell 1998, 213, 225; *SNKBZ* 1994–2002, 59:570, 581).[24] Yamanba's intense desire to manifest herself in a tangible form causes her to appear as an oni-woman. But Yamanba never calls herself an oni-woman, though she is resigned to being regarded as such by others. She emphasizes that her relationship with nature and her residence in the mountains are more important characteristics than the status others imagine or associate with her.

Yamanba is in the fifth category of noh in the five styles and sequences of noh performance.[25] It is common in the fifth category to see celebratory plays of a demon being driven away; the tempo becomes fast with a large drum in the second act, but slows down at the end of the performance. Baba Akiko argues that the first and most important reason that this yamauba is an oni is that the yamanba does not at all recognize any need to interact with people and to engage in the life of the settlement (Baba Akiko 1988, 281).

Yamanba is layered with and shrouded in religious and philosophical subtexts such as "good and evil are not two; right and wrong are the same" (Bethe and Brazell 1998, 207). The core concept of the play is the transcendental philosophy of nondualism epitomized in the *Hannya shingyō* (Heart Sutra), perhaps the best-known Buddhist text. From the viewpoint of the statement that "form is nothing other than emptiness, emptiness is nothing other than form" (*shikisoku zekū, kūsoku zeshiki*), the existence of buddhas, human beings, and yamauba is miniscule within the vastness of time and space (Baba Akiko 1988, 284–85). The protagonist sings, "Let the vibrant strains of your music and dance serve as a Buddhist sacrament for then I, too, will escape from transmigration and return to the blessed state of enlightenment" (Bethe and Brazell 1998, 213; *SNKBZ* 1994–2002, 59:571). This yamauba, created perhaps by Zeami using the philosophy of contemporary intellectuals and the zeitgeist of his time, is a seeker of enlightenment who would wander the mountains until her delusions ceased to exist, in order to escape the wheel of reincarnation.[26] Baba argues, "The noh play *Yamanba* provided a philosophy to yamauba legends, and it is the most excellent form of philosophy of the female oni" (Baba Akiko 1988, 284).

Wakita Haruko comments that *Yamanba* is crisp and has the feel of deep mountain valleys; the protagonist is a mountain spirit reflecting what a city dweller would consider as the incarnation of a mountain spirit (Wakita 2002, 45). That description perhaps corresponds to what Haruo Shirane (2012) referred to as "secondary nature." Wakita notes that elements of Yanagita's theory of the yamauba's origins discussed earlier naturally existed in the medieval period as well, and that some of these elements became the basis of *Yamanba*. From the diction of the play, Wakita interprets Yamanba as an oni-spirit (*reiki*), a creature that a human being had turned into after death. Yamanba's painful mountain rounds resemble the karma of human beings, who reincarnate through the six realms. Yamanba thinks that she will be able to escape from the rounds of reincarnation and go to a better place if Hyakuma performs a memorial service for her by means of her dance (Wakita 2002, 46). Yamanba encompasses the spirits of the dead in the mountains, which is similar to the yamauba character in *Hanayo no hime* and is in tune with the concept that contemporary Japanese had of mountains. As Monica Bethe and Karen Brazell describe, "Yamamba is depicted wandering through the hills, communing with nature, and savoring the beauty of the changing seasons; indeed she might be seen as Nature itself" (Bethe and Brazell 1978, 8–9). This nature is perhaps another way of saying what Wakita means by "what a city dweller would consider as the incarnation of a mountain spirit," and what Shirane means by "secondary nature."

YAMANBA HELPING HUMANS

Yamanba counters her dark image by stressing her positive side—for example, she helps humans with carrying wood and weaving. Yamanba recites: "At other times, where weaving girls work looms, she enters the window, a warbler in willows winding threads, or she places herself in spinning sheds to help humans, and yet women whisper—it is an invisible demon they see" (Bethe and Brazell 1998, 223; *SNKBZ* 1994–2002, 59:580). Yamanba laments that she tries to help people (*hito o tasukuru waza o nomi*), but people say they cannot see her because she is an invisible oni, referring to the preface of the *Kokinshū* (*A Collection of Poems Ancient and Modern*), which states that poetry "stirs the feelings of deities and demons invisible to the eye" (Bethe and Brazell 1998, 223n25; *SNKBZ* 1994–2002, 11:17). Although I have been focusing on yamauba's duality primarily in the pattern of yamauba narratives, duality is undoubtedly found more broadly. References to cloth and weaving—the warp and the weft, the *ji* and the *mon* (woven pattern)—connote the duality of nature. Menial tasks such as cutting grass demonstrated in other noh plays reveal the dual nature of existence in that the repetitive nature of life gives orderliness to the cosmos.[27]

The folk belief that yamauba took part in weaving and spinning may have already existed and been reflected in the noh play, or it is equally possible that the yamauba's association with weaving originated in *Yamanba* in order to give a positive impression of yamauba. In either case, I speculate that this image was strengthened through another noh text titled *Kurozuka* (Black mound, mid-fifteenth century).

THE NOH PLAY *KUROZUKA* (*ADACHIGAHARA*): THE CROSSROADS OF YAMAUBA AND ONI-WOMEN

While Yamanba laments her image as an oni, the main character of the noh play entitled *Kurozuka* is a full-fledged oni-woman possessing all the elements of yamauba described above. The play appears with different titles; it is called *Kurozuka* by the Hōshō, Konparu, Kongō, and Kita schools of noh, and is known as *Adachigahara* (Adachi Moor) by the Kanze school. The playwright is not known, but according to Baba Akiko, it could be either Konparu Zenchiku (1405–1470), Zeami's son-in-law, who inherited Zeami's subtle and allusive style, or Zeami himself (Baba Akiko 1988, 258).

Although the term *yamauba* does not appear, I believe *Kurozuka* is a critical text in that it stands at the crux of the yamauba, oni-women, and oni paradigm. The kind and helpful image of yamauba described in

Figure 1.4. The oni-woman in the noh play *Kurozuka* (*Adachigahara*). (Courtesy of Ritsumeikan University Art Research Center, *Nōgaku zu e: Adachigahara*, arcUP0962.)

"Komebuku Awabuku," "Ubakawa," and *Hanayo no hime* is revealed in the woman played by the shite of the first act (mae-shite). The oni-woman performed by the shite in the second act, who chases after the yamabushi, corresponds to the anthropophagous yamauba who runs after her prey in "Kuwazu nyōbō," "Ushikata to yamauba," and "Sanmai no ofuda." *Kurozuka*, reflecting various elements from the noh play *Yamanba*, represents a crossroads wherein the elements and images of yamauba and oni-women are jumbled together and are simultaneously disseminated, influencing various genres.

In the first act, a party of yamabushi asks for a night's lodging at a lone house in Adachigahara.[28] The owner of the house, an oni-woman in the form of an old woman, reluctantly accedes to the group's request. The chief yamabushi, Yūkei, notices a spinning wheel in her hut and asks the old woman to demonstrate how it works. She turns the spinning wheel, then tells the yamabushi group not to look in one room of her house before leaving for the mountain to get firewood. During the interlude, the yamabushi's servant, unable to resist the temptation to look, opens the door and finds piles of corpses inside. The yamabushi realize that they are staying in the oni's house that is rumored to exist in the region. In the second act, as the troupe of yamabushi flee the oni-woman's house, the oni-woman—now with her true appearance—runs after them, only to be chased away by the power of the yamabushi's incantation.

When one talks of Adachigahara, Japanese people immediately think of the legend of the oni-hag of Adachigahara (*Adachigahara no oni-baba*). An aristocratic family in Kyoto has a daughter who, although already five years old, has not uttered a word since she was born. No doctor could cure her strange illness, but one day a fortune-teller tells the family that the fresh liver of the living fetus of a pregnant woman will cure her. The girl's nurse sets off to travel in search of a fresh liver, leaving her own daughter behind with her charm. The nurse travels until she reaches Adachigahara, where she decides to stay in a hut and wait for pregnant travelers to pass by. Many years pass before a pregnant woman finally asks for a night's shelter. The nurse invites her in, stabs her, and retrieves the fetus's liver. While disposing of the dead body, she notices the charm the pregnant woman was wearing—realizing that the woman she has just killed is her own daughter, whom she left behind years ago. The nurse goes insane and becomes an oni-baba, attacking passers-by to eat their flesh.[29]

It is important to clarify that the noh play was created before this famous or infamous legend of the oni-crone of Adachigahara. The starting point of this legend is the noh play and the legend was concocted as an amalgamation of various elements such as Ishimakura setsuwa and Kishimojin worship (Kamata 2002, 26–27).[30] Komatsu Kazuhiko surmises that the legend of the oni-hag of Adachigahara may have referenced such stories as *Shuten Dōji* (*Drunken Demon*) and monster-conquering folktales, but was created after the success of the noh play *Kurozuka* (Komatsu K. 2004, 49–50).[31] Indeed, Baba calls the protagonist of the noh play the prototype of the oni-baba of Adachigahara (Baba Akiko 1988, 260).

KUROZUKA (*ADACHIGAHARA*), ONI, AND WOMEN

The title of the play, *Kurozuka* or *Adachigahara*, is the name of a place in present-day Fukushima Prefecture in northern Japan. The place-name and its association with oni comes from a poem written by Taira no Kanemori (d. 990), one of the so-called Thirty-Six Great Poets and a member of the imperial family who became a subject of the state around 950 (Matsuoka S. 1998, 85).

Michinoku no
Adachi no hara no
Kurozuka ni
Oni komoreri to
Iu wa makoto ka

In Michinoku
On the moors of Adachi
Within the Black Mound
Some demons live in hiding
They say, but can this be true?
          (Shimazaki C. and Comee 2012, 301)

This poem appears in the fifty-eighth tale of the *Yamato monogatari* (*Tales of Yamato*, ca. mid-tenth century).[32] Kanemori sent this poem to the daughters of the son of Prince Sadamoto (d. 910), the third son of Emperor Seiwa. The same poem also appears as number 559 in the *Shūi wakashū* or *Shūishū* (*A Collection of Verbal Blooms in Japanese Verse*, ca. 1005) and, according to that work, the poem was sent to the sisters of Minamoto no Shigeyuki (d. 1000), another great poet and a grandson of Prince Sadamoto.[33] In either case, the young women, the granddaughters of imperial prince Sadamoto, were living in Kurozuka of Adachi Moor in Michinoku province. In the poem, Kanemori playfully refers to the daughters as oni.

An example of describing a woman as an oni also appears in the "Broom Tree" chapter of *Genji monogatari* (*The Tale of Genji*, ca. 1010). When the Aide of Ceremonial (Tō Shikibu no jō) talks about an educated woman with whom he once had a love affair, the Secretary Captain (Tō no Chūjō) comments, "There cannot be such a woman! You might as well have made friends with a demon [oni]. It is too weird!" (Murasaki 2001, 34; *SNKBZ* 1994–2002, 20:88). Baba Akiko points out the maxim expressed in the story "Mushi mezuru himegimi" ("The Lady Who Admired Vermin"), which appears in *Tsutsumi chūnagon monogatari* (*The Riverside Counselor's Stories*, ca. mid-eleventh to early twelfth century): "Devils [oni] and women are better invisible to the eyes of mankind" (Backus 1985, 55; *SNKBZ* 1994–2002, 17:409). In the ancient period, oni were thought to be invisible. Baba writes that Taira no Kanemori addressed Minamoto no Shigeyuki's sisters as oni with affection, consoling those—like Kanemori himself—who should not be hidden or buried by society's rules (Baba Akiko 1988, 27). Here there is no suggestion of anthropophagy being attached to the ladies.

For almost 500 years, between the time this poem was composed and the appearance of *Kurozuka*, no legends of oni-women in Adachigahara existed in literature (Matsuoka S. 1998, 83). Rendering a woman as a real oni in *Kurozuka* was an ingenious use of what was originally a love poem.

Two Sides of the Oni-Woman

In the first act of *Kurozuka*, the old woman sits in her isolated house minding her own business, like a helping yamauba. This house, however, is undoubtedly an oni's house: one room is filled with corpses. Then the members of the yamabushi party, who are considered good characters, like the young heroines of "Komebuku Awabuku," "Ubakawa," and *Hanayo no hime*, unexpectedly visit her dwelling and asks for a night's shelter. The woman is reluctant but lets them in—just like the helping yamauba. Although she doesn't give a material treasure to the yamabushi troupe to help in their plight, the woman is obliging enough to entertain her guests with her spinning wheel and does try to give some comfort by fetching firewood to warm them on a cold night. The yamabushi's servant repeatedly calls her a kind woman. The acts of carrying wood and spinning have a connection with Yamanba in the noh play, who sings, "Sometimes when a woodsman rests beside a mountain path beneath the blossoms, she shoulders his heavy burden and, with the moon, comes out the mountain, going with him to the village below" (Bethe and Brazell 1998, 222; *SNKBZ* 1994–2002, 59:579). Yamanba's efforts to help the villagers—woodsmen and weavers—thus seem to be reflected in the acts of the woman in *Kurozuka*.

As the woman leaves for the mountain—the yamauba's trope—she tells the yamabushi group not to look in one room—the "taboo of looking"—and they promise that they will not. As so often happens in the folkloric taboo motif, however, this promise is broken. This is similar to "Kuwazu nyōbō," in which the woman's husband discovers the secret of the unsightly gargantuan mouth on the back of her head, and to "Sanmai no ofuda," in which the novice clandestinely looks in the room to witness his aunt revealing her terrifying yamauba appearance. The yamabushi's servant cannot resist the temptation to look, and there he finds human bones and skulls, rotten corpses bloated and streaming with pus and blood. The group of yamabushi immediately leaves the oni's den.

In the second act, realizing the traveling monks have broken their promise and seen the unsightly corpses, the woman, now an oni-woman (the protagonist of the second act wears a *hannya* [in Sanskrit *prajna*; wisdom] or *shikami* [scowling] mask), chases fiercely after them, like the yamauba in "Kuwazu nyōbō," "Ushikata to yamauba," and "Sanmai no ofuda." The hannya mask, with two sharp horns and a large mouth, represents a jealous female demon; the shikami mask, with a snarling mouth but no horns, represents an evil (masculine) demon to be defeated. With a hannya or shikami mask, the oni-woman reveals her true form; it shows her transformation or shape-shifting ability, as she changes from an ordinary-looking woman to an oni. Unlike Yomotsu-shikome, who is dispatched by Izanami on her behalf, this oni-woman is an independent agent acting on her own. The chase of the oni-woman of *Kurozuka*, however, ends in her defeat—just like the cannibalistic yamauba of mukashibanashi. Defeated by the Buddhists' prayers, she disappears. The oni-woman of *Kurozuka* is a prototype of the cannibalistic, chasing yamauba.

There are three main noh plays in which the shite wears a hannya mask: *Aoi no ue* (Lady Aoi), *Dōjōji* (Dōjōji temple), and *Kurozuka*, which are called the three oni-woman plays. A hannya mask expresses a woman's resentment and fierce obsession (The-Noh.com, n.d.). Although it has an angry expression, with two sharp horns, a wide mouth open from ear to ear, and glaring gilt eyes, "we see a trace of heart-breaking sadness hover over it, especially when the wearer hangs its head a little" (Shimazaki C. and Comee 2012, 302; see also Takemoto 2000, 5). Extraordinary anger, grudges, and jealousy were believed to transform women into oni. Michelle Osterfeld Li writes: "The shift toward oni who evoke sympathy occurs mainly in the medieval period (circa 1185–1600), when their potential for spiritual growth is considered. Even as they remain dangerous monsters, the reasons why they became oni and their potential for change start to matter" (Li 2012, 173).[34] The shite in *Aoi no ue* and *Dōjōji* are human in the beginning and turn into oni-women because of strong feelings of jealousy and resentment, but the woman in *Kurozuka* is an oni from the beginning—an oni in human form (Oda 1986, 81; Shimazaki C. and Comee 2012, 302). The fact that *Kurozuka*'s nochi-shite wears a hannya mask is, however, understandable when one considers the human, sympathetic aspect of the woman in the first act.[35]

YAMANBA IN *KUROZUKA*

The shadow of the noh play *Yamanba* can be seen throughout *Kurozuka*. The first instance is an allusion to the sixth episode of the *Tales of Ise*, used for its image of a cannibalistic oni. In the play *Yamanba*, Hyakuma fears she will be eaten by Yamanba like the lady in the sixth episode of *Tales of Ise*. In *Kurozuka*, as the nochi-shite oni-woman chases after the yamabushi group, she describes her own actions by citing a famous passage from the *Tales of Ise* in which an oni eats a lady in one gulp:

Narukami inazuma tenchi ni michite
Sora kaki kumoru ame no yo no
Oni hitokuchi ni kuwan tote
    (*SNKBZ* 1994–2002, 59:471)

Thunder and lightning fill both heaven and earth
The sky is overcast, black as a rainy night,
The fiend comes to swallow the victims in one gulp
    (Shimazaki C. and Comee 2012, 329–30)

The woman accumulates human remains in a bedroom but no explanation is given as to why. But from this association with the oni in the *Tales of Ise*, and because oni are generally known to eat humans, perhaps she planned to eat the yamabushi. Considering the fact that Hyakuma entertains Yamanba with her song in the second act of *Yamanba*, and that the oni-woman in the first act of *Kurozuka* entertains the yamabushi, one may say that the oni-woman of *Kurozuka* acts like a mirror image of Hyakuma.

A second connection between *Kurozuka* and *Yamanba* is that both the oni-woman in *Kurozuka* and Hyakuma in *Yamanba* express a strong sense of shame in relation to oni. In *Yamanba*, Hyakuma feels that it would be shameful for her to be known as a woman who has been eaten by an oni. She sings:

Ukiyogatari mo hazukashi ya
    (*SNKBZ* 1994–2002, 59:576–77)

To become the subject of a woeful tale told throughout the world—how shameful!
    (Bethe and Brazell 1998, 219)

The oni-woman in *Kurozuka* feels intense shame that her secret, her true life and demonic appearance, have been exposed to the yamabushi:

Kurozuka ni kakure sumishi mo
Asama ni narinu
asamashi ya
Hazukashi no waga sugata ya
    (*SNKBZ* 1994–2002, 59:473)

Her abode, the Black Mound, the secret hiding place,
has now been exposed.
"Oh, how disgraceful!
Odious even to myself [literally, shameful]
is the sight of me!"
    (Shimazaki C. and Comee 2012, 334)

Baba Akiko asserts that the woman of *Kurozuka* becomes an oni because the womanly feeling of shame suddenly overcomes her when her bedroom replete with pus and blood is exposed; "By this cruel final betrayal [the yamabushi breaking their promise], by the yamabushi's discovery of the most secret place where she had hidden the hoard of sacrificial offerings to her passions, she was driven by the extreme sense of shame and turned into an oni" (Baba Akiko 1988, 258–59; 264). Kawai Hayao agrees with Baba entirely: "The nō play *Kurozuka* expresses in its extreme the sense of shame induced by a broken 'not to see' taboo . . . The woman was trying to kill the man with full force of her rancor, but the emphasis nevertheless is upon her feeling of shame" (Kawai 1996, 23). Further, he notes that in *Kurozuka*, a drama for an aristocratic audience, that sense of rancor is made to vanish by the power of Buddhist prayer (Kawai 1996, 24–25).

In regard to shame, Baba Akiko has an insightful statement: "There is a word *funshi*, dying from indignation. But rather than dying from a fit of anger, wouldn't a person die from an internal struggle of *chijoku*, shame and disgrace, that simmer in the shadow of anger?" (Baba Akiko 1988, 197). Baba's comment refers to the Rokujō Haven's emotional state toward Aoi, Genji's formal wife, in *The Tale of Genji*. I believe that shame and disgrace are shared by Hyakuma and the woman in *Kurozuka*. Hyakuma dreads the fact that she will die soon, but her fear is compounded by the infinite shame and disgrace that would be hers if it became publicly known that she was eaten by an oni. When her appearance and activities are exposed, the woman in *Kurozuka* feels undying shame and disgrace—and, I would add, intense resentment. I consider resentment or indignation (*ikidōri*) as important as—perhaps more important than—shame in transforming someone into an oni. After all, that is what made her chase the yamabushi troupe. I do agree with Kawai that foregrounding resentment—a wild, violent expression of oni—would go against aristocratic, elegant sensitivity. I believe in the case of the oni in *Kurozuka* that a sense of shame, a human feeling, came back to her as a result of the yamabushi's earnest prayers. Shame, disgrace, and resentment were probably the reasons that Izanami dispatched Yomotsu-shikome to kill Izanagi, and yamauba who did not have to worry about the feelings of an aristocratic audience and who originated with the chasing woman of *Kurozuka* flung off their sense of shame and kept running after their victims.

I would like to consider the "taboo of looking" for a moment. Kitayama Osamu, clinical psychologist, argues that in the tales with a "not to look" motif, what is exposed as a result of broken promises are physiological human behaviors such as childbirth, breastfeeding, defecation, and urination. The exposure leads to a decisive feeling of separation between the one who sees and the one who is seen (Kitayama 1993, 8–9, 68). The one who sees the secret, according to Kitayama, feels a physiological disgust/repulsion, a concept put forth by Ozawa Toshio, scholar of German literature. Ozawa has compared various folktales concerning marriage between different species in many countries, and asserts that in the "not to look" taboo, there is a strong rejection—intuitive disgust/repulsion—by humans of animal spouses, and that the taboo was created to prevent such rejection (Ozawa T. 1979, 28, 126–27, 129). Fundamentally, Kitayama argues that a sense of shame is strongly related to the expectation gap between those who see and those who are seen—to put it simply, in the story of Izanagi and Izanami, that shame was caused by the enormous gap in the expectations of the two (Kitayama 1993, 61–62).

In an argument similar to Kawai's, Kitayama remarks that when the emphasis is on the viewpoint of someone who is exposed rather than on the trespasser's rejecting attitude, a feeling of shame results. Indeed, Kitayama notes that many stories of the "not to see" taboo end with the departure of someone who was seen, and that the Izanagi/Izanami myth is unusual in that Izanami exhibits anger toward Izanagi when she breaks the promise (Kitayama 1993, 62).[36] While Kitayama connects "being seen" to female figures, male figures also break the taboo. An example is the legend of Mt. Miwa; in *Nihon shoki*, Ōmononushi no kami appears as a beautiful little snake at the request of his wife Yamatotohi momosobime no mikoto. He agreed to reveal his real appearance to her on the condition that she would not be alarmed. But because she shrieked with astonishment, he left her (*SNKBZ* 1994–2002, 2:283). Having said that, female figures of this type are more frequent in Japanese myths, legends, fairy tales, and literary works. It should be noted, however, that although many female figures are the ones being seen, they are also the ones who order others not to look.[37]

It is of interest to compare the actions of Toyotama-bime, grandmother of the first Emperor Jinmu, and Izanami. In Japanese myth, Toyotama-bime goes to the shore to give birth to her child. She asks her husband, Hoori no mikoto, not to watch her during her delivery but, breaking the taboo, he secretly looks—and discovers her to be a giant crocodile (*SNKBZ* 1994–2002, 1:135–37; Philippi 1969, 156–58). After breaking the promise not to look, both husbands, Izanagi and Hoori no mikoto, act the same way toward their wives: astonished and disgusted, they run away (*SNKBZ* 1994–2002, 1:47, 135). The wives' reactions, however, are different. Izanami attacks her husband; Toyotama-bime retreats without vengeance, even sending her younger sister to become her newborn baby's foster mother. What makes their behavior so different?

I speculate that it has something to do with verbalization of their emotion or the direction of emotional ventilation. Toyotama-bime says, "I am exceedingly shamed" (*SNKBZ* 1994–2002, 1:136). She feels ashamed of how she looks, blaming her own appearance; her emotion goes inward—that is, she internalizes her feelings. Toyotama-bime shuts herself off—and indeed, she shuts the passage between the ocean and the land as well. Izanami, on the other hand, expresses, "*You* have shamed me," blaming her husband above all. She verbalizes her emotion of fury and attacks her husband. Her emotional rage flows outward. In other words, in contrast to Toyotama-bime's "*I* am shamed," Izanami vents her emotions onto someone else: "*You* have shamed me." The woman in *Kurozuka* chases off the yamabushi by saying, "My bedchamber which I so jealously concealed, / *You* exposed, stealing a look inside. / I have come to *vent my rage upon you*" (Shimazaki C. and Comee 2012, 328; *SNKBZ* 1994–2002, 59:470–71; my emphasis). The woman's emotional steam is venting outside—toward her opponent, the promise breaker—so she attacks. But while she is fighting against the priests, her power wanes, probably because of their prayers. She then feels ashamed and disappears. Ōmononushi no kami, who appeared as a little snake, left Yamatotohi momosobime no mikoto, saying that *she* had caused him shame. He even added that he would similarly shame her in return (*SNKBZ* 1994–2002, 2:283–85; Aston 1956, 158–59). So Yamatotohi momosobime no mikoto "flopped down on a seat and with a chopstick stabbed herself in the pudenda so that she died" (Aston 1956, 159).

A large number of female characters simply retreat or disappear. Kawai Hayao argues, "It is a Japanese cultural paradigm that a woman must disappear when a man looks into a forbidden chamber in order for sorrow [the feeling of *aware*] to complete the sense of beauty" (Kawai 1996, 22). It is therefore possible to interpret behaviors such as quiet retreat or disappearance as socially encouraged. In other words, just like an evil yamauba, a female who verbally expresses her rage and fury is not welcome in the general public. But perhaps it is precisely because yamauba goes against societal expectations and keeps coming back that she is so appealing.

Let us go back to the connections between *Kurozuka* and *Yamamba*. The third connection is the yamanba's weaving and the image of her turning a spinning wheel. While Yamanba of the noh play sings that she winds thread and places herself in spinning sheds, no prop for weaving appears on the stage. A spinning wheel becomes a major prop in *Kurozuka*—one of only two on the bare noh stage—and the spinning wheel becomes the protagonist's own tool. At the request of the chief yamabushi, the woman or mae-shite of *Kurozuka* starts to turn the spinning wheel. She spins the string with

Figure 1.5. The woman spinning in the noh play *Kurozuka* (*Adachigahara*). (Courtesy of Ritsumeikan University Art Research Center, *Kurozuka*, arcUP1513.)

a song of longing for the past called the *Ito no dan* (string section). Komatsu Kazuhiko states: "An element of spinning is often found in the yamanba narratives that start to appear during the medieval period. I cannot help thinking that the image of 'a yamanba turning a spinning wheel' is projected on the oni of *Adachigahara*" (Komatsu K. 2004, 50–51). I believe this is not only projected on the oni-woman but also is strengthened through this very oni-woman. I speculate that *Kurozuka* helped disseminate the visual image of yamauba's association with strings—or at least with her spinning wheel.

CONCLUDING REMARKS

In this chapter I have studied one of the major characteristics of yamauba, her duality, through some representative mukashibanashi, otogizōshi, and noh texts, and touched upon another major characteristic, the power of transformation. Although the malevolent yamauba and the benevolent yamauba look incompatible with each other, they are two sides of the same coin, and these stories possess a complementary narrative format.

In mukashibanashi, the term *yamauba* is interchangeable with the term *oni-woman* when her evil and cannibalistic side is highlighted, especially when both cannibalism and mountains appear as major factors in one story. The character tends to be called oni-woman rather than yamauba when she feels strongly ashamed of her appearance or actions, and her emotional intensity is the predominant feeling of the story. While this cannibalistic, evil yamauba is destined to be defeated by a socially approved personage, be it a priest, husband, or another man, she may have her ancient roots in Yomotsu-shikome, and her strong image as a frightening yet pathetic figure seems to owe much to the woman in *Kurozuka*. When the yamauba's positive side—helping, giving good fortune and fertility—is accentuated, only the term *yamauba* is used. In spite of her terrifying appearance (a demoness in form), the character Yamanba as portrayed by Zeami is a self-reflective, nature-loving creature. Like the yamauba in *Hanayo no hime* or any yamauba in mukashibanashi, Yamanba's life is sustained in the mountains. Mountains and her association with nature are what make the yamauba distinct from oni-women. After all, the topos of yamauba is the mountains. The various usage of the words *yamauba*, *oni-woman*, and *oni* probably originates in yamauba's roots in oni, but the interchangeability of yamauba and oni-woman in the proactive behavior of yamauba indicates the influence of patriarchy, by which men tried to confine women to the private sector. The major characteristics of a yamauba are that she lives in the mountains, brings death and destruction as well as wealth and fertility, possesses the duality of good and evil, and has the power of transformation, able to manifest herself as an ugly crone or a young beauty.

By the seventeenth century, the distinction between yamauba and oni-women was already quite blurry in performing arts texts even for a benevolent yamauba. The yamauba who appears in *Kinpira nyūdō yamameguri* (Lay priest Kinpira's travel through the mountains, early 1680s), the grandmother of a fictional super-child, Kinpira, is an oni-woman. She is ten feet tall with white hair, and she has miraculous powers. While the character's diction is heavily influenced by the noh play *Yamanba*, this yamauba identifies herself as an oni-woman without a moment of hesitation. Some yamauba also have horns. In Chikamatsu Monzaemon's (1653–1725) *jōruri* and kabuki play *Komochi yamanba* (A yamanba with child, 1712), Chikamatsu freely used diction from the noh plays *Yamanba* and *Kurozuka*. In *Komochi yamanba*, when the famous warrior Minamoto no Raikō (or Yorimitsu, 948–1021) confronts the yamanba (a former courtesan named Yaegiri) with his sword, crescent-shaped horns pop up out of her scalp and her eyes sparkle. These stories all reveal the strong and deep relationship between yamauba and oni or oni-women.

2

Mother Yamauba and Weaving
Childbirth and Bloodsucking, Spinning and Spiders

FROM THE EARLIEST APPEARANCE OF THE TERM *YAMAUBA* in writing, yamauba has been associated with childbirth and fertility, revealing an aspect of yamauba as a goddess of the mountains. As mentioned in the introduction, the entry on the sixth month of 1460 of *Gaun nikkenroku*, a diary of Zen priest Zuikei Shūhō (1391–1473), states that a yamauba gave birth to four children. "The reason why the summer of that year had lots of rain was because the yamauba gave birth to four children, namely, Haruyoshi (Good spring), Natsusame (Summer rain), Akiyoshi (Good autumn), and Fuyusame (Winter rain)" (Tokyo Daigaku Shiryō Hensanjo 1961, 125). The year's abundant rainfall, the priest suggests, was the result of the yamauba's fertility. A folktale titled "Yamauba hōon" ("Yamauba's Gratitude") from Ōita Prefecture recounts a similar tale; the yamauba comes to a married couple in a village and asks for shelter while giving birth, which the sympathetic couple gives her. After the safe birth of her baby, the yamauba asks the couple to name the baby as well as her other children. The couple feels honored, and names the first child Natsuyoshikō (Good Summer), the second Akiyoshikō (Good Autumn), and the third Fuyuyoshikō (Good Winter). The yamauba rewards the couple with two boxes—one that magically produces abundant gold and one filled with yarn (Miyazaki K. 1969, 428–30). The children's names seem to reflect an expression of reverence to a higher power and hope for good seasonal weather to come.

In Matsutani Miyoko's *Yamanba no nishiki* (*The Witch's Magic Cloth*, 1967), a retelling of a folktale from Akita Prefecture, an old woman helps a yamauba on Mt. Chōfuku give birth to a healthy, strong child who can run as soon as he is born. Appreciating the help, the yamauba gives the old woman a roll of gold brocade that lasts forever, and promises to keep the villagers healthy because they made her rice cakes. This yamauba is described

DOI: 10.7330/9781646420551.c002

as the deity of Mt. Chōfuku. As examples of yamauba giving out end-less yarn or a magical roll of brocade reveal, yamauba are often associated with strings, spinning, and weaving. The yamauba helps humans with spin-ning and weaving in the early fifteenth-century noh text *Yamanba*. Yamaoka Genrin explains that yamauba "is associated with weaving and spinning as recited in *kusemai*" (Yamaoka 1993, 46).[1] Yamauba's association with weav-ing and spinning was already established by the beginning of the early mod-ern period (1600–1867).

A mother yamauba, however, still carries the image of the dark side of her duality. Miyata Noboru speculates that female yōkai such as yamauba, *iso onna* (seashore women), and *ubume* (literally, birthing women) suck human blood in their attempt to compensate for the loss of their own blood dur-ing childbirth (Miyata 2000, 192). As far as a yamauba sucking blood is concerned, I speculate it is again related to the actions of oni. This chapter studies the mother yamauba with spinning and weaving skills, also consid-ering her relationship with spiders. As we have seen in chapter 1, in many "Kuwazu nyōbō" ("The Wife Who Does Not Eat") stories, the wife who does not eat turns into a spider. Spiders are known for their threads and for weaving webs. I conjecture that the wife's identity as a spider comes from the similar traits yamauba and spiders share.

YAMAUBA WORSHIP

"In the popular belief of rural areas, the mountain deity is believed to be a goddess who gives birth to twelve children every year," Hori Ichirō writes. "She is therefore called Mrs. Twelve (*Jūni-sama*), and her twelve children symbolize the twelve months of the year" (Hori I. 1968, 167). There are many legends and sites that tell of yamauba giving birth to children and raising them (see Yanagita 1978–1979, 1:239–55; Yoshida 1992, 29–55). Among them, Yanagita Kunio's account of the yamauba on Mt. Akiha is particularly interesting.

According to Yanagita, on Mt. Kuraki in the Okuyama district of Tōtōmi (present-day Shizuoka Prefecture), there is a boulder called Koumitawa (lit-erally, giving-birth-ridge or giving-birth-boulder) on the peak behind the Myōkōji temple. During the Tentoku era (957–961) a yamauba is said to have lived on the mountain and raised her three children: the eldest son was Ryūchikubō, the master of Ryūzumine; the second son was Shirahige Dōji, the master of a mountain in Kaminosawa; and the youngest was Jōkōbō, the master of Yamazumi inner sanctuary. She is worshipped in various places (Yanagita 1978–1979, 1:248–249). Yanagita adds that, according to *Tōtōmi no kuni fudokiden* (Reports on records of culture and geography of Tōtōmi province, 1789), the ancestors of the Hiraga and the Yabe were sent by official command to subjugate the yamauba, but one can conjecture from Akiha Yamazumi's early modern history that they were reconciled later and their descendants served the same deity (Yanagita 1978–1979, 1:248–49). Why, one wonders, did the mother of three deities, who is worshipped in various places, become the target of subjugation? *Tōtōmi no kuni fudokiden*, written by Uchiyama Matatsu (1740–1821), offers an answer: the yamauba did something harmful to the villagers.

MOTHER OF DIVINE CHILDREN AND ANTHROPOPHAGY

The account in *Tōtōmi no kuni fudokiden* goes as follows: an old man said a yamauba lived on Mt. Kuraki during the Tentoku era. She helped the villagers by spinning textiles (this sounds like the protagonist of the noh play *Yamanba*). After a while she bore three male children. The place of her childbearing is called Koumitawa, located above the area of Myōkōji temple. The names of the three children, Ryūchikubō, Shirahige Dōji, and Jōkōbō, are exactly the same as in Yanagita's account. Some time after giving birth, the yamauba harmed villagers. Hiraga Nakatsukasa and Yabe Gotō Saemon received an official order to subjugate the yamauba, who escaped to Mt. Akiha. Now people say the yamauba lives in Mt. Asama. Every year on the equinoctial day people worship the yamauba. The yamauba's site remains on Mt. Akiha (Uchiyama 1969, 400).

The account says "the yamauba harmed villagers" but does not define the harm she caused. However, two other texts, *Shizuoka-ken Iwatagun-shi* (Records of Iwata district of Shizuoka Prefecture, 1921) and *Shizuoka-ken densetsu mukashibanashishū* (Legends and mukashibanashi of Shizuoka Prefecture, 1934), state the yamauba ate children.

Shizuoka-ken Iwatagun-shi goes on to provide additional information about the yamauba, claiming that 960-plus years ago, a yamauba lived on Mt. Kuraki. She was skilled at weaving cloth out of wisteria. She used to come down to Fukusawa, Izumi, and Ochii to use the looms there to weave cloth. Perhaps because a yamauba helped women during childbirth, there is a small wayside shrine called Midwife in Ochii. In Fukuzawa there was a family called Hiyūga. The yamauba used to go there to babysit and housesit while spinning wisteria yarn. One day she ate a child of the house. The family avenged the child by giving the Yamauba burning hot stones mixed with real dumplings. When the yamauba asked for water to cool her down, the family gave her oil instead to make her condition worse. She ran to Ochii and

Kamagawa River and died. According to a variant of *Shizuoka-ken Iwatagun-shi*, the villagers were going to avenge the child but the yamauba ran away to Mt. Kuraki. The villagers could not capture her because the place was pitch dark. That is why the mountain was named Mt. Kuraki—Dark Mountain. The villagers petitioned their lord to subjugate the yamauba so he sent Hiraga Nakatsukasa and Yabe Gotō Saemon. The samurai and villagers chased the yamauba without success. Eventually the yamauba escaped to Shūyōji temple (Shūyō is the sino-reading of Akiha). According to a legend, the yamauba had three children; one was Hakuhatsu Dōji, enshrined in Mt. Toguchi, another was Ryūchikubo, enshrined in Ekōin, and the other was called Jōkō deity, enshrined in Jōkōji temple (Iwatagun Kyōikukai 1971, 1025–27). Regarding the date of the yamauba's residency in Mt. Kuraki, it was "about 960 plus years ago from now." If one speculates the year of "now" to be around 1919, giving a leeway of two years from *Shizuoka-ken Iwatagun-shi*'s first publication date of 1921, the yamauba was supposed to have lived in Mt. Kuraki around the late 950s, which corresponds to the Tentoku era, as Uchiyama and Yanagita wrote.

The *Shizuoka-ken densetsu mukashibanashishū* version is very similar to the story of *Shizuoka-ken Iwatagun-shi*, though it says that the yamauba ran to Tenryū River instead of Kamagawa River, and that she escaped from Mt. Kuraki to Mt. Akiha, rather than to Shūyōji temple (Shizuoka-ken Joshi Shihan Gakkō Kyōdo Kenkyūkai 1934, 3–4). Also, there is no mention of yamauba's divine children in *Shizuoka-ken densetsu mukashibanashishū*, but she is worshipped for her midwifery skill.[2] The story may be considered a variant of "Yamauba to ishimochi" ("Yamauba and Stone Rice Cakes"), which we saw in the introduction. Yamanba's actions in the noh *Yamanba*—weaving as well as making the sky dark—seem to be projected onto these yamauba stories. Further, the expedition to subjugate the yamauba who escaped to a mountain reminds one of Shuten Dōji stories. Shuten Dōji (Drunken Demon) is an oni chieftain who lives on Mt. Ōe, eats human flesh, and drinks blood. He was expelled from his original abode on a mountain and eventually escaped to Mt. Ōe, where he made his residence. The imperial court commands the two generals, Minamoto no Raikō (948–1021) and Fujiwara no Hōshō (958–1036), to destroy Shuten Dōji and his evil oni band. With the help of divinities and Raikō's four lieutenants, called *shitennō* (four guardian kings)—Watanabe no Tsuna (953–1025), Sakata no Kintoki (d. 1017), Taira no Sadamichi (also known as Usui no Sadamitsu, ca. 954–ca. 1021), and Taira no Suetake (also known as Urabe no Suetake, ca. 950–ca. 1022)—Raikō and Hōshō eliminate Shuten Dōji and his cohorts.[3] The oldest extant Shuten Dōji text, titled *Ōeyama ekotoba* (*Illustrations and*

Writing of Mt. Ōe), was created in the fourteenth century and, as will be described in detail in chapter 4, the stories of Shuten Dōji were widely established by the fifteenth century. Similar to Shuten Dōji, the yamauba lives on a mountain and eats children; she escapes to Mt. Akiha as she cannot stay in her original place; and the government issues an order to subjugate her. One gets the sense that these yamauba legends and tales were created and re-created by combining several existing tales. In any case, even though the yamauba is worshipped, anthropophagy seems to follow her, and the locus of the yamauba legend above points to Mt. Akiha.

Legends of Yamauba on Mt. Akiha

Akiha worship, which became enormously popular during the Edo period (1600–1867) for protection against fire, started with the enshrinement of a Shugendō practitioner from Shinano province (present-day Nagano Prefecture) as Akiha DaiGongen (Great Akiha deity) after his death; he was trained on Mt. Togakushi and resided in a monk's dwelling called Sanjakubō in Echigo province (present-day Niigata Prefecture). Tamura Sadao, who has examined numerous documents on Akiha shrines and temples, notes that the study of Shugendō is most important for Akiha worship (Tamura 2014, 22). According to the homepage of the Akihasan Hongū Akiha Jinja (Akiha main shrine at Mt. Akiha), the present-day shrine was called Akiha DaiGongen before the Meiji period (1868–1912) and is revered all over Japan as the head shrine of all Akiha shrines.[4] Akiha DaiGongen, first established in 709, had been a site of worship for both Shinto and Buddhism because of their syncretism before the Meiji period, but the government's policy of separation of Buddhism and Shinto as well as the anti-Buddhist movement at the beginning of the Meiji period forced Akiha DaiGongen to become either Shintoist or Buddhist. Akiha Shrine (Akiha jinja) on top of Mt. Akiha was created in the process (Tamura 2014, 19, 354), and now there are several Akiha shrines and temples on and around Mt. Akiha.

Tamura Sadao writes that the name "Akiha" appears for the first time in 1569, in a historical document in northern Tōtōmi, but that this document is unreliable; it may have been embellished at a later date. The literature that claims Akiha Shrine was established during the Nara period (710–794) or the Kamakura period (1185–1333) is all fabrication (Tamura 2014, 8, 113). The legend of the yamauba's arrival during the Tentoku era (957–961) and of her having three children was perhaps also retrospectively created in the late medieval or early modern period to attract more tourists and pilgrims to Mt. Akiha.

Figure 2.1. Yamauba Shrine on Mt. Akiha. (Photo by author.)

Yanagita writes that the majority of the small shrines and temples found in various villages and by the wayside, where the populace have worshipped for many years, were established in the middle of the samurai period (1185–1868) probably by itinerant *miko* (shrine priestesses, shamans) and *hijiri* (wandering monks) (Yanagita 2015, 286). As I wrote in the introduction, traveling religious practitioners such as yamabushi, hijiri, and itinerant miko, including Kumano *bikuni*, greatly helped to create and spread many of the yamauba legends during the late medieval and early modern periods.

The yamauba on Mt. Akiha also reveals the strong association of yamauba with weaving. Akihasan Hongū Akiha Jinja has a small wayside shrine called Yamauba Shrine in its compound. According to "Enshū Akihayama honji Shōkanzeon Sanjakubō Daigongen ryaku engi" (Abbreviated history of Sanjakubō Deity, manifestation of Kannon Bodhisattva, of Mt. Akiha of Tōtōmi province, 1717), there was no water on Mt. Akiha in ancient times so the chief monk of the Akiha temple prayed hard to the bodhisattvas and deities for water. They responded by creating a torrent of water in which swam a toad with the characters for Akiha written on his back— Akiha temple is named after this toad. During the Kan'ei era (1624–1645), a yamauba came to the well and wove on her loom. Hence it is called Hataori-i, a weaving well (Takei 1983, 424–25). While "Enshū Akihayama honji Shōkanzeon Sanjakubō Daigongen ryaku engi" states that the yamauba offered the cloth to the chief temple priest, according to the Akiha main shrine's legend, the yamauba offered the cloth to the Akiha deity of Akiha shrine, and since then the Akiha shrine has held the dedicatory ceremony of cloth to the Akiha deity according to the ancient style (Yamamoto 2003, 32). Although their details differ, both legends propose that the yamauba offered the cloth she wove on a loom at the well to a higher being, revealing the yamauba's strong association with weaving.

Orikuchi Shinobu believes the yamauba was originally a maiden who waited on a mountain deity, speculating that because these maidens tended to live long, people started to think of uba as old women (Orikuchi 1995, 363). It could well be that a virgin chosen for a deity became old, and stories concerning an (old) virgin were meshed with a medieval belief in yamauba's weaving, resulting in the yamauba legends on Mt. Akiha. Needless to say, weaving has been important for women since ancient times. In *Nihon shoki*, Sun Goddess Amaterasu was "engaged in weaving the garments of the Gods" (Aston 1956, 41).[5]

Mitani Eiichi (1911–2007), a scholar of Japanese literature, writes that tales of a deity visiting a village are deeply rooted in the folklore of Japan. People of olden days truly believed that a deity visited from faraway or beyond the horizon, and a virgin chosen by the villagers would weave cloth on a loom to adorn the deity. The image of a maiden welcoming a deity is, Mitani continues, detected in the legends called "Hataori gozen" ("Weaver on a Loom") and "Daishi ido" ("Kūkai's Well") (Mitani 1952, 472–73).[6] The legend of Hataori-i on Mt. Akiha seems to carry vestiges of "Hataori gozen" in that a weaver offers the cloth she has woven to a deity, and of "Daishi ido" in that water is miraculously made to gush out by divine power.

Yanagita Kunio notes that a "yamauba was originally a water deity who wove on a loom on the water's bed. But few people know this now" (Yanagita 1970a, 187). Yanagita does not elaborate, but I presume from Yanagita's degradation theory mentioned in the introduction that what he meant is that the yamauba used to be a mountain deity who was identified as a water deity, but the yamauba fell from grace—that is, from deity status. For farming folk who live in the flatlands, a mountain deity is a water deity and at the same time, a deity of the paddies. A famous hypothesis in Japanese folklore studies is that the mountain deity alternates living in the mountains and in paddies—in spring the mountain deity comes down to the paddy fields and becomes the deity of paddies. After the harvest, the deity returns to his or her permanent abode in the mountains, becoming again the mountain deity. This mountain deity is simultaneously a water deity because the deity comes down with water to moisten and enrich the fields (Gorai 2000, 67–68). While the yamauba's origins are rooted in oni, as a mysterious female residing in the mountains, giving birth to divine children, and associated with weaving, she is simultaneously considered divine—a mountain goddess. This duality encompassing both the negative and the positive—inspiring fear and awe—makes the kaleidoscopic entity of yamauba a fascinating creature.

YAMAUBA MONOGATARI: YAMAUBA LEGENDS ON MT. HONGŪ

There is a humble yamauba shrine near the inner sanctuary of Ōagata Shrine in Mt. Hongū in Ninomiya (present-day Inuyama City in Aichi Prefecture). The yamauba legends of Mt. Hongū, also known collectively as *Yamauba monogatari* (Tales of yamauba), are in a nutshell the tale of Fukutomi Shinzō shooting a yamauba who has a child. According to *Owari-shi* (History of Owari [present-day Aichi Prefecture]), written by Fukada Masatsugu (1773–1850), archive commissioner of Owari province, around the time of Bunmei (1469–1486), on a moonlit night a samurai named Fukutomi Shinzō went hunting on Mt. Hongū upstream on the Haguro River. Near a Hongū shrine, a thirty-foot-tall yamauba was combing her long black hair. Shinzō, thinking she must be the yamauba who was said to live on this mountain, shot her. She ran away, and as he tracked her blood trail he reached his friend Koike Yohachirō's house. When Shinzō asked about Yohachirō's wife, Yohachirō found her bed empty and her whereabouts unknown—but there were two poems written in blood left for him and her son. Their son, when he grew up, built a temple for his mother (Fukada 1999, 23–24). Taki Kiyoshi considers this record to be the prototype of various versions of *Yamauba monogatari* around the region (Taki 1986, 85–87).

In *Yamauba monogatari*, the way the yamauba-wife disappears, leaving her husband and son behind, has a remarkable resemblance to *Shinodazuma* (Wife of Shinoda Wood, also known as *Kuzunoha*), a fox wife legend. The *Shinodazuma* legend recounts that a fox in Shinoda Woods is saved by Abe no Yasuna, a fabled (fictional) character. The appreciative fox disguises herself as a beautiful woman named Kuzunoha, becomes Yasuna's wife, and bears a son. Accidentally revealing her true form one day, she disappears from home, leaving a poem that tells her family who she really is and where she lives. The son is said to be the famous Onmyōdō practitioner, Abe no Seimei (ca. 921–1005). Fox wife legends are seen as far back as in the *Nihon ryōiki* (*Miraculous Stories from the Japanese Buddhist Tradition*, ca. 822; see *SNKBZ* 1994–2002, 10:26–28; Nakamura Kyoko 1997, 104–5) of the early ninth century, although in *Nihon ryōiki*, no specific name is given to the man or the place where he met his wife.[7] The *Shinodazuma* legend has been popular since the early Edo period and been used for theater and fiction. The belief that Abe no Seimei is the son of a fox mother and that the mother leaves the family with a poem is incorporated in the puppet/kabuki play *Ashiya Dōman ōuchi kagami* (A Courtly Mirror of Ashiya Dōman, 1734), also known as *Kuzunoha* (fourth act); it is one of the play's climaxes. Written by Takeda Izumo I (d. 1747), the play was enormously popular, putting an end to the fluidity of Abe no Seimei's birth legend (Orikuchi 1995, 253).[8] The fact that *Yamauba monogatari* contains an element of the *Shinodazuma* legend popular in the early modern period, especially after Takeda Izumo's successful play, suggests that the work was possibly created in the early eighteenth century.

Yamauba monogatari, from Ōkuchi village of the Tanba district in present-day Aichi Prefecture, has the same story line as that of *Owari-shi* but the description is more elaborate: when Shinzō goes hunting on Mt. Hongū, upstream of Haguro, he sees a faint light in the direction of a Hongū shrine. As he approaches the light, near the six-foot-tall lamp is a thirty-foot-tall yamauba, combing her hair. Close to her is a man of similar height. Shinzō thinks, "This must be the yamauba that is said to live in this mountain. The yamauba is known to delude unrighteous people's minds." He shoots her in the chest. The lamplight goes out and the mountain shakes thunderously (*NDT* 1982–1990, 7:157–59). In this version, a negative description of yamauba is added—she is said to delude unrighteous people. Also, her supernaturalness is emphasized—the mountain shakes wildly when she is shot. The action when the yamauba appears in front of the main character—her combing her hair in the lamplight, him shooting her—resembles a mukashibanashi story type called "Yamauba to itoguruma" ("Yamauba and the Spinning Wheel"), which also reveals the strong association of yamauba and spinning wheels.

In the story of "Yamauba to itoguruma," a hunter on his way home on a mountain path at night finds a white-haired old woman (sometimes the woman is young and beautiful) spinning on a tree with a light burning.[9] Thinking it strange, he shoots her with his hunting gun, but she is not harmed—she just laughs. He returns home and tells the story to his neighbor, an old man. The old man instructs the hunter to shoot below the light. On the following day, the hunter does as instructed. The light goes out and there is a sound of something falling. The woman's corpse turns into a large owl (*NMT* 1978–1980, 7:28–31; Seki 1966, 51). Although the title refers to yamauba, the spinning creature found in all the pertinent stories of Seki Keigo's *Nihon mukashibanashi taisei* turns out to be some kind of animal, such as a monkey, raccoon-dog (*tanuki*), or spider. None remains a woman. The story seems to highlight the hunter's shooting skill, or the animal's transforming skill that leads to its own demise. Importantly, the association of yamauba and a spinning wheel has become so strong that when the animal shape-shifts to a yamauba the spinning wheel comes with her. While the yamauba is not spinning but rather combing her hair by lamplight in *Yamauba monogatari* from Ōkuchi village, Shinzō's shooting skill is highlighted.[10]

The description of the yamauba in *Yamauba monogatari jikki* (True record of the yamauba tale), written by Korobō Gaun and published in 1777, is even more elaborate. According to Taki Kiyoshi (1986), *Yamauba monogatari jikki* is the culmination of research by Korobō Gaun, who had investigated local tales of yamauba. The background of the story goes back to the Kamakura period (1185–1333), and Taki writes that *Yamauba monogatari jikki* is a combination of Owari's yamauba legend and the legend of the dragon woman of Ogase Pond in Uruma, Mino province (present-day Gifu Prefecture).[11]

The summary of *Yamauba monogatari jikki* is that in 1262 a yamauba disguised as a stunningly beautiful woman appears in front of Koike Yokurō (Yohachirō's son) at the foot of Mt. Haguro. She introduces herself as Tama, the daughter of a yarn seller in Kyoto, and says that during her pilgrimage she lost her way on Mt. Atago. A splendid-looking Shugendō practitioner appeared and carried her into the air, leaving her on Mt. Haguro. Yokurō takes her to his house and marries her (Taki 1986, 156–63). Kidnapping by a *tengu* (a long-nosed goblin donned in yamabushi attire) disguised as a Shugendō practitioner was well known during the early modern period. Further, a yamauba appearing as a beautiful woman is also well known, as in such tales as "Kuwazu nyōbō." The story continues that in 1272, when Fukutomi Shinzō goes hunting on a beautiful moonlit night on Mt. Hongū, he sees a horrendous-looking yamauba with long silver hair—she is blackening her teeth. Shinzō thinks this must be the yamauba who is said to live on this mountain; the narrator explains that yamauba is a type of serpent or scorpion, sometimes appearing as an oni, other times as a beautiful woman who seduces men. So he shoots her in the chest. The lamplight immediately goes out, the brightly shining moon disappears, peaks and valleys shake, the wind blows wildly. The blood trail of the yamauba leads to the house of Koike Yohachirō (formerly Yokurō; he adopted his father's name, Yohachirō, when his father retired). When Fukutomi Shinzō asks about his wife, Yohachirō finds her bed empty. There are two poems left for him and her son, saying that she had to leave because her true identity was revealed. The blood trail leads from there to Ogase Pond. They learn that Tama was a dragon maid (Taki 1986, 164–76).

As Taki Kiyoshi writes, the yamauba being a manifestation of a dragon maid was added as the author incorporated the legend of Ogase Pond into that of the yamauba. That the yamauba or the wife of Yohachirō introduces herself as a daughter of a family who runs a string shop in Kyoto may have come from a folk belief in the yamauba's association with string. Further, Mt. Atago, the place where she said she got lost, is famous as the residence of tengu and oni, as well as the training ground for Shugendō practitioners. As time passes, the tales, incorporating various legends, beliefs, rumors, and anecdotes, become more elaborate. The yamauba worshipped on Mt. Hongū is a mother who had to leave a happily married life because of the main character's (as well as the author's and reader's) perception of folkloric yamauba as evil characters. The worshipped mother yamauba is thus tinged with negative images.

YAMAUBA AS MOTHER OF KINTARŌ

Perhaps the most famous mother yamauba is Kintarō's mother. Kintarō is the legendary childhood name of Sakata no Kintoki, one of the aforementioned shitennō. Kintarō, a boy with superhuman strength, is a popular character in folklore, kabuki and puppet plays, children's books and songs, and even is the namesake of candies called Kintarō ame. In present-day Japan, a Kintarō figure, wearing a red *harakake* (a large bib that covers one's chest and stomach) on which the Chinese character *kin* (literally, gold; *kin* from Kintarō) is written, is customarily put up on Children's Day (May 5). It was used to be called Boys' Day in the hope that boys will become brave, strong, and healthy like Kintarō. By the beginning of the seventeenth century, a yamauba came to be considered the mother of Kintarō. Many legends say Kintarō was raised in the mountains, where he wrestled with animals. He was discovered by a great warrior, Minamoto no Raikō, changed his name to Sakata no Kintoki, and became Raikō's retainer.[12] Raikō and the shitennō then eliminated such supernatural beings as Shuten Dōji on Mount Ōe and tsuchigumo, the earth spider.

According to Torii Fumiko, *Kinpira tanjō-ki* (Record of Kinpira's birth, 1661), the old *jōruri* (puppet theater) text, is the oldest extant description of Kintoki as the son of a yamauba (Torii 2002, 32). *Kinpira tanjō-ki* states, "Kintoki is a yamauba's son. One year Raikō received Kintoki from an oniwoman in the mountain, and Kintoki entered into a master-vassal relationship" (Muroki 1966, 192). Examining various jōruri texts, Torii Fumiko surmises that a folk belief holding Kintoki to be the son of a yamauba must already have existed at the beginning of the Edo period (Torii 1993, 8). Given the widely held perception in the medieval period that the yamauba was the mother of many children or super-children, it seems unsurprising to find her in early modern texts as the mother of a strong warrior who conquers demons (see Reider 2010, chap. 4; 2016, chap. 1).

Yamauba's partner or Kintarō's father is not always mentioned, but *Zentaiheiki* (Chronicle of pre-grand pacification, ca. 1692), a popular historical narrative widely read throughout the Edo period, describes yamauba's partner as a red dragon or thunder god. The yamauba, an old woman of a little over sixty years of age, explains to Raikō that about twenty-one years ago, when she was sleeping atop Mt. Ashigara, she dreamed that a red dragon made love to her. Jarred awake by a sudden clap of thunder, she found herself pregnant, and soon after, she bore a supernatural child. After some years Raikō, on his way to the capital, found the super-child on Mt. Ashigara, named him Sakata Kintoki, and made him one of his four lieutenants (Itagaki 1988, 325–28). Yanagita notes: "Until the appearance of *Zen-taiheiki*, the main habitat of yamauba was not necessarily in Mt. Ashigara. Mt. Kintoki in Shinano province (Nagano Prefecture) has caves where yamauba and Kintoki were purported to have lived, ponds where Kintoki took his first bath . . . and this is in accord with the old tale that the yamauba makes rounds of the mountains. But when the yamauba of Mt. Ashigara became the mother of Kintoki in *Zen-taiheiki*, this place alone became famous as the dwelling-place of the yamauba" (Yanagita 1978–1979, 1:248). While there

Figure 2.2. Yamauba in *Ehon Raikō ichidai ki* (Illustrated book of Raikō's life, 1796), by Okada Gyokuzan (1737–1808). (Courtesy of International Research Center for Japanese Studies.)

were precedents for the yamauba on Mt. Ashigara, it could be said that the popularity and wide distribution of *Zen-taiheiki* made the relationship between the yamauba and Mt. Ashigara definitive.

At present, Minamiashigara City in Kanagawa Prefecture where Mt. Ashigara lies capitalizes on the Kintarō legend. The official website of Minamiashigara City announces: "If one says of Kintarō that he is 'Kintarō of Mt. Ashigara,' and talks of 'Kintarō's hometown,' this is Minamiashigara City" (Minamiashigara City 2014). Thus, the city actively incorporates Kintarō themes by creating a Kintarō logo, Kintarō's welcome tower, Kintarō bronze statues, a Kintarō festival, and so on to entice tourists to the city. A number of sites related to Kintarō are concentrated in the Jizōdō area of Minamiashigara City, bringing tourists (including the author of this book) who help revitalize the local economy. Noticeably missing there, however, is yamauba as the mother of Kintarō.

The website describes Yaegiri, a rich man's daughter, as Kintarō's mother, and writes a brief biography of Kintarō. There lived a wealthy man named Ashigara Heidayū in Jizōdō. His daughter, Yaegiri, married into the Sakata clan but she returned to her hometown to evade an internal dispute of the Sakata clan, and gave birth to Kintarō. When Kintarō was born, he was first bathed in the basin of Fall of Evening Sun near her estate. As he grew older, he became exceedingly healthy, playing with the garden stones of the estate, making Mt. Ashigara his backyard. The animals in the mountains became Kintarō's playmates. Soon Kintarō became known as an unusually strong youth of Mt. Ashigara. One day he encountered Minamoto no Raikō on Mt. Ashigara and became Raikō's retainer, changing his name to Sakata no Kintoki. He went to the capital and his name became known all over Japan as one of Raikō's shitennō who subjugated Shuten Dōji of Mt. Ōe. After Raikō's death, he visited Raikō's grave day and night for three months and then left the capital for his hometown of Mt. Ashigara—from there his whereabouts became unknown (Minamiashigara City 2014).

The word *yamauba* does appear once, though cursorily, on the official website. "The building of Jizōdō [temple hall with a Kshitigarbha or Jizo image] holds a statue of yamauba (Kintarō's mother), etc."[13] The reader is assumed to imagine that Yaegiri becomes a yamauba or something along that line. On the site of the Jizōdō, there are two large stones named Taiko-ishi (drum-stone) and Kabuto-ishi (helmet-stone) respectively, with which Kintarō is said to have played. A number of paving stones are laid out in a square shape on the site of his assumed birthplace; the caption board says Kintarō's mother's name is Yaegiri. This legend—Kintarō's mother being Yaegiri—must have been created (or rearranged) in the mid-Edo period after the appearance of an enormously popular jōruri/kabuki play, *Komochi yamauba* (A yamauba with child, 1712), authored by Chikamatsu Monzaemon (1653–1725).[14]

The yamauba in *Komochi yamauba* is one of the most important and influential mother yamauba. Similar to some mysterious but beautiful yamauba already described, she is attractive. Also, like the yamauba in *Hanayo no hime*, she used to be a human being—a gorgeous courtesan named Yaegiri. Chikamatsu Monzaemon named his character after Ogino Yaegiri (d. 1736), a very popular contemporary *onnagata* (female impersonator on the kabuki stage). In the kabuki play, Yaegiri's husband and Kintoki's father is a samurai named Sakata no Tokiyuki.[15] The name Yaegiri, which appears in the Minamiashigara City's legend, was most likely adapted from this very successful play. The caption board at the site in Minamiashigara City conscientiously states that there are several versions of Kintoki's birth and birthplace.

Chikamatsu's *Komochi yamauba* is a fantastical play with a complex plot. The summary of the pertinent part relating to yamauba is as follows: Sakata Tokiyuki has left Yaegiri to avenge his father's death and is now in disguise as the tobacco seller Genshichi. He does not know that his younger sister's lover has already avenged his father. Sakata/Genshichi and Yaegiri accidentally meet at the residence of Minamoto no Raikō's fiancée. Yaegiri tells him about his sister's successful strike and accuses Genshichi of spinelessness.

Genshichi is deeply ashamed and commits suicide, first vowing revenge on Takafuji, who framed Raikō. Raikō is in hiding partly because he has protected Genshichi's sister and her lover from Takafuji. As he dies, Genshichi swears to Yaegiri that, if she is pregnant, she will become superhuman, and also that their future son will help Raikō take revenge on Takafuji. He orders her to leave the worldly life so as to rear their child in the seclusion of the mountains. Yaegiri immediately acquires superhuman power and reveals her prowess by easily repelling encroaching samurai before leaving for the mountain. Time passes and Raikō and three lieutenants encounter the yamauba and her super-child on Mt. Ashigara. Impressed by the superhuman power of the child and well aware of the yamauba's wish, Raikō names the child Sakata Kintoki and makes him one of his shitennō. Raikō and his shitennō then conquer the demons that were threatening the capital.

The yamauba's speech to Raikō about her mountain rounds comes directly from the noh play *Yamamba*, but the story of Kintoki as the child of a yamauba comes from either the *Zen-taiheiki* or the *Kinpira jōruri*. Meera Viswanathan writes, "In *Komochi yamauba*, the yamamba metamorphoses into an entirely different being, one lacking the awesomeness and alien nature of earlier avatars. Instead, she is first and foremost mother and wife, loving, loyal, and somewhat pathetic. Her demonic nature is not intrinsic to her, but merely an unfortunate outcome of her appropriation of male concerns. She must be sacrificed so that the larger issues of politics and moral justice may be played out" (Viswanathan 1996, 252). If Yaegiri-yamauba possesses any demonic tendencies, they seem most evident when she is still human; her acts of jealousy and lust are part of her original human makeup. However, she does indeed possess a loving and caring nature. She is both motherly and loyal to her husband. This change or evolution in the yamauba's character, especially loyalty/faithfulness to her husband, partially reflects some of the social expectations of Japanese women of the time.

The Edo period is often referred to as a dark age for Japanese women (Hayashi R. 1982, 325), and women's social activities were extremely limited throughout the period (Fukuda M. 1995, 257). There are numerous references that support the supposition that Japanese women occupied a subservient role to men and were held in low regard. For example, "Onna daigaku takarabako" (Treasure box for women's great learning, 1716), a popular handbook to educate women about their duties, states: "A woman's infirmities include a lack of submission, ill temper, resentfulness, jealousy, slander of others, and stupidity. Seven or eight out of ten women are afflicted with these infirmities" (Ishikawa 1977, 46). Comparing women to yin, the book says, "Yin is night and dark. In comparison to men, women are ignorant

Figure 2.3. Yamauba in *Kokkei sharekyōgaen* (Cornucopia of humorous pictures), by Maki Bokusen (1775–1824). (Courtesy of International Research Center for Japanese Studies.)

and do not understand things right in front of them" (Ishikawa 1977, 54). Similarly, Confucian scholar Kaibara Ekken (1630–1714) detailed in the "Joshi o oshiyuru no hō" (Method of teaching women, 1710) the Three Obediences, a popular maxim of the day regarding women's conduct: "A young woman obeys her father; a married woman obeys her husband; and a widow obeys her son" (Ishikawa 1977, 12). A man could have a mistress if he wished, and divorce was essentially the unilateral prerogative of the husband. The ease with which a man could generally get a divorce was apparent in the brief divorce letter called a *mikudarihan* (three and a half lines) written by a husband to announce divorce.[16] While a woman could own property, her dowry became her husband's upon marriage.[17]

A three-and-a-half-line divorce letter is exactly what Yaegiri receives from her husband Genshichi before he leaves her so that he can avenge his father. Under these circumstances, it was expected that Yaegiri-yamauba be loyal to her husband. The "Onna daigaku takarabako" lists seven reasons for a husband to divorce his wife and one of them is "jealousy" (Ishikawa 1977, 34). Jealousy caused Genshichi to be disowned, and caused Yaegiri herself to be thrown out of the pleasure quarters. Acting on behalf of her dying husband and making his wish her own may have helped compensate for her impetuous behavior. The empowerment of women through verbal acumen and supernatural strength only increased female audience appeal. No doubt many Edo-era women secretly yearned to act like Yaegiri but found themselves restricted by social expectations and conventions. While the fantastic strength to overpower any man that Yaegiri-yamauba possesses destabilizes the social order, she is ultimately committed to realizing her husband's wishes and devotes herself to Kintarō, as a woman was expected to behave in contemporary society. Thus, a potential threat to the conventional social order is contained. Ironically, the skillful actor who played the role of Yaegiri would have been a man.

The motherly aspect of yamauba in *Komochi yamauba* gave birth to a kabuki dance subgenre (*shosagoto*) called *yamaubabuyō*, yamauba dance. Torii writes that the yamauba always appears as a beautiful woman in this dance piece (Torii 2002, 67). The first yamauba dance piece in the present style is entitled *Shitennō Ōeyama-iri* (Shitennō enters Ōeyama, 1785) (Kokonoe 1998, 257–58). In this work the author Segawa Jokō (1739–1794) amplified the yamauba's motherly affection for her child significantly with such phrases as "He is so dear to me . . . you may laugh if you want. Everything is for the sake of this child" (Kokonoe 1998, 332–33). The yamauba was performed by Segawa Kikunojō III (1751–1810), a very popular and well-known onnagata. It is easy to imagine how this kabuki dance, in which a beautiful yamauba, performed by a seductive male actor, declares her undying love for her child, could have had some degree of influence on the ensuing *ukiyo-e* (woodblock prints) version of the alluring yamauba. Kabuki actors were popular subjects of the ukiyo-e artists—their images were painted on posters, much like present-day celebrities.

During the Kansei era (1795–1801) the yamauba was portrayed in ukiyo-e as an alluring, fully mature mother who humors Kintarō (Kintoki). The most famous ukiyo-e artist of the yamauba is Kitagawa Utamaro (1753–1806), who produced about forty works on the theme of yamauba and Kintarō (Shimizu 1990, 231). His yamauba is loving and voluptuous, with long black hair and white skin. Motherly love is amply revealed in such prints as *Yamauba to Kintarō ennenmai* (Yamauba and Kintarō, dance) and *Yamauba to Kintarō genpuku* (Yamauba and Kintarō, coming-of-age). Utamaro's yamauba oozes sensuality. For example, in *Yamauba to Kintarō kamisori* (Yamauba and Kintarō, shaving hair), a tall yamauba carefully shaves Kintarō's hair, while her own hair remains unkempt and her breasts are partially revealed to spark a sensual reaction. Another example is *Yamauba to Kintarō chibusa* (Yamauba and Kintarō, breastfeeding). Kintarō is suckling his mother's large breast while touching the other nipple with his hand. Her white skin and long unkempt hair reveal her unrestrained and erotic beauty.

Figure 2.4. *Yamauba Nursing Kintoki*, by Kitagawa Utamaro (1753–1806). (*Yamauba Nursing Kintoki*, Japanese, Edo period, about 1801–03 [Kyōwa 1–3], Artist: Kitagawa Utamaro I, Japanese, early 1750s–1806, Publisher: Tsutaya Jūzaburō [Kōshodō], Japanese Woodblock print [nishiki-e]; ink and color on paper, Asano and Clark 1995, #388; Hizō Ukiyo-e taikan 7, Musée Guimet II [1990], pl. 62; Ukiyo-e shūka 3 [1978], list #723; Shibui, Ukiyo-e zuten Utamaro [1964], 209.2.1; Yoshida, Utamaro zenshū [1941], #383; Ukiyo-e taisei 7 [1931], #288; Vertical ōban; 38.6 × 25.9 cm [15 3/16 × 10 3/16 in.]; Gift of Louis W. Black, RES.51.18; Photograph © [date of publication] Museum of Fine Arts, Boston.)

Utamaro, influenced by Torii Kiyonaga (1752–1815) in the portrayal of beauties, had great success through his creation of bust portraits (*Ōkubi-e*; literally, big-head pictures); a scary-looking yamauba, advanced in age, would not suit this type of portrayal. Bluntly put, it would not sell. His yamauba are women portrayed ideally—especially from men's perspective—with sensuously arranged long black hair, small mouths, and white skin. Utamaro has transformed the yamauba into a sensual mother and a commodity to be gazed upon and admired. According to Pavel Medvedev, this genre is "a specific way of visualizing a given part of reality . . . new genres reflect changes in real social life. Those changes lead to new views of experience and to different genres of speech, social behavior, and literature" (Morson and Emerson 1990, 275–77). It was thus a combination of social, political, and commercial forces that helped give birth to the concept of the alluring yamauba.

The impression Utamaro's yamauba gave to people in Edo society must have been considerable: Torii notes that, before Utamaro, the yamauba was portrayed in picture books as a scary looking oni-woman; after him, she came to be depicted as young and beautiful (Torii 2002, 61–67).[18] Indeed, there is a great contrast between the beautified yamauba portrayed by Utamaro and those that came before him, including those by his teacher, Toriyama Sekien (1712–1788). Sekien depicts the yamauba in his *Gazu hyakki yagyō* (Pictures of one hundred demons strolling at night, 1776) as a tired-looking old creature in the mountains.

Similarly, Nagasawa Rosetsu's (1754–1799) yamauba, famous as a treasure of the Itsukushima Shrine at Miyajima, is a white-haired old hag who looks suspiciously at the beholder. These artistic renditions depict a skeptical-looking (or perhaps just tired) aged woman with disheveled white hair—in other words, the familiar image of yamauba in mukashibanashi. On one hand, the yamamba in noh was performed by an actor wearing an old woman mask and a white-haired wig—not a portrayal generally considered sexually attractive. Moreover, in the countryside, where urban culture and vogue did not necessarily sit well with older traditions and beliefs, yamauba probably retained many of their indigenous images: the fertile mother, lonely woman, or voracious hag, as local traditions dictated. On the other hand, for commercial appeal and to suggest eroticism, yamauba in the jōruri/kabuki theaters, literature, and ukiyo-e were portrayed in a sensuous manner, underscoring the eroticism of youth and motherhood. Yamauba remain nevertheless marginalized Others as they "live spatially far away from a community, and are thus known to the community only through their imagination" (Komatsu K. 1995, 178). The representations

まうば
山蜈

Figure 2.5. Yamauba in *Gazu Hyakki yagyō* (Pictures of one hundred demons strolling at night, 1776 [1805]), by Toriyama Sekien. (Courtesy of Japanese National Diet Digital Library.)

of yamauba vary according to individual imagination. With the archetypal image of the yamauba as her base, she evolved according to the needs of the people.

CHILDBIRTH, BLOODSUCKING, AND ONI

While the anthropophagous side of yamauba is wiped out or spectacu-
larly sanitized in the selected commodified yamauba of kabuki dance and
Utamaro's prints of the late early modern period, yamauba in mukashibanashi and some legends keeps her penchant for eating human flesh—and
eating flesh goes with drinking blood. Miyata Noboru, quoting the stories
from Konno Ensuke's book, writes that some yamauba suck human blood,
and that behind the yamauba and *yamaonna* (mountain woman/women) lurk
the image of childbirth (Miyata 2000, 187, 189). A story from Kumamoto
Prefecture tells of a hunter's mother who encountered a yamauba in the
mountains. Looking at the mother, the yamauba guffawed. It was said
around the area that when a yamauba laughed, she sucked human blood. The
mother screamed. Surprised by the mother's shriek, the yamauba ran away.
But the mother's blood had been sucked and she died soon after (Konno
1981, 229). A similar story of a yamauba sucking blood is told around the
border between Kumamoto and Miyazaki Prefectures. When people working in the mountains were sleeping in a mountain hut, a yamaonna came in
and sucked their blood (Konno 1981, 231). Miyata comments that in the latter story the yamauba acts like Dracula. Indeed, it does sound like Dracula,
and if there was snow in background, the yamauba might be compared to a
snow woman that appears in one episode of Ima Ichiko's excellent manga
Hyakkiyakō shō (Extracts of one hundred demons strolling at night).[19]

Miyata speculates that female yōkai suck human blood in their attempt
to supplement the loss of their own blood during childbirth (Miyata 2000,
192). In the case of yamauba, however, sucking blood seems to stem more
from baggage carried over from her oni origin or from the double image
of oni-women and yamauba, like the woman in the noh play *Kurozuka* discussed in chapter 1. Drinking blood is what oni do, as exemplified by Shuten
Dōji. Shuten Dōji loves saké, and he feasts on blood, calling it saké as well.

There is an interesting mukashibanashi story type titled "The Origin of
Fleas and Mosquitoes." The bloodsuckers in this story type are usually oni.[20]
Often, various parts of Shuten Dōji's dead body suck the blood of humans.
One such story from Iwate Prefecture goes, "At the end of the story of
Shuten Dōji, the head of the demon was cut off. The blood that spat-
tered turned into fleas, the burned ashes turned into horseflies and mosquitoes, the joints that did not burn turned into leeches that suck human
blood" (Mayer 1986, 278). Before his demise Shuten Dōji was feared for his
atrocious acts of eating human flesh and drinking blood. He continues to
threaten humans even after his death. A story from Aomori Prefecture tells
that the dying Shuten Dōji declares he will keep eating human flesh after

his death, and his blood turns into fleas, while his burned and severed flesh becomes lice (*NMT* 1978–1980, 1:367). In Tōno, Iwate Prefecture, the oni's child from the story type of "Oni no ko Kozuna" ("Kozuna, Ogre's Child") burns himself in a hut, and the ashes of his burned body become horseflies and mosquitoes that suck human blood (see *NMT* 1978–1980, 1:366–68).[21]

As a variation of the story type "Sanmai no ofuda" (see chapter 1 for synopsis), one mukashibanashi from Sado Island is titled "Yamauba Who Turns into a Flea." In this story, the yamauba meets her demise when she turns into a flea and is smashed by the bonze (Hamaguchi 1959, 181–82). While this yamauba is not given an opportunity to become a bloodsucker after her death, she still is associated with bloodsucking and this reveals the transformation powers of oni as well as yamauba. The image of oni or oni-women carried over to yamauba is strong.

Yamauba's strings, weaving, or magical cloths and yarns are also related to oni in a number of cases. Yanagita recounts the story of a family living on a mountain that finds a yamauba's *tsukune* (dialect word for a ball of hemp yarn), which produces infinite yarn (Yanagita 1978–1979, 1:240). The tsukune makes the family rich, but soon after the young wife gives birth to an oni-child (*onigo*) with two horns. Yamauba seem to be inseparable from oni.

STRINGS, SPINNING, AND SPIDERS

The account of the tsukune and oni-child brings us back to yamauba's association with strings, spinning, and the spider that is described as the protagonist's true identity in many "Kuwazu nyōbō" stories. As seen in chapter 1, "Kuwazu nyōbō" is considered to be a representative story of yamauba. Why does a spider appear in the majority of the stories? Kawai Hayao writes: "A spider's work is connected to spinning and weaving. In German, a spider is called *die Spinne*, obviously related to *spinnen*, 'to spin.' Here we can readily see a possible association of spider with the Goddess of fate who weaves the cloth of fortune. It seems rather natural as well that Yama-uba have close relations to spinning" (Kawai 1996, 31).

Yanagita Kunio conjectures that a spider was considered to be a temporary manifestation of a water deity in the olden days. The anthropophagous character of "Kuwazu nyōbō" was originally a spider rather than a yamauba (Yanagita 1969, 150–52). Yanagita cites several legends called "Water-Spiders," in which a spider pulls a whole human being and even a huge tree into the bottom of the water. A man is fishing at a pond. A spider comes out of the pond, puts its thread on one of the man's toes, and goes back to the water. The spider appears again, attaches another thread, and goes back to the pond. It repeats the same actions and gradually, the threads become thick and strong. Then the man takes the rope off his toe and attaches it to the roots of a tree beside him. Soon the spider pulls the rope into the water, uprooting the whole tree into the depths of the pond (see Yanagita 1969, 152–54; 1960, 52; 1966, 46–47; Seki 1962, 88; Yanagita and Suzuki 2004, 159–60; Kawai 1996, 31). A similar story is found in "Jōren no taki no jorōgumo" (Jorō spider of Jōrendaki waterfall) (*NDT* 1982–1990, 7:221–22). Here a huge *jorōgumo* (*Nephila clavate*, literally a "prostitute spider") that lives in the basin under Jōrendaki waterfall pulls a woodcutter to the bottom of the waterfall. Yamauba may have taken over the spider's position because of their similar attributes, and perhaps because of the yamauba's increased influence or popularity during the late medieval and Edo periods. As mentioned earlier, Yanagita considers the yamauba to have been a water deity who wove on a loom at the bottom of the water. If that is the case, the yamauba and the spider are connected through this water deity.

I would also speculate that the appearance of a large number of spiders in "Kuwazu nyōbō" comes from the mixing of yamauba and spiders because of their similar features. They both possess duality; spiders weave webs and eat the prey caught on their webs; some raise their babies on their back; others eat their own kind. Both yamauba and spiders are fertile. Like yamauba, yōkai spiders—tsuchigumo (earth spiders)—have a shape-shifting ability and they also have a strong association with oni.

SIMILARITIES BETWEEN YAMAUBA AND SPIDERS

Yamaguchi Motoko writes that spiders are known for their fecundity. Some spiders are said to raise their young on their backs. Such behaviors symbolize the positive aspects of the female as a fecund mother who affectionately nurtures her children. On the other hand, spiders create webs and catch their prey to suck their blood (Yamaguchi 2009, 90). Similar to yamauba, spiders have dual aspects.

Various kinds of spiders have appeared in literature, but a physical spider in ancient literature is by and large considered a good omen because it was believed to herald the arrival of a person one is waiting for (*SNKBZ* 1994–2002, 2:119; Sudō 2002, 70–71). The oldest extant example of such usage appears in *Nihon shoki* in the poem composed by Sotoori Iratsume on the second month of the eighth year in the reign of Emperor Ingyō (Sudō 2002, 70). The poem is preceded by an explanatory note:

The emperor went to Fujiwara and secretly observed how matters were with Sotoori Iratsume. That night Sotoori Iratsume was sitting alone, thinking fondly of the emperor. Unaware of his approach, she made a song, saying:

Waga sekoga
kubeki yoi nari
sasagane no
kumo no okonai
koyoi shirushi mo
        (*SNKBZ* 1994–2002, 2:119)

This is the night
my husband will come
the little crab–
The spider's action
tonight is manifest
        (Aston 1956, 320)

Aston noted that "it was considered that when a spider clung to one's garments, it was a sign that an intimate friend would arrive. Little crab is another name for spider" (Aston 1956, 320).

Also in *Kibi daijin nittō emaki* (Illustrated story of Minister Kibi's adventures in China, end of the twelfth century), a spider helps Minister Kibi escape from captivity in China (see Reider 2016, 102–8). One of the challenges posed by Chinese officials that Minister Kibi had to solve was to decipher the poem *Yabatai*.[22]

> In front of the Chinese Emperor, Kibi was made to read. As he looked
> at the writing, he became dizzy and lost focus; he could not see nor make
> sense of a single character on the paper. Then, drawing on his faith, Kibi
> turned to the direction of Japan and appealed to Japan's patron deity and
> Buddha—specifically, the deity of Sumiyoshi Shrine and Bodhisattva of
> Hase Temple—whereupon his eyes became clear and he could see the
> characters. Still he could not figure out in what order they should be read,
> when a spider came down from nowhere, leaving its thread on the paper to
> show Kibi how to read the text. (Reider 2016, 107)

These good spiders (from the viewpoint of humans) are truly spiders—having a spider's form.

On the other hand, the tsuchigumo or earth spider in ancient times was a human being, *tsuchigumo* being a derogatory name for those who defied imperial (central) authority—antiestablishment forces (or perhaps individuals). During the medieval period, however, the tsuchigumo appears as a yōkai in *Tsuchigumo zōshi* (Picture scroll of an earth spider, ca. early fourteenth century) and "The Sword Chapter" of the *Heike monogatari* (*Tale of the Heike*), the oldest extant works in which a spider is so portrayed.

This yōkai spider is a shape-shifter. In one scene of *Tsuchigumo zōshi*, the yōkai spider, disguised as a gorgeous lady, mesmerizes the brave imperial warrior Minamoto no Raikō with her beauty and tries to attack him by throwing a number of cloud-like white balls. These white balls are apparently spider eggs—her own eggs, reminding one somewhat of the story of Medea in Greek mythology. I have discussed elsewhere that *Tsuchigumo zōshi* plays a significant role in the emergence of the tsuchigumo as a killer female shape-shifter.[23] I speculated that this image was created primarily through tsuchigumo's association with oni—despite their different physical appearances, tsuchigumo and oni have remarkable similarities, which at least partially resulted in the production of a yōkai shape-shifting female spider. I will briefly summarize my hypothesis below.

ONI VERSUS TSUCHIGUMO, YAMAGUMO, AND YAMAUBA

As I have written about elsewhere (see Reider 2010), one feature of oni is that they are the Other: people who had different customs or lived beyond the reach of the emperor's control were considered to be some form of oni. Indeed, one could argue that any person who is forced to live on the periphery of mainstream society or who voluntarily does so is marginalized and thus considered oni (Komatsu K. and Naitō 1990, 11). The story of Shuten Dōji, who was chased from his original abode and eliminated by an imperial order, is a good example.

It is commonly accepted among scholars that tsuchigumo refers to the less-cultivated indigenous people of Japan who inhabited the islands after their creation by heavenly deities but before the arrival of the imperial family's ancestors, who claimed authority to rule Japan as the descendants of heavenly beings (Tsuda 1963, 188–95).[24] Regarding the origin of the tsuchigumo's name, Urabe Kanekata, a Shinto priest of the thirteenth century, writes that "according to *Settsu fudoki* (Topography of Settsu province), in the reign of Emperor Jinmu, there was a villain called *tsuchigumo*—he was given the contemptuous name of 'earth spider' because this person always dwelled in a pit" (Urabe 1965, 132). A tsuchigumo is thus depicted in ancient literature as a villainous human being whose customs and manners differ from mainstream conventions, who defies central authority, and has different physiological features than other people. In that sense, the earth spider is considered to be one of the most ancient types of oni (Baba Akiko 1988, 170).

Another aspect of commonality between oni and tsuchigumo is their perceived power to cause illness in ancient and medieval times. For example, Takahashi Masaaki identifies an oni as a deity responsible for causing epidemics, in particular smallpox (Takahashi Masaaki 1992, 4); a *mushi* (insect, bug, worm) was also believed to cause illness. Peter Knecht writes: "Under the influence of Chinese medical treatises, early medieval Japanese practitioners of medicine argued that the causes for human diseases are certain entities active inside the human body. These causes were conceived as oni, but at that time oni were not yet the terrifying figures they became later. However, in later interpretations it was thought that a kind of *mushi* (an imaginary 'insect') was active in the different parts of the body. Challenged by some outside being, these *mushi* were believed to cause a disease together with the intruder" (Knecht 2010, xiv).

Knecht, Hasegawa Masao, Minobe Shigekatsu, and Tsujimoto Hiroshige have noticed that a strong relationship existed between diseases caused by mushi and oni, and have reported an interesting contagious disease called *denshi-byō* (illness caused by *denshi*), in which a person is emaciated by the time of death. The modern diagnosis of this illness is close to pulmonary tuberculosis. Fascinatingly, this denshi was considered both a mushi and an oni from Japan's ancient through early modern periods, and consequently a remedy was sought from both medicine and religion (Knecht et al. 2012, 278–324). As Japanese medical studies of mushi and oni were heavily influenced by Chinese medical studies, Knecht, Hasegawa, and Tsujimoto examine premodern Chinese medical treatises concerning illnesses that were believed to be caused by *ki* (the sino-reading of oni); among them were contagious diseases such as *eki-byō* (epidemic), *gyaku-byō* (malaria), and *chū-byō* (later called denshi-byō), Interestingly, when mushi took over diseases caused by oni, oni's characteristics were transferred as well (Knecht et al. 2018, 19). In "The Sword Chapter" of the *Tale of the Heike*, Minamoto no Raikō suffered from gyaku-byō or *okori* (malaria) one summer, and it turned out that illness was caused by the tsuchigumo (or more precisely, *yamagumo*, mountain spider, as will be discussed later). It is said that the first appearance of mushi-related illness was in the twenty-fifth year of Ōei (1418), and abundant examples of mushi-caused diseases are recorded in the fifteenth and sixteenth centuries (Knecht et al. 2012, 325). I speculate that oni and mushi as medical terms were still fluid in Japan's medieval time and also that through their symbolic similarities as enemies of imperial authority and followers of different customs, and perhaps some resemblance as vectors of illness, tsuchigumo came to adopt some of the characteristics of oni—namely, transformational skills and cannibalism.

Tsuchigumo's association with oni is assumed to have become tangible enough to be visualized in *Tsuchigumo zōshi* during the medieval period. Just as oni infamously eat humans in one gulp, the spider, on its way out of the decayed mansion in *Tsuchigumo zōshi*, eats "the old woman in one gulp." And as oni transform into men or women to get their targets, the spider shape-shifts to a beautiful woman and dazzles Raikō in order to capture him. The *Tsuchigumo zōshi* text seems to offer a close relationship between oni and tsuchigumo or perhaps a fluid intermingling of the two creatures. One noticeable point in regard to *Tsuchigumo zōshi* is that despite the title, the word *tsuchigumo* does not appear in the text. The spider is introduced as yamagumo. Some scholars speculate that the title *Tsuchigumo zōshi* might be a later addition (Ueno 1984, 106). In "The Sword Chapter" the spider is also called yamagumo. While this seems to indicate a fluid stage of tsuchigumo appearing as yōkai, it could also indicate a bifurcation point when yama-gumo transformed into something like yamauba, the mysterious female creatures in the mountains. This tsuchigumo-yamagumo is fecund and nurturing like a real female spider; when Raikō cuts open its flank, numerous small spiders about the size of seven- or eight-year-old children noisily trot out. They must be her children, whom she carries with her. At the same time, this creature is a man-eater like an oni or evil yamauba. From her belly come pouring out 1,990 heads of people she must have eaten.

It is interesting to note that in one "Kuwazu nyōbō" from Ōita Prefecture, the cannibalistic character is said to have transformed into a tsuchi-gumo (*NMT* 1978–1980, 6:187). Another "Kuwazu nyōbō" from Niigata Prefecture describes a yamagumo that turns into a man's wife (*NMT* 1978–1980, 6:209–10). Yet in another version of "Kuwazu nyōbō" from Ehime Prefecture, the wife turns out to be Shuten Dōji (*NMT* 1978–1980, 6:192–93). Although oni are not associated with spinning or weaving, behind the yamauba lurks the image of oni.

FEARED AND WORSHIPPED YAMAUBA

In this chapter I have discussed worshipped yamauba, their procreation, and their association with weaving. Also, their relationship with oni and spiders were examined. A yamauba giving birth is strongly tied to villagers hoping for good weather, but sometimes it carries a dark image. Some yamauba worship originates from yamauba's childbirth and villagers' fear of her curse. Ōyamatsumi Shrine located in Kahoku town (present-day

Kami City), Kōchi Prefecture honors Ōyamatsumi no mikoto, a deity born between Izanagi and Izanami, who is in charge of mountains; she presents the ambivalent status of the yamauba—or the villagers' attitude toward yamauba. The *shintai*, or object of worship believed to contain the spirit of the deity of Ōyamatsumi no mikoto, is an eerie-looking skull. According to a local legend, while a yamauba was passing by the area, she suddenly went into labor and gave birth to her children in a mountain cavern. It was the buckwheat-sowing season and the villagers unknowingly burned the mountain that day (to burn off vegetative cover for fertilization as well as to exterminate pests). The fire spread rapidly, engulfing the cavern and burning the yamauba to death. After that, various misfortunes befell the village. The villagers thought the disasters were caused by the yamauba's curse, so they took the yamauba's skull from the cavern and worshipped it as a mountain deity, whereupon the misfortunes stopped (*NDT* 1982–1990, 12:159). Komatsu Kazuhiko writes that worshipped supernatural beings are deities and unworshipped ones are yōkai (Komatsu K. 1994, 283); this yamauba became a mountain deity because of the prayers of villagers who feared her curse.

While yamauba on the kabuki stage and ukiyo-e prints are safe to look at as entertainment and commodities, the yamauba who are believed by local villagers to live in the nearby mountains are enigmatic beings regarded with a mixture of reverence and fear.

3

Reading Minds and Telling Futures
"Yamauba and the Cooper," "The Smile of a Mountain Witch,"
and Throne of Blood

THE YAMAUBA'S MIND-READING ABILITY is little known. However, a
yamauba has a long history of mind reading and these stories have wide
distribution (*NMT* 1978–1980, 10:117). Similar to the appearance of the
term *yamauba* in religious quarters in the early Muromachi period, the
mind-reading ability of an evil creature, though not described as yamauba, first appears in religious writing. This chapter examines how the yamauba's mind-reading ability came into being by studying the story type
"Yamauba to okeya" ("Yamauba and the Cooper") and its preceding setsuwa, and speculates how the protagonist—a mind-reading yamauba—of
Ōba Minako's (1930–2007) modern short story titled "Yamauba no
bishō" ("The Smile of a Mountain Witch," 1976) was created. Among
possible sources for Ōba's yamauba is "Star Eye" by Zacharias Topelius
(1818–1898). Further, this chapter examines the yamauba's other uncanny
ability—telling one's future. Komatsuzaki Susumu and Komatsuzaki
Tatsuko write that a yamauba is "an oni-woman who has a mouth on the
top of her head that eats rice balls and miso soup, or someone who eats
an entire ox. But on the other hand, in the stepmother stories, she is kind
to give a night's lodging to a girl who is lost ('Komekko nukakko'), and
some yamauba can foretell the future and use this ability for good people
('Naranashi tori' ['Picking Wild Pears'])" (Komatsuzaki and Komatsuzaki
1967, n.p.).[1] While "Naranashi tori" is a good example, I believe the most
famous case is the forest witch in Akira Kurosawa's famed film, *Throne of
Blood* (1957).

DOI: 10.7330/9781646420551.c003

MIND-READING YAMAUBA:
"YAMAUBA TO OKEYA" AND *SATORI*

A mukashibanashi that tells of a mind-reading yamauba is called "Yamauba to okeya," classified by Seki as number 265 under "Stupid Animals" (*NMT* 1978–1980, 7:101–7). Seki summarizes this type as follows:

> Cooper (wood-cutter, or charcoal-maker) in a mountain hut is bend-
> ing canes in his hut in the wood. *Yama-uba* (*yama-otoko*, beautiful badger
> [raccoon-dog], *tengu* [flying goblin], or monkey) comes and guesses what
> the cooper is thinking. (a) Cooper's round cane suddenly springs off,
> making the ashes in the fireplace fly up and hit the *yama-uba*; (b) when he
> breaks a stick, a piece of stick flies up and hits the *yama-uba*; or (c) a burn-
> ing bamboo cane springs up and hits the *yama-uba*. *Yama-uba* is frightened
> at this sudden happening and she says, "a human being does what he does
> not think he does." Then she goes away. (Seki 1966, 54)

Although the title of this story type denotes yamauba, only two stories among this group have the yamauba character reading the human mind; the rest of the stories have other beings as the mind reader. In many tales printed in Seki Keigo's *Nihon mukashibanashi taikei*, the mind reader is a *satori*, a mind-reading yōkai that lives in the mountains.[2]

Back in the eighteenth century, Toriyama Sekien (1712–1788), a ukiyo-e artist, wrote in his "Konjaku gazu zoku hyakki" (Pictures of demons now past, continued, 1779) about satori, which is also known as *satori no wappa* (satori boy): "In the deep mountains of Hida and Mino, there is *kaku*. People in the mountains call it *satori*. It has dark skin with long hair. It speaks human language and can read people's minds. It does not purpose-fully harm people. If a man tries to kill it, *satori* knows beforehand and is said to flee" (Toriyama 1992, 114). The illustration shows that the satori is a furry creature. Inada Atsunobu explains that *kaku* are large mon-keys, and they were called satori (sensing, perceiving) because they could sense or *satoru* people's minds (Toriyama 1992, 114). Indeed, Yanagita, who named this story type "Yamauba to okeya," comments on the yam-auba's mind-reading tale: "The folktale is also included in *Zoku zoku Kyūō dōwa* [Exemplum by Kyūō, further continued, 1838] and is known as *satori* man in Kantō and Chūbu regions. On page 199 of *Kai mukashibanashi shū* [Folktales from Kai province] the mind reading character is known as *omoi* (thinking) . . . An example of a woman [reading a man's mind] exists like in this tale. But because it is hard to give a name for this type instan-taneously, I will temporarily call it 'Yamauba and the Cooper'" (Yanagita 1933, 36).

In other words, Yanagita is surprised to find a female counterpart of the satori man and expediently gave the name "yamauba" to this group type. The story introduced by Yanagita is from Iwate Prefecture:

> Once there was a cooper. He went to the mountains to cut bamboo and made a bonfire for himself. There came a yamauba and warmed herself at the fire without saying a word. The cooper thought to himself, "a yamauba came. It's not good." Yamauba immediately said, "You just thought, 'a yamauba came. It's not good,' didn't you?" The cooper then said to himself, "how can I kill this yamauba?" The yamauba again guessed it right, "You are thinking that you want to kill me, aren't you?" The cooper got worried, "It's awful. This yamauba can see through my mind." "You are worried that I know everything you are thinking," the yamauba said out loud. He then without thinking tried to pick up a round cane from the fire, when suddenly the bamboo that had been over the fire for a long time sprang off and made the ashes in the fire fly up and hit the yamauba. The yamauba was frightened at this sudden happening. Crying out "Hot!" she ran away, saying "Humans do things that they are not thinking of. I have to be careful." After that, it is said that yamauba hardly approached humans. (Yanagita 1933, 36)

The yamauba comes to the cooper perhaps to warm herself at his fire, and probably also to entertain herself by reading his mind and saying his thoughts out loud to see his reaction. But in the end, she runs away from the man because she is frightened by an event caused by the man's unpremeditated serendipitous action.

The other story with a yamauba as a mind-reading character appears in *Kikimimi sōshi* (1933), a collection of folktales from northern Japan. This tale is named for its protagonist, Hikotarō:

> A man named Hikotarō was in a mountain hut, bending canes to be used for winnowing baskets. There came a yamauba and warmed herself at the fire Hikotarō had made. Hikotarō thought to himself, "this is a yamauba. I'll throw ashes at her . . ." The yamauba said, "Hikotarō, you are thinking about throwing ashes at me, aren't you?" Hikotarō was surprised to hear it and thought, "this is not good. But if she attacks me, I will cut her with a sharp hatchet that I bought recently." Again the yamauba said, "Hikotarō, you are thinking that you will cut me with a sharp hatchet that you bought recently, aren't you?" "This is really bad," Hikotarō thought, "I will be eaten up by this monster soon." The yamauba guessed it right again. Amazed, he quietly bent the cane over the fire, when a round cane suddenly sprang off and made the ashes in the fire fly up and hit the yamauba. The yamauba was frightened at this sudden event and said, "Hikotarō, you

do things that you are not thinking of!" She fled from the hut to a field of
bamboo grass. As Hikotarō followed her groaning sound in the field, he
found a huge yamauba lying on the ground. He was scared and immediately went back to his hut and packed his stuff on his back and went home.
(Sasaki K. 1964, 66)

The story line is the same as any other tale of the story type "Yamauba to
okeya." The mind-reading character comes to a man but in the end he or
she runs away. The title "Yamauba to okeya" seems misleading given that
only a few stories have a yamauba rather than a satori for their main character. It turns out, however, that a mind-reading yamauba did appear more
than once before the nineteenth century, before the publication of *Zoku
zoku Kyūō dōwa*.

PREMODERN SETSUWA OF MIND READING

An account of the story type "Yamauba to okeya"—although the mind-
reading character is a boy, not a yamauba—is found in a medieval com-
mentary on the *Lotus Sutra* titled *Ichijō shūgyokushō* (Annotation on jewel
of one vehicle, written by a Buddhist monk Eikai in 1488). A story in the
third chapter goes: "A woodworker was making buckets, when a demon
(*mamin*) disguised as a boy (*dōji*) appeared and said what the cooper was
thinking. The cooper [tried to] concentrate on his work but missed, bending the cane over the fire. The cane sprang off and hit the boy's forehead.
The boy ran away" (quoted in Tokuda 2016b, 2:45). Gorai Shigeru explains
that the *wappa* of *satori no wappa* is a *dōji* or *warawa*, a boy (or man) with a
parted hairstyle who serves an important personage. This dōji or warawa
could be the equivalent of a tengu; in other words, satori no wappa means a
boy (man) or tengu who can see into people's minds (Gorai 1984, 33).[3] This
boy or dōji perhaps later became a satori no wappa (or a tengu). According
to Gorai, mukashibanashi are made from sources such as myths, legends,
and religious writings by replacing religiosity with humanity or materialistic
reason, and changing stores of gratitude to interesting tales. This change
appears to have happened during the Muromachi period and flourished in
the Edo period (Gorai 1984, 9–10, 31–32).

   In 1585, almost 100 years after the completion of *Ichijō shūgyokushō*, Tenkai,
a Buddhist monk of the Tendai sect, wrote a similar story in *Jikidan innenshū*
(Collection of direct sermons on cause and effect). A notable difference is
that the mind-reading character is an old woman, not a boy. Tenkai explains
the *Lotus Sutra*'s teaching of serendipity by citing what he calls a "usual old
tale" (Tenkai 1998, 99): "One night a woodworker living in a mountain hut

was making wooden circular boxes. There came an old nun (*rōni*). The wood-worker thought she was a demon and tried to shoot her. But she said what he was thinking out loud. Then he thought to kill her with a sickle, but again she guessed what he was thinking. Suddenly the wood that had been over the fire sprang off arbitrarily and hit the old woman. Surprised, the old woman (*rōjo*) ran away" (Tenkai 1998, 99; Tokuda 2016b, 45).[4] Surmising from Tenkai call-ing this mind-reading story a "usual old tale," I believe this type of story must have been widely known by this time. Later, in some tales of the Edo period, this mind-reading character is named a yamauba.

In the early Edo period, a mind-reading story with the term *yamauba* written in the characters meaning "gentle crone in the mountains" (see the section titled "Yamabushi Subjugating Yamauba" in the introduction) emerges in the sixteenth story of volume 1 of *Fusō saigin* (Fusō's reexpla-nations of Zen kōan, 1654).[5] The author, Fusō Daiton (d. 1645), cites the mind-reading tale as an emblematic story to explain the training of what his school calls "Buddha's subjugating evils." "A cooper lived in a mountain hut in Kiso, Shinano province. There came a yamauba and said what he was thinking out loud. Frightened, perhaps, the cooper missed when bending the cane over the fire, and the cane sprang up and hit the yamauba. Neither cooper or yamauba knew what happened" (Fusō 1976, 35; Tokuda 2016b, 45). The process of the change from a boy to a yamauba is very similar to the way the term *yamauba* appeared during the medieval period in religious quarters—changing from an evil oni to an oni-woman to a yamauba—as described in the introduction.

Gorai believes that the source for the group of stories called "Yamauba mondō" ("Yamauba's Dialog"), which includes "Yamauba and the Cooper," is the satori no wappa (Gorai 1984, 36). Satori no wappa, tengu, or mountain father probably later became yamauba. Interestingly, in Yanagita Kunio's *Nippon no mukashibanashi*, the story of "Yamachichi no satori" ("Satori, a Mountain Father") is printed after "Kuwazu nyōbō" and "Ushikata to yamauba" (see Yanagita 1960, 52–53). The mountain father in "Yamachichi no satori" can be easily switched to a mountain mother, yamahaha, or yamauba. The contemporary popular science fiction writer Komatsu Sakyō (1931–2011) wrote a short story titled "Yamauba-tan" ("Story of Yamauba," 1978), in which yamauba is explained as the wife of a mountain father, alias *satoru no bakemono*, a monster who lives in mountains and sees into people's minds (Komatsu Sakyō 2015, 409). The yamauba could be a wife of the mind-reading man or a mind reader herself, absorbing satori's major trait.

Tokuda Kazuo also regards the "Yamauba and the Cooper" stories as part of satori setsuwa; and he further speculates that satori-like yamauba setsuwa had existed perhaps in the fifteenth century around the time the noh play *Yamanba* (early fifteenth century) was created. Indeed, the way Yamanba in the noh play appears in front of the entertainer's group as if the Yamanba knew the entertainer's mind reveals that stories of the satori-like yamauba must have been around in Zeami's time (Tokuda 2016b, 43–46). While it is a pattern of the noh drama that the shite or main character appears to a traveling priest, in many cases the place the shite appears is somewhat related to the shite. In the case of *Yamanba*, the related place for her could be any mountains in Japan; Yamanba appears to Hyakuma as if she knew exactly what Hyakuma's destination was and her route through the vast mountains.

When one pauses a moment to consider yamauba's major attribute of anthropophagy and their usual demise at the end of a story, yamauba's mind reading poses a question. As Kelly Hansen writes, "The fact that *yamanba* are frequently overcome through trickery also works against the notion of mind reading as a common trait of the *yamanba*" (Hansen 2014, 169). The yamauba in "Ushikata to yamauba" (see chapter 1) would have survived if she had been able to read minds. The same logic applies to yamauba's fate in another well-known tale, "Sanmai no ofuda" (see chapter 1): she was easily tricked. If the yamauba had had the ability to read the man's mind, she would not have met her demise in these tales.

The yamauba in "Kuwazu nyōbō" (see chapter 1) seems to distinguish herself on this point because the way she appears to the man—her future husband—somewhat resembles the way the protagonist of the noh play *Yamanba* appears to the entertainer. A man mutters to himself or his friend about how he wants a wife who does not eat, and a yamauba disguised as a beautiful young woman shows up at his house. She appears in front of him as if she has read his mind. It could be that the yamauba heard his voice when she was nearby. Or it could be the man's muttering summons the word spirit (*kotodama*)—an ancient concept that certain words when spoken activate spiritual power, a form of man's communication with deities (see Cornyetz 1999, 178; Thomas 2012).[6] The man's utterance could have activated a mountain deity, yamauba, though this interpretation probably is reading too much into the story because even if she were a mountain goddess or she simply had the ability to read the man's mind, that power is then immediately dropped. After it is dropped—provided that the reader/audience recognized the ability to begin with—the story continues as if nothing has happened. No one thinks (or is supposed to think) about it, and she dies in the end.

Yamauba's mind-reading ability is thus not compatible with her anthropophagous trait. Generally speaking, each story type presents an aspect of yamauba. A mind-reading yamauba does not chase after a man with the intent to kill him; she comes to a man's fireplace because she wants to warm herself and/or to enjoy teasing the man. On the other hand, a voracious, devouring yamauba who meets her demise after chasing her prey is not equipped with a mind-reading ability. As Meera Viswanathan notes, "The yamamba is never all these things simultaneously; instead, as the figure of the yamamba intervenes in a number of texts, her character becomes reformulated, fragmented, and disjointed in its accommodation of revisionist views" (Viswanathan 1996, 242). The opening tale of Ōba Minako's modern short story "The Smile of a Mountain Witch" may be considered one such revisionist work in that Ōba combined two different, seemingly incompatible types of traits—mind reading and devouring—into one tale in her prologue, and her yamauba in the main story sacrifices herself for the happiness of her family.

"THE SMILE OF A MOUNTAIN WITCH"

Retelling and Re-creating Yamauba Stories

The opening tale of "The Smile of a Mountain Witch," which is a tale within the main story, reads like a prologue.

> I would like to tell you about a legendary witch who lives in the mountains. Her straggly grey hair tied with string, she waits there for a man from the village to lose his way, meaning to devour him. When an unknowing young man asks to be put up for the night, the owner of the house grins, a comb with teeth missing here and there clutched between her teeth. As he feels a cold chill run up and down his spine beholding this eerie hag of a woman, her yellowed teeth shining under the flickering lamp, she says, "You just thought 'What an uncanny woman she is! Like an old, monster cat!' didn't you?"[7]
>
> Startled, the young man thinks to himself, "Don't tell me she's planning to devour me in the middle of the night!"
>
> Stealing a glance at her from under his brows, the man gulps down a bowl of millet porridge. Without a moment's hesitation she tells him, "You just thought in your mind, 'Don't tell me she's planning to devour me in the middle of the night!' didn't you!" He thinks to himself, "what a spooky old hag! This monster cat of a woman must be one of those old witches who live up in the mountains I hear so much about. Or else she wouldn't read my mind so well!"
>
> In any case, these old mountain witches are able to read a person's mind every time, and in the end the victim runs for his life away from her

abode. The old witch pursues him, and the man just keeps running for his life. At least this is the form the classic mountain-witch tales assume. (Ōba M. 1991, 194–95; Ōba M. 2009, 461–62)[8]

Ōba Minako spends two of the seventeen pages of her story on the folkloric yamauba's ability to read one's mind. She then introduces her modern-day protagonist, a mind-reading homemaker who lives in the flat-lands. Although Ōba describes her version of the folkloric yamauba tale as "the form the classic mountain-witch tales assume," it is not how the mind-reading yamauba is remembered in the folktales I have described above, in which a man's encounter with a mind-reading character is always followed by the mind reader running away from the man saying, "Humans do things they don't think of." The yamauba Ōba introduces in the opening, however, does not flee from humans; on the contrary, she chases after the man. This is in concordance with the anthropophagous yamauba's well-known behavior, but it does not fit the form of mind-reading folktales.

Obviously Ōba did not mean to write yamauba's *saiwa* (retelling) in the opening of her story. According to *Kōjien*, saiwa is an act of expressing mukashibanashi or legends using contemporary language (*Kōjien* 1978, 1046).[9] Matsutani Miyoko (1926–2015), author of children's books and a well-known collector of Japanese folktales, says that when the saiwa writer liberally adds his or her own ideas to the work, it becomes difficult to know whether the work should be called *saiwa* or *sai-sōzō* (re-creation) (Matsutani 1979, 247–48). Kinoshita Junji (1914–2004), playwright and literary critic, believes that the work becomes sai-sōzō when a writer freely interprets the folktale, using his or her own style of expression.[10] Yamada, scholar of informatics on the creation, dissemination, and transformation of culture, coined the term *saisō* for this: "*Saisō* is 're-creation.' That is to say, *saisō* is to put together existing material, copy it, and add something to the copied material to create something new. In *saisō*, a creator uses whatever materials are available for his expression. *Asobigokoro* (playfulness) is indispensable. Isn't it ingenious the term 'recreation' has a meaning of 'amusement'?" (Yamada 2002, 14). Perhaps the opening tale of "The Smile of a Mountain Witch" is Ōba's saisō of yamauba folktales leading into her main story.

Ōba remarks that "when reading old stories, one notices the same stories are transmitted a little differently depending on region . . . A certain section of the same story was probably dropped according to the mood of listeners and the storytellers themselves; likewise, some sections must have been changed to incorporate the transmitters' dreams. The real pleasure of *monogatari* [tales; literally, telling things] lies in how the story has been changed by the transmitters, and I'd say that the process of changing itself is the truth of *monogatari*" (Ōba M. 2010b, 343–44). In the opening, Ōba presents a strong image of the folkloric yamauba with mind-reading skill as her major attribute, so that the yamauba in her main text becomes credible, what the narrator calls a "genuine yamauba."[11] Of course, that is exactly where Ōba's imagination and creativity shine.

Ōba's modern yamauba in her main story, which comes immediately after the prologue, lives in the flatlands during the Shōwa period (1926–1989). She has a husband and two children. She uses her ability to please those whom she likes until the end of her life; she dies at the age of sixty-two, content, although she has always been entirely misunderstood by those she loved. This yamauba may have been pursuing the happiness that would come in the shape of a husband—if she married she could lead a life away from her mother and would no longer have to deal with societal pressure to marry—and that could be one reason why Ōba added the folkloric scene of yamauba chasing a man in her prologue. In any case, Ōba's Shōwa yamauba possesses many major traits of the folkloric yamauba. The unnamed protagonist eats so much, though it is not human flesh, that she becomes obese. She has horns in her dreamy, hidden form; "it would be the sensation of slitting the skin around the temples in order to let horns grow, horns which are itching to grow out, but cannot" (Ōba M. 1991, 201). She possesses the duality of yamauba; "she would see that half her face was smiling like an affectionate mother, while the other half was seething with demonic rage. Blood would trickle down from half her mouth while it devoured and ripped the man's flesh apart. The other half of her lips was caressing the man who curled up his body in the shadow of one of her breasts, sucking it like a baby" (Ōba M. 1991, 201). Although at times she wishes to release the more sinister half of her split personality, her domestic disposition to please her family always seems to win out.

POSSIBLE SOURCES OF ŌBA'S MIND-READING YAMAUBA

While mind-reading yamauba folktales are important, I speculate that an inspiration for Ōba's narration of her yamauba's childhood came from her reading of old tales, including stories of foreign origin. There are many fairy tales that portray supernatural beings with telepathic ability. "As a young schoolgirl," Michiko Wilson writes, "Ōba Minako (1930–2007) was totally absorbed by *mukashi-banashi* (ancient folktales), *otogi-zōshi* (classical Japanese fairy tales), and *otogi-banashi* (fairy tales in modern Japanese) as well as classical Western fairy tales by Hans Christian Andersen and the

Grimm brothers" (Wilson 2013, 218). Ōba must have been familiar with
fairy tales of various countries including "Hoshi no hitomi" ("Star Eye"),
written by Zacharias Topelius, a Finnish author often called the Andersen
of Finland. Star Eye can read people's minds. She can look through doors
and walls. Translated by Manzawa Maki (1910–2009), the book titled *Star
Eye*, which contains the eponymous short story, has been enormously popular in Japan since its first appearance in the mid-twentieth century as children's literature.[12]

A synopsis of "Star Eye" is as follows. On Christmas Eve, a Laplander
baby is thrown off a sled as her parents dash away to escape a pack of
wolves. The baby's innocent eyes have a wonderful power, and the wolves
leave her alone in the snow on the wild, lonely mountain. A Finnish settler
finds the baby before dawn on Christmas Day and takes her home. The
settler's wife welcomes the baby and raises her lovingly. But when Star Eye
is around three years old, her foster mother notices that she can see into
her mind. Although she loves Star Eye as much as her own children, she
becomes angry at the girl. While the Finnish settler is away on business,
she imprisons Star Eye in the cellar, thinking she is a witch child. A wicked
neighbor thinks the same—with the foster mother's consent, she takes Star
Eye to the mountain and leaves her there. It is again Christmas Eve, three
years later. The foster mother abandons Star Eye in the mountain, but Star
Eye's penetrating eyes can see through God's abode from the mountain. On
Christmas Day, the settler comes home. He tells his wife he dreamed that
Star Eye was God's blessing and that they should take good care of her.
Learning that Star Eye has been abandoned on the mountain, he rushes to
look for her—but she is nowhere to be found. Afterwards, the neighbor is
killed by wolves and the Finnish couple are impoverished.[13]

Star Eye bears a remarkable resemblance to the protagonist of Ōba's
fiction. In one episode when Star Eye is about three years old, her foster
mother is sitting at her spinning wheel, thinking of her husband's horse that
has lost the shoe of its left hind foot. Star Eye remarks to her toy horse:
"Mother is thinking that you have lost your shoe on your left hind foot"
(Topelius 1927, 151). In "The Smile of a Mountain Witch," Ōba's modern
yamauba repeats what her mother is thinking out loud. "When she was
still at a tender age and had not yet quite learned to use the bathroom, she
would be so engrossed in play that she often had accidents. She would say
to her mother who came running, 'Oh you naughty girl. You've got to tell
Mommy on time before it's too late,'" and the narrator says, "As her mother
burst out laughing, she would go on, saying, 'Really I'm no match for this
child!—What can I say!'" (Ōba M. 1991, 196). Star Eye's foster mother loves

Star Eye and feels pity for her because she knows Star Eye cannot help it—Lapp children are believed to use witchcraft. But "much as the good foster-mother loved the child, she did not take kindly to this strange power" (Topelius 1927, 149–50). Likewise, in "The Smile of a Mountain Witch," the mother loves the child but finds her difficult to deal with: "Utterly amazed at her daughter reading her mind time after time, [she] would give in, saying, 'This child is very bright, but she really tires me out!'" (Ōba M. 1991, 196).

I assume that many people have had an uneasy experience or two in their lives thinking someone may have seen into their minds. If one feels that one is being watched (seen through) all the time, it would be very frightening—just as the mother of Ōba's modern yamanba and Star Eye's foster mother felt. It would be equally exhausting for the mind reader to be able to see into people's hearts. As a mind-reading ability is paranormal, not everyone has it, and it could very well frighten people—the association of mind reading with witchcraft is unsurprising.

While folktales may have first inspired Ōba, perhaps her own experience, such as her interaction with her mother, who passed away at the age of sixty-two, may also have influenced the creation of her character—her character's disposition, at least, if not exactly her mind-reading ability. Ōba notes, "My Meiji-born mother was a fairly new type of woman. She spoke frankly and demanded her children to do the same" (Ōba M. 2010b, 334). Speaking one's mind and mind reading are not the same, of course, but both can make the other party uncomfortable. In her later years, Ōba's mother seemed to have regretted teaching her children to be so frank. Ōba writes, "Perhaps when I abused someone by speaking my mind—as my mother always instructed me to do, or stubbornly refused to accept someone's opinion," her mother looked unhappy. Ōba continues, "There was a time that my mother suddenly changed. She stopped scolding us, and instead, started to gaze into the far distance like *a distant mountain*" (my emphasis). This may be reflected in Ōba's modern yamauba, who dreamed of living in her native mountain landscape. Likewise, Ōba herself seems to have behaved like the yamauba: "Because my mother understood the subtle workings of the human mind and her children acquired the ability intuitively, I learned to back out when someone was in a bad mood" (Ōba M. 2010b, 334). That Ōba considers herself a yamauba is well described in her short story "Majo ni atta yamanba" ("Yamauba Who Met a Witch") (Ōba M. 2010a, 434–39) and other works.[14] These characters all behave differently from those in the mainstream—such as having a mind-reading ability or speaking their minds out loud—and are meshed together to help create the remarkable character of the yamauba of "The Smile of a Mountain Witch."

Selfless Yamauba of "The Smile of a Mountain Witch"

Ōba's modern yamauba presents a more amiable side of yamauba. Unlike her version of the folkloric yamauba in the prologue, who reads men's minds in order to entrap them (and eat them), Ōba's Shōwa yamauba in the main story uses her ability to please her loved ones, especially her husband, molding herself into the person they wish her to be. Her ability culminates in her final act of taking her own life so that she will not continue to be a burden to her family in terms of financial and physical care. Even after the woman's death, her daughter feels content because her mother's face is the picture of happiness, her final effort to comfort her daughter and her husband.

One may consider that Ōba's yamauba lacks self-conviction: she goes with the flow, protecting herself from social complication; or she lives a selfless life with remarkable endurance in Japanese patriarchal society. The precedents of women serving their husbands and children in the patriarchal family system could broadly include fictional yamauba such as Yaegiri-yamauba of *Komochi Yamauba*, who is loyal to her husband and motherly to her child, or the yamauba of the kabuki dance, who dotes on her child without reservation. Even though Yaegiri-yamauba and her ilk live in the mountains, they conform to social norms and have no doubt that what they do—going into the mountains to rear their child as ordered by their husband, taking care of the child and presenting him to the lord—is the right thing. Surely the contemporary audience's interest lies more in the actors' performance, but still, the characters are created within the construct of a patriarchal social system.

Ōba's yamauba behaves like a loving mother and caring wife, like her theatrical precedents. What is unique about Ōba's narrative is, however, telling the tale of the yamauba *critically* through the yamauba's perspective—her *hon'ne* (true feelings and opinions). As Michiko Wilson writes in her insightful article (2013), Ōba's modern yamauba suppresses her hon'ne to please people who are dear to her. This perspective reveals to the reader not simply the suffering of a mountain witch living as a woman in contemporary Japanese society, but the suffering of a woman in a man's world. Mizuta Noriko comments that "while reflecting the image of yamauba orally transmitted in folktales, the story describes a wife and mother of a nuclear family in contemporary Japan. The work is simultaneously double-structured to portray the psychological depiction of women serving their husbands and children in the patriarchal family system in the past" (Mizuta 2002, 28).

Ōba's yamauba of the Shōwa period uses her ability exclusively for her family's domestic happiness, not her own. The narrator of "The Smile of a Mountain Witch" comments in the prologue: "These beasts [such as cranes, foxes, snowy herons] that disguise themselves as human women invariably make extremely faithful spouses; they are very smart and full of delicate sentiment. Yet, their fate somehow is inevitably tragic" (Ōba M. 2009, 463; Ōba M. 1991, 195–56). The sad death of Ōba's yamauba is in concordance with the traditional ending of such supernatural beings.

Although the status of Ōba's yamauba is not specifically described, she is believed to be a homemaker, as was the norm at the time of publication in 1976. In the 1970s the term *kotobuki taisha* (auspicious resignation from a company) was used as a conventional matter of course—women were expected to resign from their work upon marriage or prospective marriage (before reaching the age of twenty-five) because women's happiness was equated with marriage (see Hori T. 2018; Ishinabe 2014). The term reveals the social/historical thoughts of the time—the female role (and her happiness) was firmly believed to exist solely at home, within a household. Beliefs about women's status have changed since then. The Japanese Equal Employment Opportunity Law was passed in 1985 and implemented in 1986. After the collapse of the Japanese bubble economy in the early 1990s, when lifetime employment in a company was no longer the norm, a wife's financial contribution to a household became increasingly important. The number of households in which husband and wife both work surpassed that of single-income households in 1997. While this indicates women's advancement in society as part of the workforce, it also reflects Japan's entering an era of economic stagnation in which a double income became necessary (Honma 2018). At the beginning of the Reiwa era (2019–), the term *kotobuki taisha* is considered obsolete. If someone were to write a sequel to "The Smile of a Mountain Witch" that reflects present Japanese society, the yamauba of the Reiwa period may use her mind-reading ability to solve murder mysteries or expose government corruption.

FORTUNE-TELLING YAMAUBA: THE OLD WOMAN IN "NARANASHI TORI" ("PICKING WILD PEARS")

While reading minds could be an advantage or disadvantage to the party who possesses that power, telling the future could be advantageous or disadvantageous to the party whose fortune is told. As mentioned earlier, Komatsuzaki Susumu and Komatsuzaki Tatsuko (1967) point out that some yamauba can foretell the future and use this ability to help good people, as seen in "Naranashi tori" ("Picking Wild Pears").

In "Naranashi tori," classified as the story type 176 by Seki Keigo (1966, 121), a mother is sick in bed and her condition is getting worse. The family is too poor to buy medicine. One day she says she wants to eat wild pears grown in the mountains. The eldest of her three sons goes to the mountain to pick wild pears for her. On the way he meets an old woman sitting on a big boulder; she gives him advice about how to get to the place where the wild pears grow. But he forgets her advice and is eaten by the monster of the pond on the mountain. The second son meets the same fate. The old woman gives the same advice as well as a sword to the youngest son. He follows the old woman's advice and succeeds in picking fruit and rescuing his elder brothers with the sword. The brothers safely return home with many wild pears and their mother recovers from her illness (Kanzawa 1967; *NMT* 1978–1980, 4:35–44). While the old woman in "Naranashi tori" gives advice to three brothers, it is up to them whether they use that advice to accomplish their task. In other words, whether the fortune-telling yamauba is considered beneficial or harmful depends on how the characters utilize her foreknowledge.

Interestingly, Kanzawa Toshiko, the author of *Nashitori kyōdai* (Wild pear–picking brothers, 1967), which is part of an illustrated book series on which Komatsuzaki Susumu and Komatsuzaki Tatsuko commented, does not call the old woman a yamauba in her book; she is described simply as "an old woman." Likewise, in the stories of "Naranashi tori" included in Seki Keigo's *Nihon mukashibanashi taisei*, (*NMT* 1978–1980), the character with foreknowledge is also referred to as an old woman, or sometimes as an old man, a bird, a gourd, and so on, but none of them are called a yamauba. It is Komatsuzaki Susumu and Sakamoto Hideo who call the old woman a yamauba in their explanation of Kanzaki's "Naranashi tori" story. Indeed, according to the survey conducted by Komatsuzaki and Sakamoto, children did not think the woman was a yamauba until they were told this by their teachers.[15] One student expressed the opinion that the old woman was a deity because she knew so many things and helped the brothers. The children were surprised to hear that this old woman was a yamauba, because the yamauba they knew about were scary and the one in this story was kind. Only one source—Seki Keigo's English article "Types of Japanese Folktales" (Seki 1966, 121)—calls the character yamauba.[16] But this woman certainly is old and lives in the mountains; she seems to know all about the mountain. So it is understandable that she would be called a yamauba. And as she knows everything about the mountain, she may indeed be a manifestation of a mountain goddess.

SHAMANISTIC YAMAUBA IN *HANAYO NO HIME*

A yamauba with the ability to tell the future already appears in *Hanayo no hime* (*Blossom Princess*, ca. late sixteenth century or early seventeenth century).

The yamauba says to Blossom Princess, the heroine of the story: "You are a fortunate person but meet hardship like this because someone hates you. Still, in the end, you will be happy. Come here. I'll give you this small bag because you've done something for me. Open it when you marry a young man" (Reider 2016, 183). As discussed in chapter 1, the yamauba in *Hanayo no hime* is a helper and a fortune giver. She is also a fortune-teller, a shamanistic being. Okada Keisuke notes that the relationship between an oni and a yamauba is based upon the notion of a mountain deity and a maiden who serves the deity. In the text of *Hanayo no hime*, when the heroine prays for the mountain deity, she encounters a yamauba, and then the oni. As the narrator uses the word *kijin* (oni and deities), this oni himself suggests a mountain deity. The yamauba can also be considered a maiden who serves the mountain deity (Okada 1976, 160–61; 1977, 69–70).

Further, Yamagami Izumo speculates that old women in the legends of abandoned old folks in the mountains (see chapter 5) were originally elderly shamanesses living in the mountains; the abandoned women and the old women living in the mountains possessed the same character and supernatural power of sorcery. The contradictory stories of yamauba eating children and giving birth to children and raising them to be superheroes are indicative of her extraordinary power of sorcery and fortune-telling (Yamagami 2000, 380).

THE WITCH IN *THRONE OF BLOOD*

A more ominous and perhaps internationally known fortune-telling yamauba is Akira Kurosawa's witch in his film *Kumonosu-jō* (*The Castle of the Spider's Web*, 1957), known in the West as *Throne of Blood*. The film is based on Shakespeare's *Macbeth* (1606) and portrays the rise and fall of an ambitious nobleman. In Kurosawa's hands, the three weird sisters in *Macbeth* become one *mononoke* (evil spirit or witch). Kurosawa's witch is our yamauba—a combination of the woman in *Kurozuka* and Yamanba in the eponymous noh play. She lives in the center of Spider's Web Forest (Kumode no mori). The strong relationship between yamauba and spiders seen in chapter 2 is instrumental in understanding Kurosawa's fortune-telling yamauba.

In the film, Washizu's (Macbeth) ambition and desire to become ruler at all costs is wickedly incited by the prophecy of the witch in Spider's Web Forest. The witch's prophecy envelops the play's characters and audience like a spider spinning a web, and eats at Washizu's mind as it feeds on his and his wife's ambitions. The witch of the forest is the weaver of the net; with her symbolic spinning wheel, she instigates the characters' ensuing actions.

THE CASTLE OF THE SPIDER'S WEB AND THE SPIDER'S WEB FOREST

The translation of the original Japanese title is *The Castle of the Spider's Web*, the name of the castle where Washizu resides as ruler after killing his master. Kurosawa comments on the title, "When I went into the way castles were constructed in those days, some of them made use of the wood which was grown as if it had been a maze. Therefore, the wood was named 'the wood of spiders' hair,' meaning the wood that catches up invaders as if in a spider's web. The title *The Castle of the Spider's Web* (*Kumonosu-jō*) came to me in this way" (Manvell 1971, 104). The key is "the wood that catches up invaders *as if in a spider's web*" (emphasis in the original). In his film, Kurosawa has Miki (Banquo) say, "The infamous Spider's Web Forest. Stretching out like a spider's web, protecting Spider's Web Castle against all foes."[17] The wood catches all foes—including Washizu in the end.

According to Blumenthal, the forest is "both the battleground where the conflict rages and the very incitement to conflict . . . It is the life at the centre of the film." He equates the forest with Washizu's mind (Blumenthal 1965, 191). It indeed represents the warrior Washizu's mind; he is trapped by his own ambition and desire, and the forest's web will not let him go. Eventually the ignited Spider's Web Forest implodes on Washizu. The forest represents a mechanism for perpetual human desires through Washizu, the prey caught in the spider's web. The Castle of the Spider's Web is located near the Spider's Web Forest, standing at the edge of the web. The forest does not grow naturally, however. The weaver—the evil spirit or witch—who resides in the middle of the Spider's Web Forest spins its web. She is a human-eating hag—like "the hag who appears in the noh play named *Black Mound*" (Manvell 1971, 103).

FROM THE WOMAN IN *KUROZUKA* TO THE WITCH OF *THRONE OF BLOOD*

Of adapting Shakespeare's *Macbeth*, Kurosawa says: "In the case of the witch in the wood, I planned to replace it with an equivalent to the hag which appears in the noh play named *Kurozuka* (Black mound). The hag is a monster which occasionally eats a human being. I realized if we were to search for an image that resembles the witch of the West, nothing exists in Japan other than this. The other parts, however, I went on developing during the actual stage of interpretation" (Manvell 1971, 103). In other words, Kurosawa had a clear image of how he was going to portray the witches in *Macbeth* in his own film: as the oni-woman who secretly accumulates human bones and skulls, rotten corpses, and so on in her bedroom in the noh play *Kurozuka*. The image of a witch in the West is

Figure 3.1. The evil spirit of *Throne of Blood*.

easily relatable to a Japanese oni-woman because of her major attribute of anthropophagy.

As written in chapter 1, there are only two props on the noh stage of *Kurozuka*: one is a simple wooden frame, symbolizing her lone house, in which the old woman or mae-shite (the lead actor of the first act) sits. The frame barely holds her. She comes out of her hut, and a little later a spinning wheel, the other prop, is brought onto the stage. Sitting on the otherwise bare stage, the woman slowly spins the wheel and laments her current poor environment.

In the film, when the two generals, Washizu and Miki, encounter the old witch in Spider's Web Forest, she is seated at a spinning wheel in a simple framed hut, the two props used in *Kurozuka* (Toida 1964, 19). Lost in Spider's Web Forest, Washizu and Miki come to the hut, which is only partly visible because a huge tree is blocking the site. Washizu, saying that the unfamiliar hut is "the work of an evil spirit," tries to shoot an arrow, when they hear a strange chanting coming from the dwelling. They dismount their horses and approach the hut from the side, the closest point to the generals. The generals (and the audience) go around the tree and are greeted with a full view of an eerie old woman sitting at a spinning wheel—in a long shot, the camera shows her profile from the right side, with the spinning wheel closest to the camera. The camera then zooms in so the audience's eyes will naturally focus on the mysterious old female figure. Her chanting continues. Soon, however, the audience's eyes will shift to the huge spinning wheel (much larger than the one used in *Kurozuka*) that the uncanny hag is spinning. It is the wheel's slow and steady movement in an otherwise static scene that compels the audience to focus attention on it.

In *Kurozuka*, the woman reluctantly starts to turn the spinning wheel at the request of the chief yamabushi. As she begins turning the wheel, she chants of her longing for the past:

> *Maso-o no ito o*
> *kuri-kaeshi*
> *Mukashi o ima ni*
> *Nasabaya*
>   (*SNKBZ* 1994–2002, 59:463)

> Pure linen thread let me spin
> turning it round and round,
> How I long to spin
> the past into the present!
>   (Shimazaki C. and Comee 2012, 314–17)

The woman recites about the transient nature of this world and the cycle of reincarnation; she sings of an illusory, elegant world of the past in the capital, alluding to the *Tale of Genji* in the style of *ito-tsukushi*, enumeration of strings. The woman in the noh play turns the spinning wheel to make a living, to entertain guests, to express her longing for the past and her desire to be released from the transient world. This is a sad, subtle, and poetic scene in which her projected thoughts and memories run like a revolving lantern or kaleidoscope—she moans for her irretrievable past. The witch of Kurosawa's *Throne of Blood*, on the other hand, spins out the generals' future—the thread of fate—as she also recites on the impermanence of this world, themes in concordance with *Kurozuka* and many other noh plays.

DESIRES, IMPERMANENCE, AND THE WHEEL

While spinning the wheel, the witch chants, "Why should men receive life in this world? Men's lives are as meaningless as the lives of insects. The terrible folly of such suffering." She chants further about the transient nature of life and the futility of human desire: "A man lives but as briefly as a flower, / Destined all too soon, / To decay into the stink of flesh. Humanity strives, / All its days, / To sear its own flesh, / In the flames of base *desire*" (emphasis added). As many critics say, one of the major themes of the film is Buddhist teaching on *mujō*, the impermanence and transient nature of this world—the brevity of worldly gains and fame, and the instability of sentient beings (see, for example, Goodwin 1994, 169–91; McDonald 1994, 124–38). The chorus chants at the beginning and at the end of the film: "Look upon the ruins, / Of the castle of delusion, / Haunted only now by the spirits, / Of those who perished. A scene of carnage, / Born of consuming *desire*, / Never changing, / Now and throughout eternity, / Here stood Spider's Web Castle" (emphasis added).[18]

Desire is the cause of suffering. The Four Noble Truths, the essence of the Buddha's teaching, instruct that: (1) in all life there is suffering; (2) suffering is caused by desire; (3) suffering can be ended because the cause is known; and (4) the way to end suffering is to follow the Noble Eightfold Path.[19] Desire is the second of the Four Noble Truths that the historical Buddha delivered in his very first sermon at Deer Park in Sarnath near Varanasi in India. This sermon is called the First Turning of the Wheel of Dharma. Dharma or Buddha's Law are the Buddha's teachings of the path to enlightenment; the first sermon symbolizes the historical Buddha's "action of setting the Wheel of the Law in motion" (Fisher 1993, 20). While Buddha taught the Four Noble Truths in order to help release humans from the cycle of reincarnation, the witch in the film is turning the wheel to sets ambitious men into motion toward destruction. Instead of showing a path to enlightenment, Kurosawa's witch's wheel goes around and gets nowhere, only stirring human cravings.

The Castle of the Spider's Web is a testimony to the result of unleashed human desire, which continues the cycle of suffering—a cycle like a wheel. The wheel is one of the oldest symbols of Buddhism. The Wheel of Suffering represents the cycle of rebirth of a human or the transmigration of sentient beings through the six realms: hell, starving ghosts, beasts, raging spirits, men, and deities. Thus, while the wheel in the film is spinning the thread of fate for man, the wheel simultaneously represents the Wheel of Suffering in which humans are trapped.[20] I believe Washizu and Miki are fundamentally good men, but when a yamauba tells one's fortune or gives advice, it is up to the characters how they react. In the case of Washizu and Miki, they became slaves to the yamauba's judgment.

After the witch and the hut vanish, the camera pans over the surrounding mounds of dead bodies. As McDonald (1994) notes, these mounds are superimposed on the image of the pile of corpses that the traveling Buddhist priests found in the forbidden room—the old woman's bedroom in *Kurozuka*. The piles of bodies and bones surrounding the hut in the film are the result of human folly, showing the fate of those who died in battle. This is a forbidden sight—Washizu's mind is exposed, like the skeletons in a closet that should not be seen. For Washizu and Miki to encounter the witch in Spider's Web Forest is tantamount to opening the door of the forbidden room in *Kurozuka*. Washizu and Miki learn what they are not supposed to know. Innocent travelers in *Kurozuka* become the hag's side dish and are devoured. Likewise, Washizu, Miki, and an assassin sent by Washizu become the witch's prey. The evil spirit of the forest catches her victims with the web from her spinning wheel.

When the generals finally come out of the forest and see the castle, Miki says, "Finally free of that spider's web." That freedom, however, is an illusion. The evil spirit that prophesizes the generals' fortunes watches and sees all.

From Yamauba in the Noh Play *Yamanba* to the Witch of *Throne of Blood*

While Kurosawa uses the hag in *Kurozuka* for the witch in his film, the noh mask he chose for his witch was not the hannya mask used for *Kurozuka* but a yamanba mask used for the noh play *Yamanba*.[21] A yamauba's major trait, like an oni-woman's, is anthropophagy. Significantly, the visual image of the evil spirit of the forest in the film—an old woman with a face like a yamanba mask and disheveled white hair—is that of a yamauba. As a lover of noh theater, Kurosawa must have known *Yamanba*.

When Washizu and Miki lose their way in the forest, it is ominously foggy and dark. Suddenly rain pours. Lightning strikes and thunder crashes.[22] The generals then hear unidentifiable shrieks—pealing laughter. Washizu says to Miki, according to Donald Richie's translation, "An evil spirit—a spirit of the forest is holding us here" (*mononoke ja, mononoke no shiwaza ja*) (Kurosawa 2003). Indeed, the evil spirit is holding the generals with her Spider's Forest Web spun out of her spinning wheel.

Like the witch in the film, Yamanba, the protagonist of the noh play *Yamanba*, is endowed with supernatural power. She darkens the sky to stop a group of entertainers so that they stay the night at her place. Yamanba requests a dance and song from Hyakuma Yamanba, who became famous by impersonating Yamanba and dancing Yamanba's dance. At night, while urging Hyakuma to dance, the real Yamanba dances, describing her life in the mountains. Yamanba's dance is fitting, because the witches in Shakespeare's *Macbeth* often dance before they exit the stage.[23] Importantly, at the end of the noh play, the chanters sing that Yamanba "soars up peaks, resounds down valleys. Until now she was here, or so it seemed, mountain after mountain, making mountain rounds, her destination never to be known" (Bethe and Brazell 1998, 225). That is how the evil spirit of the film disappears; she vanishes suddenly after her first appearance. It should also be noted that when the evil spirit appears the second time, she is running through the mountains, as Yamanba in the noh play does on her mountain rounds.

The noh play's Yamanba does mountain rounds in her attempt to be released from the cycle of reincarnation. The witch in the film, on the other hand, keeps sentient beings trapped in her spinning wheel, or aloofly watches humans and their folly. When the witch appears the second time to respond to Washizu's call, she stands on the mound of corpses. She is literally on top of it—smiling, as she knows that Washizu will soon be part of the mound. She seems to know everything. In that sense, she is like a goddess of the forest.

The witch of Spider's Web Forest, by igniting ambitious thoughts in Washizu, exposes the fundamental desire, foolishness, and madness that continue the cycle of incarnation, keeping humans trapped in the world of suffering. Kurosawa's film portrays the lives of an ambitious man and wife during the period of civil wars in Japan, when a lower-ranking retainer overthrows his lord. At the story's epicenter lies the witch—our yamauba. The evil spirit foretells the future, weaves Spider's Web Forest, traps and manipulates the minds and bodies of Washizu and Miki. She makes the forest work against the Castle of the Spider's Web, "the castle of delusion," an illusion she has created. The wheel in Buddhism symbolizes the Buddhist Law that destroys ignorance and breaks the cycle of life and reincarnation. The witch's wheel, on the other hand, warps the Wheel of Dharma. It reflects human ignorance and the cycle of suffering. The wheel spins out the thread of fate. By the witch's hand, it produces a spider's web that grows into the Spider's Web Forest to catch every sentient being. They all perish in the end, as nothing lasts forever. The witch of *Throne of Blood* encompasses the Yamauba of the noh play, the woman of *Kurozuka*, spiders, and spinning. Kurosawa's witch is a wonderful saisō—re-creation—of yamauba.

MIND READING, FUTURE TELLING, AND RE-CREATION

Yamauba's telepathic ability, which is usually not registered as one of her common traits among modern Japanese people, does not originate with yamauba, but rather with an evil creature used to explicate religious teachings during the medieval period. Eventually the mind-reading trait became yamauba's via satori, most probably as a female counterpart of a satori man. The telepathic ability of yamauba does not go well with the fate of yamauba in many famous anthropophagous yamauba folktales, but these two traits rarely appear in the same tale. In the prologue of "The Smile of a Mountain Witch," however, Ōba combined the two types of yamauba and re-created, through saisō, her yamauba. "The Smile of a Mountain Witch" is an entertaining story and a critique of contemporary patriarchal Japanese society. Perhaps the most significant contribution of the work from the perspective of the study of yamauba is, however, that Ōba foregrounded yamauba's less-known or little-known mind-reading attribute.

Another uncanny "seeing" ability of yamauba is her power to see the future, as in the case of the old woman in "Naranashi tori" or the forest witch in Akira Kurosawa's *Throne of Blood*. The man-eating yamauba does not possess an ability to see the future. The white-haired woman who resides in the heart of Spider's Web Forest spins out the thread of one's future, as with the self-fulfilled prophesy for Washizu and Miki. She could be a goddess of death in that she leads Washizu to self-destruction by inciting his ambition. Both Ōba's yamauba and Kurosawa's old witch are wonderful products of creative imagination, revealing how a prototype is continually re-created by reapplying the yamauba's attribute(s).

4

Yamauba, Yasaburō Basa, Datsueba

Images of Premodern Crones, Yamauba's Flying Ability,
and Re-creation of a Prototype

YAMAUBA AND ONI-WOMEN, REVISITED

Some scholars argue that flying is a trait of yamauba. According to Takashima Yōko, scholar of literature and cultural anthropology, yamauba shares with Western witches the ability to fly (Takashima 2014, 116). Takashima's description of yamauba's flying ability is based on earlier scholarship by Takahashi Yoshito (1995) and Ōwa Iwao (1996). In turn, they draw upon Miyata Noboru's work (1987) on the legend of Yasaburō Basa (Yasaburō's old mother).[1] Note, however, that Miyata calls Yasaburō Basa a kijo (oni-woman, female ogre/demon), not a yamauba, although he does write that such kijo legends are based on the yamauba legends narrated in mountainous areas (Miyata 2000, 203).

Furthermore, both Takahashi and Ōwa make use of "Rōba oni no ude o mochisaru zu" (Old woman leaving with the oni's arm, 1889), a woodblock print by Tsukioka Yoshitoshi (1839–1892). The print portrays a scene from the kabuki play *Ibaraki* (first performed in 1883) in which the eponymous oni transforms himself into an old woman to retrieve his arm from Watanabe no Tsuna (953–1025) (Isao 2001, 81).[2] Takahashi's caption for this print is "An illustration of a yamauba" (Takahashi Y. 1995, 50). Takahashi uses the terms *yamauba* and *oni-woman* interchangeably in his book.[3] Ōwa Iwao asserts, more explicitly, "Folkloric yamauba of our country eat human beings, and like witches, fly in the sky" (Ōwa 1996, 94). He then explains Tsukioka Yoshitoshi's print as an image of an oni-woman and yamauba from Niigata Prefecture named Yasaburō Basa. The caption that Ōwa gives for Tsukioka's illustration is "Yasaburō Basa portrayed by Tsukioka Yoshitoshi" (Ōwa 1996, 95).

DOI: 10.7330/9781646420551.c004

Figure 4.1. "Rōba oni no ude o mochisaru zu" (Old woman leaving with the oni's arm, 1889), by Tsukioka Yoshitoshi (1839–1892). (Courtesy of Japanese National Diet Digital Library.)

In chapter 3, we saw that Akira Kurosawa adapted the image of the oni-woman from the noh play *Kurozuka* as the counterpart of the three weird sisters of *Macbeth*, and that he adopted a yamauba mask for the appearance of the forest witch. The image of a witch in the West is certainly that of a scary anthropophagous hag like the witch in "Hansel and Gretel," a fairytale of German origin; a widely acknowledged image of witches is also that they fly at night riding on a broom. But does the Japanese yamauba fly like Western witches? Oni can fly, indeed. This is exemplified by the oni who assaulted Watanabe no Tsuna (described below) and by Shuten Dōji, the oni chieftain.[4] But can a yamauba also fly? What is Yasaburō Basa to begin with, and how does Yasaburō Basa relate to yamauba setsuwa? Yasaburō Basa and yamauba seem to be related to another frightening female figure, Datsueba (literally, clothes-stripping, old woman). How are Yasaburō Basa, yamauba, and Datsueba related? This chapter addresses these questions by focusing on the legends of Yasaburō Basa and their variants, as well as on the concept of the creation, dissemination, and transformation of narratives and imagery.

LEGENDS OF YASABURŌ BASA

According to *Niigata ken densetsu shūsei* (Koyama N. 1996; Collection of the legends of Niigata Prefecture, hereafter *Densetsu shūsei*), there lived in Nakajima a hunter named Yasaburō.[5] He was a dutiful son. But his mother was known for her cruelty and desire for human flesh, and so the villagers feared her as an oni-baba. Whenever there was a funeral, his mother would exhume the body of the dead from the graveyard and eat it. One evening Yasaburō was attacked by a monster who grabbed him by the neck, but Yasaburō immediately took up his sickle, struck the monster, and severed its arm. The monster ran away. When Yasaburō returned home with the monster's severed arm, he found his mother lying in bed. When Yasaburō's mother saw the arm, she dashed away on foot (*tobidashite*) out of their house. It was not until the following morning that Yasaburō, having tracked the trail of bloodstains, discovered his mother was the monster. For two hundred years after that, Yasaburō's mother lived on Mt. Yahiko (in present-day Niigata Prefecture). In the first year of Hōgen (1156), however, Tenkai, a Shingon Buddhist monk of high virtue, remonstrated with her. She repented her evildoing and became a deity named Myōtara Ten'nyo, who protected good men and women and punished evil people (Koyama N. 1996, 177–78).

Miyata Noboru's account of the legend of Yasaburō Basa is almost identical to that in *Densetsu shūsei*.[6] The main character is again referred to as an oni-baba, not a yamauba. She lives for two hundred years, eating corpses and kidnapping children. But there are some minor differences. In Miyata's version, for example, Yasaburō's profession or where he lives is not mentioned. Also, when Yasaburō is attacked, the nature of the monster's departure is not mentioned. Importantly, when Yasaburō returns home with the monster's severed arm, his mother sees the arm, grabs it, and flies (aerially) away (*tobisari*) out of the hole in the gable to Mt. Yahiko (Miyata 2000, 201–2).[7] If Miyata had written it as "dashed (on foot)" instead of "flew (aerially)," I wonder if Takashima, Takahashi, and Ōwa would have considered flying ability to be a major trait of yamauba.

YASABURŌ BASA AS ONI-WOMAN

As we have seen in chapter 1, the terms *yamauba* and *oni-women* are used interchangeably in folktales when the woman is cannibalistic. In literature, extraordinary anger, resentment, and jealousy transform women into oni, but in many folktales oni-women do not express jealousy or anger. Could the Yasaburō Basa legends be such a case?

It turns out that one Yasaburō Basa story included in *Yahikoson-shi jiten* (Dictionary of the history of Yahiko village, 2009) explains that Yasaburō Basa became an oni precisely because of her resentment. Here, Yasaburō Basa appears as Kurozu Yasaburō's grandmother (or mother in another version). The Kurozus were an old family of blacksmiths who had left the Kumano region to follow the Great Deity of Yahiko to Yahiko village. When arranging the ridgepole-raising ceremony for the construction of the Yahiko Shrine in the third year of Shōryaku (1079), there was an argument over who would preside on the first day of the ceremony: the master blacksmith (Yasaburō), or the master carpenter. The Yahiko chief administrator decided that the master carpenter would serve on the first day. Yasaburō's grandmother (or mother) resented this arrangement so much that she cursed the administrator and the carpenter, and performed all manner of evil acts.

One day when Yasaburō was returning from hunting, Yasaburō Basa tried to take his spoils from him, but he fought back and cut off her arm. Later she attempted to kidnap Yasaburō's five-year-old son but was unsuccessful. Finally, she became an oni and left on the wind. She was able to fly freely, and went on to commit various heinous crimes in one province after another. In the first year of Hōgen, the monk Tenkai saw her lying against a large tree trunk at the foot of Mt. Yahiko. Understanding that she was Yasaburō Basa, Tenkai remonstrated with her. She repented of her sins, became a good deity, and was worshipped as Myōtara Ten'nyo, protector of children and good people. After that, Myōtara Ten'nyo lived at the foot of a large cedar tree, and when she heard about the death of an evil person, she snatched the corpse and its clothes and hung them on the branches of the tree, which came to be known as Baba-sugi (Old woman's cedar tree) (Yahikoson Kyōiku Iinkai 2009, 384).[8] Even Kishimo (in Sanskrit, Hārītī), a child-eater who became a protector of children like Yasaburō Basa/Myōtara Ten'nyo, did not think of eating her children. With their descriptions of her eating humans and committing horrendous crimes, these accounts show that Yasaburō Basa is indeed an oni-woman.[9]

Sasaki Raita, a scholar of Japanese literature, provides a very similar story. In the third year of Shōryaku (1079), a master carpenter and a master blacksmith quarreled over the seating order at a ceremony to celebrate the completion of the construction of Yahiko Shrine, and it was decided that Yasaburō the master blacksmith should sit below the master carpenter. Yasaburō's mother resented this treatment of her son so much that she became an oni. She would ride on black clouds and commit various evil deeds (Sasaki R. 2008, 205).

DATSUEBA AND IMAGES OF PREMODERN CRONES

Datsueba's Association with Yasaburō Basa and Yamauba

The image of Yasaburō Basa, an oni-woman who lived at the foot of a large tree and snatched the corpses of evil people, hanging their clothes on the branches of the tree, overlaps with that of Datsueba. The frightful-looking Datsueba sits under a large tree at the Sanzu River (Sanzu no kawa, Sanzugawa, or Sōzuka), which divides this world from the next.[10] Before the dead cross the Sanzu River, she mercilessly strips their clothes off, and hangs them on the large tree. When the dead are naked, Datsueba strips them of their skin. The stripped-off clothes and skin of the deceased symbolize their evil acts. The more evil they have been, the more the branches bend under the weight. Koyama Naotsugu, editor of the *Densetsu shūsei*, comments on Yasaburō Basa: "A statue of an ugly female, sitting with one knee up, is installed in the main hall of the Hōkōin, a temple of the Shingon sect of Buddhism, located next to Yahiko Shrine. This is the statue of Myōtara Ten'nyo, who was formerly Yasaburō Basa and was said to have become a deity after her repentance. A large Japanese cedar tree named Baba-sugi stands behind the Hōkōin. Designated as a natural monument, Baba-sugi is more than one thousand years old. This is the tree on which Yasaburō Basa was said to hang corpses" (Koyama N. 1996, 177). That Yasaburō Basa's statue sits with one knee up seems to identify her with Datsueba.[11]

As Caroline Hirasawa writes of the sculptures of Ubason (literally, revered crone, the deity worshipped at the Uba hall) housed in the Tateyama Museum in Toyama Prefecture, the posture of "one knee raised and the other leg crossed under its body" is "a pose also assumed by female *kami* sculptures (*shinzō*), [and] images of a deity called Datsueba" (Hirasawa 2013, 161). As I explain below, I feel that Yasaburō Basa/Myōtara Ten'nyo, Datsueba, and yamauba occupy three distinctive spaces: Yasaburō Basa/Myōtara Ten'nyo above the ground, Datsueba underground, and yamauba the mountainous middle ground.

According to Kawamura Kunimitsu, Datsueba first appeared in an apocryphal sutra called *Bussetsu Jizō bosatsu hosshin innen jūōkyō* (The sutra on the Bodhisattva Jizō's aspiration for enlightenment and the Ten Kings, hereafter *Jizō jūōkyō*).[12] An unattractive old female oni referred to as *ōna no oni* with the same role as Datsueba appears in *Dai Nihonkoku Hokke genki* (Miraculous stories of the Lotus Sutra in Japan, ca. 1043, hereafter *Hokke genki*) (Kawamura 1996, 35).[13] In *Jizō jūōkyō*, Datsueba's counterpart, called Ken'eō, receives clothes from Datsueba and hangs them on the branches of the tree called Eryōju, but he does not appear in other major literature such as *Hokke genki* or *Konjaku monogatarishū*.[14] In a text that was hugely popular and influential during the medieval and early modern periods, *Kumano kanshin jikkai mandara* (Mandala viewing the heart and ten worlds of Kumano, hereafter *Kumano mandara*), Datsueba is typically depicted alone and enormous, perhaps reflecting her importance or popularity. It is thus Datsueba who appears by the Sanzu River to strip the clothes from the dead and hang them on the tree branches.[15]

Datsueba appears in many depictions of hell, but Kawamura Kunimitsu writes that the most widely disseminated version is *Kumano mandara* (Kawamura 1996, 33). From the end of the medieval period to early modern times, Kumano bikuni, or itinerant nuns from the Kumano region who performed *etoki* (literally, picture explanation or decipherment) actively preached on the *Kumano mandara*, which visualized heaven and hells and "edified female audiences in particular with Buddhist teachings, while raising funds for temples and shrines in the Kumano Mountains" (Kaminishi 2006, 138).[16]

Datsueba is portrayed here with her clothes worn loosely, baring her drooping breasts and bony torso. She sits on a boulder in an illustration in the well-circulated *Kumano mandara* (Ogurisu 2014, 22).[17] She shares these features, in addition to her sitting posture with one knee up, not only with Myōtara Ten'nyo but also with the yamauba as illustrated in a late sixteenth- or early seventeenth-century otogizōshi titled *Hanayo no hime* (see figure

1.2).[18] Some Datsueba have disheveled white hair, just like the yamauba. While Datsueba is frightening to mortals, she has a dichotomous aspect. Kawamura observes that she strips clothes off the dead, but she also gives clothes to human beings before they are born, and so she is a goddess of birth and death (Kawamura 1996, 35–37). Shikama Hiroji also notes the duality of Datsueba. Datsueba stands (or sits) between this world and the other world. She symbolizes a being that punishes evil as well as saves people (Shikama 2013, 25–26).

Hirasawa writes, "Worship of an old woman *kami* (*ubagami*) took place throughout Japan and produced similar images . . . Folklore studies take this type of *kami* image as representing the mountain goddess (*yama no kami*) or old woman of the mountain (*yamanba*)" (Hirasawa 2013, 162; also see Kawamura 1994). Generally speaking, *ubagami* refers to an elderly woman who has been deified. For example, the spirit of a wet nurse (*uba*) for a high-born child will often be enshrined nearby if she has thrown herself into a body of water with the noble child.[19] Some ubagami are elderly shama-nesses and/or itinerant priestesses who, trying to flout the prohibition on women entering a sacred area, were instantly turned into stones, which were then worshipped as ubagami.[20] An ubagami worshipped at a village border is often known as *Shōzuka no bāsan*, which is a variant of *Sōzuka no bāsan* (the old woman of the Sanzu River) (Ōshima 2001b, 179).

The wooden Datsueba statue installed in Shōjuin temple in Shinjuku ward in Tokyo was known during the late Edo period as the "venerable crone of child-rearing" (*kosodate rōbason*) for her miraculous power to heal any kind of pediatric disease (Shikama 2013, 28). Legend has it that the statue was so famous for its cough-healing powers that people from all over Edo came to pay their respects in 1849, creating an enormous thriving market in the district (Shinjuku-ku Kyōiku Iinkai 1997).[21]

Hirasawa also notes the popularity of Datsueba in 1849 in relation to Ubason in Tateyama, Toyama Prefecture: "The white cloth carpeting the path across the bridge was dedicated to Ubason—and to yet another of her doubles, the female demon Datsueba who resides on the shore of the Sanzu river and removes the clothing of the dead as they arrive for judg-ment. The Datsueba cult became extremely popular around the An'ei era (1772–1781) to the extent that there were efforts to suppress it in Kaei 2 (1849). This Datsueba fad coincides with development of the Ubason-Datsueba cult at Tateyama" (Hirasawa 2013, 169).

Some of the recurring descriptions of Datsueba's activities—hanging clothes on branches, sitting on a boulder—may have been influenced by familiar images of a premodern old woman. A legend from the town of

Figure 4.2. Statue of Datsueba in Shōjuin temple, Shinjuku ward, Tokyo. (Photo by author, 2017.)

Mizuho, in the Ōchi district of Shimane Prefecture, tells of a yamauba who lived in a cavern at the foot of Mt. Nunohoshi. She wove her clothes and then aired them by hanging them over tree branches in the mountains (*NDT* 1982–1990, 11:174). Kawamura proposes that the Datsueba/old female goddess personifies a woman who lived a long time after completing her role as a mother, or a single woman who was never a mother; the image can be applied to any woman regardless of age, and was the harsh reality for women of the Muromachi period (Kawamura 1996, 38). Indeed, the image of Datsueba seems to be reflected in the description of yamauba in *Hanayo no hime*, who outlived all her children. She explains her situation to the princess: "My grandchildren and great-grandchildren were taking care of me, but they hated me so much and would not let me in their house. So, I made the mountain my home, picking up nuts for food" (Reider 2016, 181).

MEDIEVAL PROTOTYPICAL FEMALE FEATURES

Kawamura points out that the *Kumano mandara* includes hells specifically for women, such as the Blood Pool Hell (*Chi no ike jigoku*) (Kawamura 1996,

39). The Blood Pool Hell is described in the Blood-bowl Sutra (*Xuepen Jing*; in Japanese, *Ketsubonkyō*, late twelfth or early thirteenth century), which explains that women are punished in the Blood Pool Hell because "the blood produced by their bodies spills on the ground and offends the earth gods or ends up in rivers from which the water to make tea for holy men is drawn" (Glassman 2008, 177). Tokieda Tsutomu, who researched the spread of the *Ketsubonkyō* in eastern Japan, convincingly argues that from the medieval period onward yamabushi were heavily involved in conducting memorial services using the *Ketsubonkyō* for women who died in childbirth (Tokieda 1986, 595–98). At the close of the medieval period, traveling nuns "began to take over the propagation of the *Ketsubonkyō* cult and make it their own. These nuns carried paintings that revealed in lurid detail the world of the Blood Pool Hell and also offered the promise of salvation" (Glassman 2008, 181).

Ikumi Kaminishi points out that Kumano bikuni, who fostered and disseminated *Kumano mandara*, "sought laywomen, the last group to be prosélytized in Buddhism, as the prime target of their religious propaganda. Donations were expected from independently wealthy female patrons." Further, "in their *etoki*, women's biological conditions were incorporated into a moral discourse. The moral of the story was that mothers could escape the vicissitudes incurred by their female bodies if their sons and daughters donated money to Buddhist temples or erected Nyoirin's statue. Through this measure, a woman 'buys' an incarnation in Buddha Amida's paradise in the future. This misogynistic view has been propagated in Buddhism since its inception, but the Kumano *bikuni* turned the misogyny to their advantage" (Kaminishi 2006, 156, 160). Misogynistic Buddhist writings penned by men were encouraged by both men and women, and Kumano bikuni, many with yamabushi as husbands, helped drive home the condemnation of women's biological features among their female audiences. I should like to note that the proto-yamauba described as evil in early religious writings, such as the evil ubai (in Sanskrit, *upāsikā*; devoted lay female follower of Buddhism) in *Daisenji engimaki* (Legends of Daisenji temple, ca. early 1320s) or the old nun in *Jikidan innenshū* (Collection of direct sermons on cause and effect, 1585) (see the introduction and chapter 3) may be related to old itinerant nuns, or connected to the yamabushi's ambivalent view of women. In any case, depictions of an old woman in charge of death and birth became intricately entwined with these characters as well as with the imagination of preachers and audiences, creating similar reimagined portrayals of the image of women. Depending upon the location and individual perspective, these characters become goddesses or demons; and behind the dissemination of these stories of medieval prototypical female figures lies the influence of yamabushi, traveling bikuni, and religious practitioners.[22]

Yasaburō Basa/Myōtara Ten'nyo, Datsueba, and yamauba all possess the duality of good and evil; I believe premodern women put their hearts into these frightening-looking medieval crones so that the supernatural beings' compassionate side would render them some happiness or lessen their pain in life. These three supernatural beings have the power to judge people in accord with their actions. They look scary and stern, probably because they can see the truth of humans' hearts and actions, and reward or punish them accordingly. Their image symbolizes ordinary old women who, precisely due to their long life, have experience in the ways of the world, and knowledge of the vicissitudes of life, with all its happiness and sadness. Their accumulated years of life are reflected in their appearance, and their age has given them the power of persuasion over women.

PROCESSES OF ADAPTATION AND RE-CREATION OF A PROTOTYPE

COMMONALITIES BETWEEN THE YASABURŌ BASA STORY AND PREMODERN SETSUWA

Let us return here to the question of flying yamauba and Yasaburō Basa. As a number of scholars have pointed out (see, for example, Tanigawa 2005, 302), Yasaburō Basa is remarkably similar to the oni in the story "Ryōshi no haha oni to narite ko o kurawamu to suru koto" ("How the Hunters' Mother Became an Oni and Tried to Devour Her Children"), which is included in the twelfth-century *Konjaku monogatarishū* (*SNKBZ* 1994–2002, 38:76–78; Ury 1979, 163–65). In this story (hereafter called "Hunters' Mother"), two brothers go into the mountains to hunt deer. While they are waiting for their prey in the depths of the night, something grabs one brother's topknot. He immediately thinks an oni is trying to eat him. He asks his brother, who is in a tree fifty yards away, to shoot this monster. The brother shoots with accuracy, severing the monster's arm. When the two return home with the arm, their aged mother is writhing in pain in her secluded room. When she sees the arm, she rises from her bed, saying, "You—You—." The brothers throw the arm at her, shut the door, and leave. Soon after, their mother dies and they confirm that the arm was their mother's. In both "Yasaburō Basa" and "Hunters' Mother," some monstrous being grabs a son by the neck or topknot late at night in the mountains, and the son severs the monster's arm. When the son returns home with the monster's arm, he finds his mother lying in bed. She sees the arm from the bed, and demands it. The son belatedly learns that his aged mother is a human-eating oni. The fact that the "Hunters' Mother" tale appears in the *Konjaku monogatarishū* suggests it must have already been well known by the late Heian period. Indeed, it could very well be the seed for the Yasaburō Basa legends. While the aged mother in "Hunters' Mother" later dies in bed, however, Yasaburō Basa goes out on a corpse-eating spree. There is no description in the tale of how the old mother-oni gained access to the treetop to grab her son's topknot, so one can only imagine that she either climbed the tree or flew.

In "The Sword Chapter" ("Tsurugi no maki") of *Heike monogatari* (*Tale of the Heike*, fourteenth century), there is the famous episode of Watanabe no Tsuna's encounter with an oni at Modoribashi Bridge in Kyoto. Here the oni can fly. At Modoribashi, Tsuna comes upon a beautiful woman about twenty years of age who asks him to escort her home. Tsuna agrees and just as he lifts her onto his horse, she reveals her true identity as a monstrous oni. Grabbing Tsuna's topknot and flying into the air, the oni declares that he is going to take Tsuna to Mt. Atago. Tsuna deftly manages to cut off the offending arm, causing the oni to fly away. Sometime later, the same oni, disguised now as Tsuna's foster mother, visits his house, and asks Tsuna to show her the oni's arm. No sooner does Tsuna do so than she reveals her true oni identity, grabs the limb, and flies away with it. The oni in both stories grabs the victim by the neck or topknot, but the victim severs the oni's arm and returns home with it. The oni then retrieves his arm. In the latter story, the oni flies away from Tsuna's house with his arm, perhaps to Mt. Atago. In "Yasaburō Basa," Yasaburō Basa reclaims her hand and dashes/flies away from the house to Mt. Yahiko.

Tsuna's Modoribashi episode became the source for the noh play *Rashōmon*, written by Kanze Kojirō Nobumitsu (1450–1516). In the noh play, too, the oni clearly flies away after his arm is severed. Neither the oni in Tsuna's Modoribashi episode nor that in the play *Rashōmon* has a specific name. However, by the beginning of the Edo period, this nameless oni was considered to be Ibaraki Dōji, one of the right-hand men of the oni chieftain Shuten Dōji. In the popular eighteenth-century version of Shuten Dōji's story called the Shibukawa edition, the oni whose arm Tsuna severed is identified as Ibaraki Dōji. The Shibukawa edition is almost identical to a picture booklet published during the Kan'ei era (1624–1643), and so one can suppose that by the early seventeenth century the oni was commonly identified as Ibaraki Dōji (see Matsumoto R. 1963, 172). Tsukioka Yoshitoshi's woodblock print of 1889, "Rōba oni no ude o mochisaru zu," which depicts a scene from the kabuki play *Ibaraki*, reflects this belief. More than a century later, Takahashi Yoshito and Ōwa Iwao called the oni illustrated in "Rōba oni no ude o mochisaru zu" Yasaburō Basa and yamauba in their works *Majo to yōroppa* (1995) and *Majo wa naze hito o kūka* (1996), respectively.

IBARAKI DŌJI, SHUTEN DŌJI, AND YASABURŌ BASA

I mentioned at the outset that oni can fly, as exemplified by Shuten Dōji, the chieftain of oni. Here I speculate that Shuten Dōji stories are also connected to Yasaburō Basa. The connecting points are Shuten Dōji's identity as Yasaburō in some Shuten Dōji legends, and a description of Yasaburō Basa as a background component in the creation of the noh play *Yamanba*. Yasaburō Basa lived for 200 years terrorizing the villages around the foot of Mt. Yahiko. It is interesting to note that, according to *Ōeyama ekotoba* (Illustrations and writing of Mt. Ōe, ca. fourteenth century), the oldest extant Shuten Dōji text, the oni chieftain also lived on Mt. Ōe for 200 years and terrorized Japan, until his death at the hands of Minamoto no Raikō. In the aforementioned Shibukawa text, Shuten Dōji was born in Echigo province (present-day Niigata Prefecture), the birthplace of Yasaburō Basa. Interestingly, a legend in the Echigo region states that Shuten Dōji hid himself on Mt. Yahiko and that his comrade, Ibaraki Dōji, lived in the Karuizawa section of the nearby city of Tochio (Tokuda 2001, 86–87; also see Tanigawa 2005, 312–17).[23] Yasaburō Basa is Yasaburō's old mother, and Yasaburō Basa's habit of kidnapping and eating humans is similar to that of Shuten Dōji. Just like Shuten Dōji, Yasaburō Basa became an oni and left with the wind, flying freely and committing heinous crimes in various provinces.

As I have written elsewhere, it is generally accepted that there are two versions of Shuten Dōji texts: the Ōeyama (Mt. Ōe) version and that of Ibukiyama (Mt. Ibuki) (see Reider 2016, 11–12). One of the major differences between them is the location of the oni's fortress. In the Ōeyama version, the fortress is located on Mt. Ōe, whereas in the Ibukiyama version it is situated at Mt. Ibuki. Satake Akihiro argues that the Ibukiyama version was formed by incorporating into the Ōeyama version the subjugation of a warrior named Kashiwabara Yasaburō (d. 1201). Because of his military exploits in the war against the Heike, Yasaburō was appointed estate steward (*jitō*) of Kashiwabara manor (hence, Kashiwabara Yasaburō). According to an entry for the first day of the eleventh month of Shōji 2 (1200) in a Japanese historical chronicle titled *Azuma kagami* (Mirror of the east, ca. thirteenth century), the emperor commanded Sasaki Sadatsuna

(1142–1205), the military governor of Ōmi province, to subjugate Yasaburō because he exploited his position as steward to further his own interests. Yasaburō escaped to Mt. Ibuki to avoid capture and terrorized nearby villages for eighteen months before he was finally killed in 1201 by Sasaki Nobutsuna (1181–1242), the fourth son of Sasaki Sadatsuna (Satake 1977, 19–23, 119). Yasaburō was on the run in and around Mt. Ibuki from his escape until his capture, during which time he became known as the legendary figure Ibuki Yasaburō. Ibuki Yasaburō appears in *Sangoku denki* (Stories from three countries, 1407), a collection of setsuwa written by Gentō (dates unknown), as well as in the otogizōshi stories titled *Ibuki Dōji*. Ibuki Yasaburō and Kashiwabara Yasaburō are the same person (Satake 1977, 27).

According to *Sangoku denki*, a shape-shifter (*henge no mono*) named Yasaburō lived on Mt. Ibuki of Ōmi province. He dwelled deep in the mountains during the day and went out to steal treasures from people of various provinces at night. Because he devastated Japan, the emperor commanded the military governor of the province, Sasaki Bicchū-no-kami Minamoto no Yoritsuna (also known by the sino-reading Raikō) to subjugate Yasaburō.[24] Yoritsuna struggled to find Yasaburō, a supernatural being who appeared and disappeared at will. But after several years, and with the help of divine power, Yoritsuna finally encountered and killed Yasaburō. The evil spirit of Yasaburō then became a poisonous serpent, causing famine and harming Ōmi province for nine years. To appease Yasaburō's spirit, divine status was bestowed upon him, whereupon Yasaburō became a water deity protecting the area around Mt. Ibuki (Satake 1977, 16–17; Nagoya Sangoku Denki Kenkyūkai 1983, 145–51).

In one version of the *Ibuki Dōji* otogizōshi, Yasaburō was a great shape-shifter and villain. He secretly visited the beautiful daughter of a rich local man named Ōnogi, and the daughter soon became pregnant. Ōnogi entertained Yasaburō with a feast and lots of saké to the extent that Yasaburō died from acute alcohol poisoning. Before his death, Yasaburō offered a prediction to Ōnogi's daughter that her child with him would be endowed with supernatural powers. After a thirty-three-month pregnancy, she duly bore a child, Ibuki Dōji (Satake 1977, 10–12). In another version of the otogizōshi *Ibuki Dōji* (*SNKBT* 1989–2005, 54:185–213), Yasaburō of Mt. Ibuki was a saké-loving scoundrel who served the Great Ibuki deity, an incarnation of the legendary Eight-Headed Serpent. He married the beautiful daughter of a powerful family, Ōnogi. Ōnogi learned about Yasaburō's wrongdoing, such as his eating three or four beasts and domestic animals alive every day, and decided to kill Yasaburō while he was inebriated. Yasaburō died from Ōnogi's stab wound, but Ōnogi's daughter gave birth to a child who turned out to be as wild as his father. Like his father, the child had a great liking for saké, so he was called Shuten Dōji (Drunken Demon). As Satake writes, Ibuki Dōji later became Shuten Dōji (Satake 1977, 35).

Indeed, in yet another version of this otogizōshi story entitled *Ibukiyama Shuten Dōji* (Shuten Dōji on Mt. Ibuki), the serpent was a deity of Mt. Ibuki and the father of Shuten Dōji, who loved saké (*MJMT* 1987–1988, 2:357–78). Yasaburō thus later became identified with Shuten Dōji's father or Shuten Dōji himself. It is certain that the stories of Shuten Dōji were widely established in the fifteenth century. The evidence is to be found in such works as *Ōeyama ekotoba* and the record of a noh performance at the Daijōin temple at Nara in 1427 that includes *Ōeyama*, a noh play featuring Shuten Dōji (Sasaki R. 2008, 206). As Takahashi Masaaki writes, the background of Yasaburō legends lies in the legends of Shuten Dōji (Takahashi Masaaki 1992, 181).

YASABURŌ BASA'S INFLUENCE ON THE NOH PLAY *YAMANBA*

While Shuten Dōji legends influenced and, in turn, were influenced by Yasaburō Basa stories, Yasaburō Basa tales seem to have influenced the noh play *Yamanba*. At least, according to Isshiki Tadatomo (also known as Minamoto no Tadatomo, d. 1597), a military lord and poet, the Yasaburō Basa tales inspired Zeami to create the noh play *Yamanba* (Isshiki 2008, 84–85; Tokuda 2016a, 41). Isshiki recounts an old tale about Yasaburō Basa in his collection of tales and essays known as *Getsuan suiseiki*. While Isshiki does not use the word *kajiya* (blacksmith), his account is more akin to the mukashibanashi version of Yasaburō Basa stories titled "Kajiya no baba" ("Blacksmith's Old Mother"). The general plot goes as follows. A traveler or hunter sleeps in a tree. Many wolves or cats climb on top of one another to ascend the tree in order to attack him, but the traveler defends himself with his sword. The wolves then cry out for someone to send for the "blacksmith's old mother" for help. Soon a big wolf appears, but the traveler cuts off the wolf's foreleg. When the traveler returns home, or goes to blacksmith's house, he finds that his old mother or the blacksmith's mother has had her arm cut off. In one version, he kills the old woman, who then turns into a wolf. In another, he shows her the wolf's foreleg. When the old woman takes it and goes away, he finds the bones of his true mother under the floor (Seki 1966, 49–50. For the Japanese text, see *NMT* 1978–1980, 7:10–31).[25]

Isshiki recounts that across the sea from Sado Island was Mt. Yahiko, and at the foot of the mountain lived a lowly man named Yasaburō with his old mother. One day a Buddhist monk was passing along a mountain path on Mt. Yahiko when the sun set all of a sudden. Coming across a small temple, he went in to rest. While he was there, people came to cremate the body of a recently deceased person. After everyone attending the funeral had left, an oni rose from the pyre and tried to eat the monk. The monk earnestly prayed and drove the oni away with a dagger, cutting off the oni's arm. Realizing he was no match for the monk, the oni left, saying, "I will ask Yasaburō's mother on Mt. Yahiko for help." No sooner had the oni disappeared then daylight came back. The man took the arm, went to Yasaburō's house, and told them what had happened. Yasaburō's mother dashed out from the house saying, "This is my arm," took it, and flew off from the roof, riding on a gust of wind and black clouds (Isshiki 2008, 85). Isshiki notes, "'Encouraging compassion by entering the house of the evil' (*Kiman, kendon no mono no ie ni hairite, hito o nayamasu. Kaerite jihi no mono*), they say. Zeami incorporated this concept into his noh play, *Yamanba*." (Isshiki 2008, 85). Sasaki Raita annotates "this" to mean the compassionate side of the dual character of yamauba (Isshiki 2008, 85n18); Isshiki thus believes that Zeami's portrayal of Yamanba was a consequence of his connecting the compassionate side of yamauba to Yasaburō Basa.[26]

In the first half of the sixteenth century, Yasaburō Basa was already connected to *Yamanba*. Why, then, is Yasaburō Basa not called a yamauba rather than an oni? While Yasaburō Basa may have been a source for the noh play *Yamanba* in the early fifteenth century, it was widely recognized in the early modern period that the oni or old woman who cut off Tsuna's arm was Ibaraki Dōji or Shuten Dōji. Before the appearance of the word *yamauba* in the Muromachi period, yamauba-like beings were generally portrayed as oni or oni-women, so it is natural that the "Hunters' Mother" story and Tsuna's Modoribashi episode, both of which appeared earlier in history, used the term *oni*. The man-eating character in later works could presumably have been called a yamauba, but the term *oni* was used persistently, probably because the motif of an oni retrieving its arm is so strongly associated with the oni setsuwa. New setsuwa were continually created by adding to or deleting from preexisting ones, utilizing various narrative patterns.[27]

"YAMAUBA NO NAKŌDO" ("YAMAUBA GO-BETWEEN"), A VARIANT OF YASABURŌ BASA

A variant of Yasaburō Basa from Niigata Prefecture reveals a complex case of oni-yamauba—or, more descriptively, she is like an oni or cannibalistic yamauba and a helping yamauba combined in one character.

This Yasaburō Basa is categorized under the story type called "Yamauba no nakōdo" ("Yamauba Go-Between"), and it refers to both an oni-baba and a yamauba as well as Yasaburō Basa. In any case, she loves her grandchild so much that she eats him. After this, she becomes an oni-baba and lives on Mt. Kunigami, part of the Yahiko mountain range. She comes down to a village nightly to kidnap children. One day she approaches a young man to eat, but the man looks at her bare feet and gives her shoes. Overwhelmed by his kindness, she says she will arrange a bride for him and *flies* to Kyoto. (The yamauba must have flown to kidnap a bride from a large city.) She kidnaps Kōnoike's daughter and makes her the man's bride. The couple has children. The Kōnoike family, rich merchants known as the wealthiest family in Japan during the Edo period, learns that their daughter is alive, and gives the couple lots of money (*NMT* 1978–1980, 10:313). (Use of the name Kōnoike attests that the story was created after the Kōnoike family became rich and famous, during or after the Edo period.)

From a Jungian viewpoint, Kawai Hayao points out that she "loves her grandchild so much that she eats him" is "a vivid demonstration that an excess of affection for one's child may deprive him of his life" (Kawai 1996, 33). We have seen in chapter 2 a yamauba who eats a child she is babysitting. In this Yasaburō Basa variant, she eats her own grandchild. The old woman possesses duality—destructive and helpful aspects—in one character, without any intervention by a high priest like Tenkai. After her cannibalistic behavior, instead of becoming a deity for children and good people, she becomes like a god of matchmaking.

In another mukashibanashi of this story type from Niigata Prefecture, a man-eating yamauba brings a wife to a poor but good young man. This yamauba lives on a mountain ridge. No villager dares to cross the mountain because of the yamauba. A poor but filial young man who lives with his grandma is asked to go to the neighboring village across the mountain in exchange for money and rice, and he accepts the offer because his grandma will be taken care of in the event that the yamauba eats him. On the ridge, the yamauba is impressed by the man's filial piety and decides not to eat him. Saying she will arrange a marriage for him, the yamauba kidnaps Kōnoike's daughter and makes her the man's bride. The Kōnoike family learns of the daughter's whereabouts when she writes a letter to her parents. The parents tell her to return but the daughter refuses. Resigned, the Kōnoike family gives the couple lots of money (*NMT* 1978–1980, 10:313). In these stories, it is understood that the yamauba flies to the city to kidnap a bride from a rich family.[28]

CONCLUDING REMARKS

Above, I have pondered the ambivalent images of premodern crones represented by yamauba, Yasaburō Basa, and Datsueba, and yamauba's ability to fly—a query triggered by my questions about the relationship between yamauba and legends of Yasaburō Basa. The relationship between yamauba and Yasaburō Basa is deeply rooted in the fact that oni were a major origin, or predecessor, of yamauba. Yasaburō Basa was from the beginning an oni-baba: a man-eater and antisocial evil creature. She then made Mt. Yahiko her residence, and acquired the title of yamauba. It is typical of an evil yamauba that the terms *oni-baba* and *yamauba* are used interchangeably. So Yasaburō Basa can be considered both a yamauba and an oni-woman. As oni can fly, so too can an oni-woman like Yasaburō Basa. Much as Yasaburō Basa and Ibaraki Dōji fly, yamauba are also portrayed flying, although this is not one of their major traits.

If we look at the noh play *Yamanba* itself, at the end of the text Yamanba "soars up peaks" (Bethe and Brazell 1998, 225; *SNKBZ* 1994–2002, 59:582). The puppet as well as kabuki play *Komochi yamanba* (A yamanba with child, 1712), written by Chikamatsu Monzaemon, uses the same description for the yamauba who is the mother of super-child Kintoki: she "soars up peaks" (Chikamatsu 1959, 221). The yamauba who appears in *Kinpira nyūdō yamameguri* (Lay-priest Kinpira's mountain round, ca. early 1680s) is even more dynamic in her flying power. The yamauba has received "supreme supernatural power, travels through the three-thousand realms and, as she continues her mountain rounds, travels to the sky over the clouds. She is called the oni-woman" (Muroki 1969, 151). Here the yamauba flies an almost infinite distance.[29]

A flying yamauba becomes more noticeable in contemporary illustrations. For instance, Maruki Toshi (1912–2000), best known for her paintings of Hiroshima atomic bomb scenes, depicts a yamauba flying over mountain peaks, carrying her three children in her arms.[30] Conceivably, flying symbolizes freedom. Whether flight is used for good or evil, it is a reflection of human desire. Flying ability projected by humans onto yamauba (or any other figures, for that matter) may reflect human perception of yamauba as a supernatural creature.

The question about yamauba's flying ability led me to an examination of the relationship between three old female figures, Yasaburō Basa, yamauba, and Datsueba. The oni-woman Yasaburō Basa, who became Myōtara Ten'nyo, is similar to Datsueba, a terrifying hag who strips clothes or skin off of the dead at the bank of the Sanzu River, and yet gives clothes or skin to newborn babies. The representational similarities and primordial sense of duality among these females—Yasaburō Basa/Myōtara Ten'nyo, Datsueba, and yamauba—presumably reveal or reflect the collective image of old women in the Muromachi and Edo periods. Decrepit and frightening as they are, they are also given the power of beneficence. In the minds of the common people, these figures are connected, overlap, and are sometimes conflated.

Edward Drott writes that the aged were highly esteemed throughout Japanese history, "but actually it is not until the late Heian period (ca. 1050–1185)—a period I designate as the cusp of the medieval—that we witness a sudden proliferation of legends centering on *okina* gods"; the figure of the *okina* is "a mysterious old man featured in noh's ceremonial Shikisanban dances and revealed in many noh plays to be a god" (Drott 2016, ix–x). Although there is a venerable okina, no exact counterpart of a venerable crone figure is found in the medieval period. In folk beliefs, ubagami, which are inseparable from Datsueba or yamauba, may be a close proximity to a female version of the okina figure. Stories of old women, goddesses, or evil creatures continue to be told and retold. Old narratives involving various tales such as those of Tsuna and the Shuten Dōji setsuwa evolve, creating ever-new stories and images.

5

Aging, Dementia, and Abandoned Women
An Interpretation of Yamauba

YAMAUBA DOES NOT STRICTLY INDICATE an advanced age—voluptuous women living in the mountains could be yamauba or yamahaha, as we saw in chapter 2. However, the dominant image of yamauba is that of an aged woman, as discussed in chapter 4. In premodern times, an extraordinarily long-lived creature, or even an object, was believed to become an oni, as revealed in such stories as "How the Hunters' Mother Became an Oni and Tried to Devour Her Children" from the *Konjaku monogatarishū*, also discussed in chapter 4, and the *Tsukumogami ki* (Record of tool specters, Muromachi period) (see Reider 2016, chap. 7). Komatsu Kazuhiko writes that the term *tsukumogami* signifies longevity, suggesting that it refers to someone or something that has acquired special powers as a result (Komatsu K. 1994, 330).[1] The aged tool specters in *Tsukumogami ki* become oni, antisocial to human beings, and eat humans and animals. The exceptionally long-lived yamauba of *Hanayo no hime* is seen as an oni and is feared in accord with this belief. There is a strong connection between longevity and oni or yamauba. This chapter considers a possible modern interpretation of the longevity of the yamauba figure, and examines issues on aging and family conflict through the stories of Obasute-yama (abandoned women in the mountains), narratives still popular in contemporary Japan.

YAMAUBA'S ANTISOCIAL BEHAVIOR AND DEMENTIA

Intense emotions such as shame and rage can turn a woman into an oni, as seen in chapter 1. The woman in the noh *Kurozuka* feels undying shame, disgrace, and resentment that her appearance and activities have been exposed. Yamanba in the eponymous noh play must have felt a tinge of shame (or annoyance) to be known as an oni-woman who eats human

DOI: 10.7330/9781646420551.c005

beings. Otherwise, she would not have sought the good offices of the entertainer's group to spread the word that she actually helped villagers. Shame and rage are the cause of Izanami dispatching Yomotsu-shikome to kill Izanagi. What if, however, one behaves abhorrently and brazenly without any emotional struggle?

The story "Hunters' Mother" offers a clue. The narrator comments at the end of the story: "Senile and demented, their mother had become an oni and followed her children into the mountains to devour them. When parents become extremely old they always turn into oni and try to eat even their own children" (Ury 1979, 165).[2] The senility and dementia of the hunters' mother is explained as the cause of the old woman's cannibalistic behavior.

Komatsu Kazuhiko, who studied yamauba in the village of Monobe (present-day Kami City) in Kōchi Prefecture, writes that the yamauba in the area is a kind of spirit the villagers believe in, and that the yamauba plays certain societal roles. One such role is to explain the cause of old folks' diseases, expressing the idea that madness results from possession by a yamauba (Komatsu K. 1979, 351). According to a story of the area, a woman at Shin'ya became old and could not work outside, so she often looked after her grandchild at home. This old woman had started to sniff children whenever she met them. Her family thought it strange and people gradually began to loathe her. One day her family became so busy that the parents reluctantly asked the old woman to take care of their child while they were away working in the mountains. When they came back home in the evening, they found their child had been eaten by the old woman. Surprised, frightened, and angry, with the help of their neighbors, they piled firewood on a boulder, threw the old woman over it, and burned her to death (Komatsu K. 1979, 344–45). Komatsu Kazuhiko notes that while this story gives the impression of a mukashibanashi, the villagers of Monobe believed it was true. According to them, the old woman became insane and ate her own grandchild because a yamauba had possessed her. The yamauba who possessed the old woman here is considered to be an invisible entity. But according to another villager, the old woman gradually became a yamauba-like being because she was ill natured (Komatsu K. 1979, 345). In this case, the old woman is equated with the yamauba herself.

In another story, the grandmother of a household in a village in Kōchi Prefecture started to say incomprehensible things as she became older. Her family thought it was due to her old age. One day she went to the mountain to get firewood. Soon after she returned, she quarreled with her son over a trifling matter, then suddenly attacked him with a sickle. Her son was seriously injured and she cut off two of her own fingers. After that, the old woman became insane and was incarcerated until her death. A diviner-priest revealed that this event was due to a yamauba possessing the old woman (Komatsu K. 1979, 345).[3]

As life expectancy becomes longer in contemporary Japanese society, the term *dementia* becomes more familiar in everyday life. While at present Japan is known as a super-aged society, where more than one in five members of the population is sixty-five years old or older, the average life expectancy from ancient through the modern period was low, with a high infant mortality rate. Even in 1947, Japanese life expectancy was only about fifty years for men and fifty-four for women (Tokudome et al., 2016).[4] Under these circumstances, elderly people were rare. I speculate that elderly people with severe dementia were even rarer, and they would have been marveled at.

An elderly person can have a number of cerebral microemboli (ministrokes) when his or her family members are not present, and the personality of the person who has had a stroke sometimes changes. Also, a devastating event such as the death of someone dear can cause changes in the mind, post-traumatic stress disorder, or a serotonin deficiency. In the case of the yamauba possession in Kōchi Prefecture, it is possible to conjecture that the old woman described as having been possessed by a yamauba had suffered a stroke. When she regained her lucidity, the yamauba possession was said to have stopped; she was de-possessed. Each time an elderly person has a stroke, her physical and mental conditions deteriorate, and eventually she could lose herself and wander away from her home as a yamauba.

"Japan's dementia crisis hits record levels as thousands go missing," Justin McCurry reported in 2016. "The national police agency said 12,208 people with dementia were reported missing in 2015," and that "most had wandered off and were found within a day to a week, but 479 were found dead and 150 have yet to be located" (McCurry 2016). The number has increased steadily; in 2018, 16,972 people with dementia were reported missing; 508 were found dead (Asahi shinbun degitaru 2019). Yanagita Kunio noted that there were women who went into the mountains of their own volition (Yanagita 1968, 378–80). It is probably not too far-fetched to imagine that some of these women were in the later stages of dementia—they wandered off to the mountains and could not find their way back home. Actually, dementia is not limited to elderly people; although the number affected is significantly smaller, early-onset or young-onset dementia causes symptoms before the age of sixty-five. One major type, early-onset Alzheimer's, affects patients in their thirties, forties, and fifties. People with dementia—young and old—could have gone missing from their homes and been seen in the mountains. Dementia could be thus explained as the yamauba's doing. As written in the introduction, yōkai have been often called upon to explicate incomprehensible phenomena: what is inexplicable and mysterious, and perceived as negative, may have taken on the shape of yamauba.

GLUTTONOUS YAMAUBA AND DEMENTIA

Some yamauba—those that appear in "Kuwazu nyōbō" ("The Wife Who Does Not Eat") and "Ushikata to yamauba" ("The Ox-Leader and the Yamauba")—have enormous appetites. As we saw in chapter 1, a gargantuan appetite could imply memories of famine in villages. It might also suggest a suppressed female desire for a plethora of food, or a trace of Yomotsu-shikome, who has a divine proclivity for eating. An eating disorder such as bulimia nervosa or anorexia nervosa might be a reason as well.

Another possible explanation, I speculate, could be dementia—or what is presently termed frontotemporal dementia (FTD) in particular. The cause of FTD, in which the frontal and temporal lobes of the brain shrink, is unknown. The most common symptoms involve dramatic changes in behavior and personality, including increasingly inappropriate actions, lack of judgment and inhibition, and—importantly in reference to the voracious yamauba—overeating (Mayo Clinic n.d.). Changes in eating behavior may include "gluttonous or binge-like eating" and "rapid eating or stuffing food in the mouth, taking food from others' plates, or belching" (Dickerson 2014, 183).[5] This behavior brings to mind the way the yamauba in "Ushikata to yamauba" eats. FTD is often early-onset dementia, generally manifesting itself in patients forty to forty-five years old (Mayo Clinic n.d.). "It is probably the second most common cause of dementia in people younger than 65. Yet it has been reported with pathological confirmation in patients as young as 21 and as old as 85" (Dickerson 2014, 177).[6] While signs and symptoms of dementia vary depending upon the individual, young people are not exempt from dementia. FTD accounts for up to 20 percent of presenile dementia cases (Snowden et al. 2002, 140). The wife in "Kuwazu nyōbō" comes to mind, as she still looks young when she clandestinely eats food excessively. People with dementia do not recognize that their behavior is without decorum. Their perceptions are their realities—they do not believe they are doing anything wrong. From the viewpoint of the surrounding people, possibly including some of their caregivers, however, such behavior is not like the people who they used to know.

YAMAUBA AND "OBASUTE-YAMA" ("ABANDONED WOMEN IN THE MOUNTAINS")

Many elderly people stay mentally and physically healthy, happily surrounded by their family members. Ideally, as one advances in age, one's wisdom also advances. Respect for elders is especially encouraged in Confucian philosophy and was often observed in early modern Japan. A village headman of Higo province (present-day Kumamoto Prefecture) left a memorandum for his descendants, and one of the items encourages respect for the elderly. It reads: "Select a senior in the village and have him visit elderly people over seventy-four or seventy-five or eighty occasionally; at the end of the year or at the beginning of the year, have him send a small gift of paper handkerchiefs or one bagful of coal to those elderly folks. When the elderly people reach ninety years old, our lord would graciously bestow a congratulatory gift, so the senior should go and tell the members of the elder's family of the regards" (Kodama 2006, 125).

What would happen, however, if no one in the family wished to take care of the elderly person because supporting the old man or woman becomes burdensome, or because the caregivers do not feel any positive emotional connection with the elderly person—even if she or he does not suffer from dementia, like the yamauba in *Hanayo no hime*? The yamauba in *Hanayo no hime* outlived all her children, and her grandchildren and great-grandchildren hated her so much that they would not let her in their houses. The yamauba was ignored and abandoned by her own folks. She went to the mountains precisely because she was abandoned and forced to survive by herself. Hers is a story of "Obasute-yama" or "Ubasute-yama," an abandoned woman in the mountains.

Mukashibanashi "Obasute-yama"

Stories of "Obasute-yama" or "Ubasute-yama" exist all over Japan. "Obasute-yama" stories are often classified into four types (see Reider 2016, chap. 6).[7] The first type involves a middle-aged man, with a son, who plans to abandon one of his own parents by carrying him or her in a *mokko* (rope basket) to the mountain. But just as the man is about to leave his parent on the mountain, his son remarks that he is going to bring the mokko back to use again later. Realizing that the next time will be his turn, the middle-aged man brings his elderly parent back home.

The second type concerns the wisdom of an old person in solving difficult problems. A lord imposes a law to abandon old folks, but a man with strong filial feelings hides his parent in the cellar. One day, a neighboring

Figure 5.1. Tsukioka Yoshitoshi (1839–1892), *The Moon and the Abandoned Old Woman,* 1891, from the series *One Hundred Aspects of the Moon.* (Woodblock print; ink and color on paper, 14 5/16 × 9 5/8 inches [36.4 × 24.4 cm]. Courtesy of The Dayton Art Institute, Museum purchase with funds provided by Jack Graef Jr., Linda Stein, Susan Shettler and their families in memory of Jack and Marilyn Graef, 2019.9.100.)

country's king threatens to invade the lord's country unless the lord solves some difficult questions. The lord, unable to answer, issues a proclamation that anyone who can solve the problems will be rewarded. The man asks the questions of his hidden elderly parent, who easily solves the problems. The lord learns of the old parent's wisdom and rescinds the edict to abandon old people.

Yanagita notes that these two types have foreign origins. The latter originates in an old Indian legend that appears in a Buddhist scripture titled *Zōbōzōkyō* (Yanagita 1970b, 296), which influenced *Nihon ryōiki* (*Miraculous Stories from the Japanese Buddhist Tradition*, ca. 822) and *Konjaku monogatarishū*. Likewise, Wakamori Tarō considers it to have a foreign origin, also in Buddhist writings: *Hōon jurin* (in Chinese, *Fa yuan zhu lin*) written by Dao Shi (d. 683) in 668 (Wakamori 1958, 215). The wisdom of old folk is highlighted in these stories.

The third type is the breaking of branches to mark a trail on the mountain. On a journey to the place of abandonment, an old parent breaks branches off trees to guide the son safely home. Moved by his parent's love for him, the son takes the parent back home. The fourth type is the attainment of wealth by a deserted old woman. An old woman who is abandoned by her son on the mountain becomes wealthy with help from an oni or mountain deity, and her son and his wife are punished. An example story of the last type, as told in Iwate Prefecture, goes as follows:

> A son has a wife, who initially is nice to her mother-in-law. As years go by, the wife increasingly treats her mother-in-law as a hindrance and speaks ill of her to her husband. Looking at her elderly mother-in-law chewing up lice from her hair, the wife slanders the mother-in-law to her husband, saying that his mother steals and eats their precious rice. She then tells her husband to make a hut in the mountains, leave his mother there, and set fire to the hut. He does as instructed by his wife, but his mother escapes from the hut and warms herself by the fire with her legs wide open. Several oni children come there, see her genitals and ask what they are. The old woman replies that they form a mouth that eats oni. Believing the old woman, the oni's children offer her their *uchide no kozuchi* (wish-granting mallet) to save their lives. With the oni's mallet, the woman builds a town and becomes its lord. The wife learns the status of her mother-in-law and tries to do the same. But instead of getting rich, she burns to death in a hut in the mountain. (Sasaki K. 1964, 43–45)

The old woman is disliked to the point of being abandoned, but as if to compensate for or redeem the negative treatment she receives from her family, after desertion she is endowed with the power to produce material wealth to make herself and other people, usually compassionate strangers, happy. Like the old woman in the story, the yamauba in *Hanayo no hime* has miraculous powers that include fortune-telling, as seen in chapter 3.

In many mukashibanashi, the old folks are taken back to their homes and the custom of desertion is abolished. This happy ending may reflect a characteristic of mukashibanashi. Fukuda Akira writes that the general theme of complete mukashibanashi is the "infinite happiness of human beings" and the subject is the "acquisition of extraordinary happiness" (Fukuda A. 1984, 5). Even in the stories where no one comes back to retrieve an old woman, she still becomes rich when a wish-granting mallet is given to her. Yanagita Kunio conjectures that mukashibanashi of this type are perhaps born out of similar stories like "Obasute-yama" of Sarashina in Shinano province, which is well known as the 156th episode of *Yamato monogatari* (*Tales of Yamato*, ca. mid-tenth century) (Yanagita 1970b, 301).

"OBASUTE-YAMA" IN OTHER LITERARY TRADITIONS

The 156th episode of *Yamato monogatari* is the oldest extant narrative of "Obasute-yama" and has exerted an enormous influence on later stories. A man whose parents died when he was little has been taken care of by his aunt; she is like a mother to him. But the man's wife hates her intensely. "In time the old woman grew still more decrepit and bent. His wife thought of the poor old aunt as a nuisance and often wondered why she had not yet died" (Tahara 1980, 109; *SNKBZ* 1994–2002, 12:391). A story in *Konjaku monogatarishū* follows *Yamato monogatari*: "The wife, who in her heart detested her, hated especially the way the old woman was being deformed by age." The old woman's body "had bent almost in two. Finally, the wife could take no more. Why, the hag did not even have the grace to die!" (Tyler 1987, 315; *SNKBZ* 1994–2002, 38:462–64). In Japanese literary narratives, one of the main reasons the old woman is abandoned is her unsightly physical appearance; an unpleasing look intensifies the animosity of the caregiver, often the wife of her son, toward the old woman. This is interesting when one considers the importance of outer appearance in female characters in fairy tales worldwide. Often beautiful appearance is emphasized in a heroine, with little heed given to her other qualities, such as intelligence or personality.

Edward Drott writes on aged bodies of otherworldly figures in medieval Japan:

> On the one hand, readers or auditors were often encouraged to empathize with elders and reflect on the fact that all will encounter such miseries

should they live long enough. On the other hand, certain works presented the aged body as an unsettling other, to inspire fear or disgust and encourage the faithful to engage in practices that could rescue them from attachment to the human form or from horrific figures like the *datsueba*. These two didactic modes were often bifurcated along gender lines, with auditors encouraged to empathize with aged male bodies but presented with aged female others to inspire revulsion. (Drott 2016, 47)

It appears that old women rarely fare well in Japanese literature or art. In the *Tale of Genji* old women are mocked, as exemplified by the description of Gen no naishi no suke. In most noh plays they are the symbol of shame, perhaps with the exception of the old woman in *Takasago*. Ono no Komachi (ca. ninth century), one of the Six Great Poets, comes to mind when one thinks of a famed beauty whose appearance deteriorates with age. It is interesting to note that in both *Sotoba Komachi* (Komachi on stupa) and *Sekidera Komachi* (Komachi at Seki-dera), the protagonist Ono no Komachi describes her aged appearance with shame. In *Sotoba Komachi*, she grieves: "Now I am foul in the eyes of the humble creatures / To whom my shame is shown / Unwelcome months and days pile over me" (Keene 1955, 265; *SNKBZ* 1994–2002, 59:119); and "the color lost from the twin peaks / Of her brow / Oh shameful in the dawning light" (Keene 1955, 268; *SNKBZ* 1994–2002, 59:124). In *Sekidera Komachi*, Komachi laments, "All the trees in Hazukashi Grove / would not suffice to conceal my shame" (Tyler 1992, 235; *SNKBZ* 1994–2002, 58:471–72). On the other hand, in plays such as *Koi no omoni* (Heavy load of love) and *Aya no tsuzumi* (Damask drum), in which an old man falls in love with a beautiful lady of high status, there is no description of the old man's appearance as shameful or unsightly. In the noh play *Sanemori*, an old warrior dyes his hair to hide his advanced age before his departure for the front. When his opponents wash Sanemori's severed head, however, his gray hair emerges and his true appearance is revealed. Here again, though, there is no mention of his appearance as shameful. Elderly women seemed to have been doubly disadvantaged, with weakening physical strength as well as the societal perception of their "shameful" appearance.

Let us go back to *Konjaku monogatarishū*; the wife dislikes her mother-in-law so much that she urges her husband to get rid of the old woman. The conflict between daughter-in-law and mother-in-law runs deep. Still, in the end, the remorseful man goes back to retrieve the old woman—a happy ending, like a mukashibanashi.

Although it is often the wicked wife who is given the cruel role of forcing her husband to abandon his parent, the enforcer can be someone else, like a niece. In *Toshiyori zuinō* or *Toshiyori mumyōshō* (Essays on poetry by Minamoto Toshiyori [1055–1129], ca. 1113), the character who decides to abandon the elder, and who carries out the task, is a niece who was adopted as the elder's child. The aunt/mother had supported her niece/daughter for a long time, but as she became old, her niece/daughter just did not want to take care of her (*SNKBZ* 1994–2002, 87:151–52). Moreover, there is no description of her niece/daughter bringing her back home. Indeed, Kenshō (1130–1209), a poet-priest, writes in his influential essays on poetry titled *Shūchūshō* that the old woman is left abandoned (see Kenshō 1990, 176). Whether it is a wife, niece, or daughter, the wicked one is always a woman. Perhaps this is partly because women were traditionally given the caregiver's role, but this role also reflects a misogynistic societal view firmly rooted in Buddhism and Confucianism in general.

In the case of the noh play *Obasute* (*The Deserted Crone*, ca. early fifteenth century), for an old woman's deeply heartrending fate is told by a villager. After being deserted, the crone turns into a stone because of her attachment to this world. Of course, the noh *Obasute*, created by Zeami (1363–1443), is a highly literary work and one cannot necessarily take the story literally; although, because Zeami was skilled at incorporating contemporary rumors or tales into his work, there is a possibility that a legend about a woman who turned into a stone was popular around that time. As a play in the third category of noh of the five styles and sequences of noh performance, *Obasute* is graceful and elegant.[8] The highlights of the play are the songs and the dancing—a movement in the section of *kuse*, or aural highlight, and a slow, graceful dance called *jo no mai*—representing a purified and clean world detached from earthly cares. There, the abandoned woman enjoys the bright moonlight and autumn nature, while expounding on Buddhist teachings. Her desertion on the mountain is revealed at the beginning and ending of the play as the source of her sadness, and indeed, although her transformation into a stone is intensely sad and pitiable, the audience has a profound experience as the spirit dances to the beauty of the moon in a state of complete self-effacement. The joy of dancing while praising the natural beauty of the full-moon night, Buddha's salvation power, and the sadness of being abandoned are contrasted in the play (Hara 2004, 33–34). Crones in literary works such as the noh play *Obasute* and *Hanayo no hime* are given a hue of awakening, as well as of resignation.

I should like to add that in the play the old woman considers her appearance shameful. She (represented by the chorus) recites: "Unmindful that even long ago I was cast aside, abandoned, I have come again to Mount Obasute. How it shames me now to show my face, In Sarashina's moonlight, where all can see!" (S. Jones 1963, 269; *SNKBZ* 1994–2002, 58:456). *Obasute, Sekidera Komachi,* and *Higaki,* all in the third category of noh, are called *Sanrōjo* (three old woman plays). They require great skill to perform. In *Higaki* as well, the protagonist laments her aged appearance as shameful (see *SNKBZ* 1994–2002, 58:442). Edward Drott comments that "the court literary tradition suggested little hope of ameliorating the tragic dimension of aging . . . These plays depict no overt redemption. The actors must provide the audience with a sense of grace and beauty even as they remain grounded in the ultimate embodiment of despair—the aged female form—a form that, unlike the *okina,* found few instances of miraculous elevation or deification" (Drott 2016, 143).

Did the Custom of "Obasute-yama" Really Exist?

The stories of old women who were forced to make mountains their residence—abundant in mukashibanashi and literary classics—are often taken as a reflection of the Japanese folk custom of abandoning old people. Some scholars conjecture that elders were abandoned because in the village, where food was scarce, people who consumed precious food without laboring were considered burdens, useless and redundant to the family and to village life (Nishizawa 1973, 29, 65; Keene 1961, xii–xiii). Modern works on the subject such as Inoue Yasushi's 1955 essay "Obasute" (Inoue Y. 1974; for an English translation, see Inoue Y. 2000), Fukazawa Shichirō's award-winning story "Narayama bushikō" ("The Songs of Oak Mountain," 1956) (Fukazawa 1981; for an English translation, see Keene 1961, 3–50), and two films of the same title based on Fukazawa's work—one directed by Kinoshita Keisuke in 1958 and the other by Imamura Shōhei in 1983—have vividly portrayed "Obasute-yama" stories (or an impression of such tales). After the latter film, known in the West as *Ballad of Narayama,* received the Palme d'Or at the Cannes Film Festival in 1983, even people living overseas came to think the custom of abandoning old folks used to exist in Japan. "Mistreatment of seniors is nothing new. It is an issue that has resonated throughout the ages," David Spiegel writes. "The 1983 Cannes Festival winner, *Ballad of Narayama,* looked at the Japanese practice of 'ubasute,' which involved the taking of elderly women to remote locations to die of starvation, dehydration, and exposure" (Spiegel 2012, 174).

However, there is no evidence to prove that such customs existed. According to Yanagita Kunio, the stories are titled as such to attract the attention of the audience, and they are actually intended to encourage filial piety (Yanagita 1970b, 294). Likewise, Wakamori Tarō rejects

"Obasute-yama" stories' origin in a real custom of abandoning old people, noting that the stories focus on a belief in the existence of some eerie beings in the deep mountains or in mountain valleys (Wakamori 1958, 215; also see the introduction).

Yoshikawa Yūko comments that "Obasute" stories are not tales of actually abandoning old people; rather they are textualizations of the rituals of disposing of *taiyaku* (great misfortune) held when one attains the age of sixty (*kanreki*, when one returns to the first year of the sexagenary cycle), and of the benefit of such rituals. It should be noted that in folktales the age of old people is generally between sixty and sixty-two. Yoshikawa notes that the two commonalities of mukashibanashi about Obasute are the age at which old folks are deserted—either sixty or sixty-two years of age—and the ending of the custom of desertion at the story's conclusion. The age of sixty or sixty-two is one's *yakudoshi*, and a celebration or ritual of kanreki is held in order to exorcise or dispose of one's accumulated defilement and crimes. This celebration or ritual becomes both a commemoration of one's life and a prayer for longevity. Yoshikawa concludes that folklore reflects the rituals and the benefit of the rituals, rather than the actual custom of abandoning the old (Yoshikawa 1998).

Similarly, Ōshima Tatehiko writes that although scholars have long considered the lore and legends of Obasute as a reflection of some customs, including the abandoning of old parents, there is no confirmation that there was an actual custom of abandoning elders in the mountains of Japan. Ōshima notes that beyond the custom of kanreki and taiyaku, mukashibanashi and the legends of Obasute are deeply related to funeral customs such as the aerial sepulture (fūsō) and the double-grave system (ryōbosei). As written in the introduction, one deceased person has two graves in the double-grave system: one for burying the body and one for survivors to visit and pray for the deceased. The site of abandoning old women in "Obasute" stories would correspond to the burial site or aerial sepulture, where the actual dead body is buried (or abandoned). The word *Obasute* is considered to have come from the term *Ohatsuse*, originally meaning a burial site. Obasute was a place-name for a graveyard called Ohase or Ohatsuse (Ōshima 2001a, 4–5; Miyata 1997, 20).

Indeed, after examining the population registers (*shūmon aratamechō*) of the early modern period, Laurel L. Cornell concludes that "female geronticide does not seem to have existed" (Cornell 1991, 84). Cornell reasons that the "Obasute" stories "appear so prominently in the portrayal of the Japanese elderly in traditional times" because "while geronticide may not have existed in people's behavior, it did exist in their hearts and minds." She speculates that "given what ethnographers report about tension between mothers-in-law and daughters-in-law, the peasant husband and his wife must have wished, often, that they could abandon grandmother on the mountain" (Cornell 1991, 87). What has existed in human hearts has been reflected in tales. These tales would not have been transmitted and disseminated if there were not those who sympathized or empathized with such feelings.

"OBASUTE-YAMA" FROM A POEM TO NARRATIVES: CREATION, DISSEMINATION, AND TRANSFORMATION

Although the 156th episode of *Yamato monogatari* is the oldest extant narrative of "Obasute-yama," the first mention of Mt. Obasute in Heian literary works is a poem. The poem, written by an anonymous author, is "Waga kokoro / nagusamekanetsu / Sarashina ya / Obasuteyama ni / teru tsuki o mite" (Gazing at the moon / Shining on Mount Obasute / in Sarashina / my heart is / not consoled), and it is placed in the category of "Miscellany" in the *Kokinshū* (*A Collection of Poems Ancient and Modern*, ca. 905) (*SNKBZ* 1994–2002, 11:334; Rodd 1984).[9] The Obasute episode in *Yamato monogatari* is said to tell the circumstances under which the poem was recited. Interestingly, the poem in the *Kokinshū* does not have any reference to abandoning old folks. Ozawa Masao and Matsuda Shigeho conjecture that this poem may have been composed by someone who traveled in the region, expressing the traveler's earnest feelings about journeys in ancient times (*SNKBZ* 1994–2002, 11:334).

Hara Yukie notes that Ki no Tsurayuki (d. 945), one of the compilers of the *Kokinshū*, places the same poem in the category of "Love" in his *Shinsen wakashū* (Newly selected anthology of poems, completed between 930–934), and that this fact indicates the Obasute poem was interpreted according to the feelings and circumstances of the recipient of the time (Hara 1997, 20). In other words, it does not necessarily suggest that the Obasute poem reveals the custom of abandoning aged people. It could be the case that the circumstances of the poem were created later to suit the tastes of the audience.

Commenting on the similarities between the mukashibanashi of the fourth type and *Yamato monogatari*, Yanagita points out that in both stories a man abandons his old mother in the mountains because his mean wife urges him to do so. The difference is that in *Yamato monogatari*, after deserting his mother, the man goes home, looks back toward the mountain, and recites a poem about the bright moonlight; then he returns to the mountain and brings her home. The *Yamato monogatari* story ends there. In contrast, the mukashibanashi version has no poem, the old mother becomes rich on the mountain, and the wife is punished. Yanagita explains that to emphasize the wondrous, happy ending of the abandoned crone, it was necessary to add a punishment for the wicked wife in the mukashibanashi, and the pensive poem did not remain in the story (Yanagita 1970b, 300–302). He further writes that there are some mukashibanashi that include poems, while in other cases a poem existed first and the narrative was added later. Some say Obasute belongs to the latter category, but generally speaking, the storyteller writes the poem included in the story. It does not mean that the Obasute custom really existed (Yanagita 1970b, 303). Having seen in chapter 1 how Taira no Kanemori's playful poem addressing a lady was used in the noh play *Kurozuka* as the expression of a real demon, I wonder whether the original poem in the *Kokinshū* was likewise used by later people, perhaps reflecting human hearts and minds, and also to attract people's attention. It is conceivable that what was only rumored in remote regions could be told in the capital as a true story—people in the capital would believe that things such as abandoning old folks could happen in deep mountain villages. Investigating how the images and narratives have been portrayed in various texts over time is a study of adaptations and re-creations of a prototype. "Obasute-yama" stories may have been transformed into something quite different from the original source poem.

AGING, YAMAUBA, AND HEALTHY LIFE EXPECTANCY

The elderly women discussed in this chapter are considered yamauba, crones in the mountains, regardless of whether or not they entered the mountains of their own volition. In the summer of 2019, I gave a talk on yamauba in Kyoto. The majority of the audience were senior citizens. It was edifying to hear these comments from one audience member: "Senior women have no choice but to become yamauba. They have the duality of good and evil, facing society with their instinct, and grieve their karma," and "Yamauba seem to reflect the duality of gentleness and severity of real, existing aged women."

In 2010 Japan became a super-aged society (Kōsei Kagaku Shingikai and Jiki Kokumin Kenkōzukuri 2012, 5). The proportion of people aged sixty-five or over was approximately 27 percent of the Japanese population in 2015, and is estimated that demographic will account for 38.4 percent in the year 2065 (Naikaku-fu 2017).[10] The number of elderly at and over sixty-five years old with dementia was one in seven in 2012, but it is expected to increase to one in five in 2025 (Naikaku-fu 2017). According to a survey by the Ministry of Health, Labor and Welfare, healthy life expectancy for Japanese women was 74.79 years, and 72.14 years for Japanese men in 2016.[11] The average life expectancy of Japanese women in that year was 87.14 years, and 80.98 years for Japanese men; the gap between life expectancy and healthy life expectancy was 12.35 years for women and 8.84 years for men (Kōsei Rōdōshō 2018a).[12] The number of elderly people with dementia increases after the years of healthy life expectancy and caregivers who become physically and mentally exhausted may wish to abandon the elderly. More than 60 percent of the caregivers of elderly persons who require primary nursing care live with the family, and 68.7 percent of those caregivers are female (Naikaku-fu 2017).

As the workload for caregivers remains heavy, the burden on municipal and governmental finances for elderly welfare is growing quickly—expenditure on benefits for the elderly is rapidly rising. "The national health-care expenditure was Jpn Yen 40 trillion [ca. US $333 billion] in 2014, accounting for more than 40 percent of the national budget" (Tokudome et al. 2016). It is a major national issue. The council of the Second Health Japan 21, commissioned by the Japanese government to promote the health of Japanese people, lists extending healthy life expectancy and decreasing the gap between healthy life expectancy and life expectancy as a central objective for the ten-year period that started in 2012 (Kōsei Kagaku Shingikai and Jiki Kokumin Kenkōzukuri 2012, 22–24).

Responding to the great number of older people, various media including television are full of entertaining and educational programs about healthy lifestyles. Many activities and programs to encourage elderly people to lead a healthy life are available at the local, regional, and national level. Social circles and programs in local communities relating to people's interests—such as exercise and hobbies—are perhaps the most accessible.

While there are negative aspects that come with advanced age, there are many positive sides as well. "Ethnographic interviews with women in today's Japan find that many look forward to old age. What a relief 'no longer to have to keep a low profile and display feminine reserve.' Instead they can be bold, drink, and speak their mind, regardless of the company" (Walthall 1998, 156). Obasute stories that appear in mukashibanashi relate old people's wisdom, and parents' compassion for their children. Wisdom and mellowness are supposed to increase as one advances in age. Indeed, Watanabe Kazuko (1927–2016), a Catholic educator and popular author, writes that growing old provides an opportunity for a human being to become more personal and individual; in the time one has left, physical strength and energy all steadily decrease, and this necessarily makes elderly people focus on things that are very important to them, rather than trying to do everything. Further, old age gradually changes human relationships from quantity to quality, and this makes one spiritually rich (Watanabe 2012, 114–16).

As written in the introduction, from the viewpoint of gender studies, Mizuta Noriko notes yamauba as gender transcendent. According to Mizuta, the yamauba often had excessive fertility, and she lacked the feminine traits ascribed to women of the sato: chastity, obedience, and compassion. She refuses to be assigned a household role such as mother or daughter and will not be confined, and she exists outside the sato's gender system (Mizuta 2002, 10, 12–15). It is an insightful observation. This autonomous or independent spirit of the yamauba, who do not care about conforming to social and cultural norms, is what modern women writers of Japan have admired about them. We should note, however, that some yamauba from various narratives also reveal a being intricately intertwined with the life of the sato. In other words, while the prototypical yamauba or the protagonist of the noh play *Yamanba* may stand aloof from the life of the sato, some yamauba are deeply rooted in that life—they may have come to be considered yamauba due to their long lives and/or family conflicts, and may have to heavily rely on people living in the sato.

Behavioral changes in a formerly discreet and kind person are not easy for family members to accept and cope with. Often the person her- or himself is not at all concerned, but when antisocial behaviors continue long enough, the afflicted person's positive image becomes dim. It is critical to reduce the gap of years between healthy life expectancy and life expectancy so that senior citizens can enjoy and rejoice in their advanced age, the fruitful autumn of one's life. This is a major key to living a full life.

6

Yamamba Mumbo Jumbo
Yamauba in Contemporary Society

CHAPTER 5 DISCUSSED SOME ELDERLY PEOPLE who were deeply rooted in the life of a sato (settlement, village) but came to be considered as yamauba. Some of them might heavily rely on people living in the sato and were called yamauba without their knowledge. In contrast, there was (or still is?) a group of young folks who also lived in the sato and welcomed the designation yamauba. Labeled *yamanba-gyaru* (mountain witch gals) or simply *yamanba*, they uniquely fashioned themselves and appeared in major megacities, Shibuya in Tokyo in particular, in the late 1990s through the early 2000s. Kuraishi Tadahiko, a folklorist, observed that the appearance of yamanba-gyaru in Shibuya was fitting, considering the yamauba's proclivity to appear in marketplaces (quoted in Shibuya Keizai Shinbun Henshūbu 2002). This chapter examines the yamanba-gyaru phenomenon in connection with the folkloric yamauba's appearance in marketplaces, and also looks into contemporary depictions of yamauba in various literature and media, including film and manga.

YAMAUBA AND VILLAGE MARKETS

Japanese ethnographers and ethnologists have long considered three emic concepts to understand Japanese folk culture—*haré*, *ké*, and *kégaré*. Sugimoto Yoshio explains that haré represents situations in which formal, ceremonial, and festive sentiments prevail. On these occasions (*haré no hi*), people dress in their best clothes (*harégi*) and eat festive meals (*haré no shokuji*). In contrast, ké stands for routine life in which people do things habitually, conventionally, and predictably. As they consume energy in ké-based daily lives, they arrive at a condition of kegare in which their vitality wanes. Some analysts argue that haré occasions are organized to animate, invigorate, and

DOI: 10.7330/9781646420551.c006

restore the population's depleted vivacity (Sugimoto 2014, 263). According to Kuraishi Tadahiko, folkloric yamauba appear at the time of haré—a special time and space such as festivals and ceremonial occasions. A marketplace is a time-space of haré. People from the flatlands and mountains meet for largely commercial purposes, and the place of meeting evolved into a marketplace (Kuraishi 2002; Shibuya Keizai Shinbun Henshūbu 2002).

There are many accounts that tell of yamauba visiting village marketplaces. For example, Yanagita Kunio states that "a yamauba came to the market of Nitta of Minamiazumi district (present-day Azumino City) or Sengoku of Kitaazumi district of Nagano Prefecture only at the end of the year. It was rumored that the market closed soon after the appearance of the yamauba because people scattered to avoid the yamauba. While market attendees may have been afraid of the yamauba's presence, the coins the yamauba used to pay for their marketplace transactions were believed to bring good luck" (Yanagita 1978–1979, 1:279). In Makigahora, Kiyomi village of Ōno district (present-day Takayama City) in Gifu Prefecture, it was said that when a yamauba came to the market held on December 24 to buy saké, she would not appear in the village again until the spring. When the yamauba bought saké, she asked the peddler to put 90 liters of saké in her saké bottle, which looked like it would hold far less—only 380 milliliters or so. The saké peddler said, "Your bottle won't hold 90 liters, it will take at most 380 ml.," to which the yamauba responded, "Whatever you say, just pour it in." The man started to pour the saké into the bottle, whereupon, surprisingly, the saké went in as if the container were bottomless (*NDT* 1982–1990, 7:165).

I believe that a magic container that can hold an infinite amount of goods is a familiar theme in East Asia. A bag that the Laughing Buddha carries in one Chinese folktale titled "The Monk with the Bag," for example, could contain an unlimited number of trees; when the Laughing Buddha was young, he put all the trees on a mountain into his small bag, shocking and upsetting the widow-owner of the mountain who gave him permission to cut the trees. The trees were used for a religious purpose, to rebuild a temple, and the Laughing Buddha had the trees grown back on the mountain in three years (Eberhard 1965, 80–81). On the other hand, the saké the yamauba bought from the peddler was for her own enjoyment. This yamauba is a mountain deity and the saké is a paid offering for herself, or perhaps it is simply an entertaining story to tell about the yamauba's liking for saké and her honesty in paying the bill. Her fondness for saké is shared by Shuten Dōji, or any Japanese deities (and many Japanese people), for that matter. Saké is an indispensable beverage at the gatherings at the end of the year, as well as for New Year's to welcome guests, including the year's deities.

A year-end market where some yamauba appeared was "a place not only [for the yamauba and villagers] to buy necessities and to prepare for the New Year, but also to welcome ancestor spirits that visit their houses as New Year deities . . . Young men in the village who confined themselves in the mountains and became qualified as deities would disguise themselves as deities and visit the market; later, people thought of them as *yamabito* (or *sanjin*, mountain people). In ancient times, the market was held at the foot of a mountain or a riverbed near a mountain and *yamabito* (mountain people) and villagers interacted at the market . . . The legends describing that *yamabito* and yamauba appeared at the market originated in this custom and belief" (Makita 1972, 443).

Exactly when such legends started to appear is not known. Beliefs in the appearance of a yamauba in the market were, however, already established by the early modern period, as is attested in *Yamanba katabiraki* (Record of yamauba's kimono, 1714). The account goes as follows. Around the time of the Tenshō era (1573–1592), a wealthy man named Dainagon in Shitami village (present-day Chikushi City of Fukuoka Prefecture) ordered his servant to go to the year-end market at Amagi of Chikuzen province (present-day Asakura City of Fukuoka Prefecture) to sell the cotton in a bag. On his way to the market, the servant took a nap. When he woke up, it was already too late to reach the market so he dejectedly returned. When Dainagon opened the bag of cotton, however, instead of cotton there was a single-layered kimono roughly woven with variegated yarn of blue, yellow, black, and white. The kimono was acknowledged as a yamauba's goods, and was treated as a treasure for 200 years ("Yamauba katabiraki" 2001, 119–21). While this record shows a close relationship between yamauba and marketplaces, it also reveals the yamauba's weaving skill, as discussed in chapter 2.

MARKET, SHIBUYA, AND YAMANBA-GYARU

In the late 1990s, yamanba-gyaru appeared in Shibuya Central Street (Shibuya sentāgai, a famous shopping arcade) area near bustling Shibuya Station in Tokyo, and at the Shibuya 109 Building, a fashionable department store. The age of yamanba-gyaru ranged from mid- to late teens, and they crowded the area, drawing attention with their unusual, eye-catching appearance. According to Shibuya Keizai Shinbun Henshūbu, Shibuya Central Street is a border space—a confluence of two different orders—and a place of haré from the folkloric viewpoint. It is a busy place

Figure 6.1. A yamanba-gyaru in Shibuya. (Photo by author, 2007.)

that guarantees the visitors' anonymity—a place where fashions that differ from standard or traditional aesthetics are accepted and acknowledged; it is where a folkloric yamauba from a different realm could enter. Yamanba-gyaru, with their antiestablishment fashion, could exist with peace of mind in Shibuya Central Street (Shibuya Keizai Shinbun Henshūbu 2002; Kuraishi 2002).

Figure 6.2. Shibuya scramble crossing and 109 Building. (Photo by author, 2019.)

Yamanba-gyaru Fashion and Ganguro

What is the outward appearance of yamanba-gyaru? Their attributes are: (1) white, blond, silver, or gray hair, highlights in their hair, damaged hair, or spiked hair; (2) white lips; (3) panda-like eye makeup, white or glitter around the eyes, and/or artificial eyelashes; (4) platform shoes. Always part of their presentation are the color of their hair and their *ganguro* makeup (Yoshie

2010, 91). The ganguro (literally, black face), which is the basis of yamanba-gyaru, requires an explanation.

In the mid-1990s, the fashion of young sales associates in the Shibuya 109 Building—miniskirts, platform boots, hair dyed brown, and slightly tanned skin—attracted lots of attention and rapidly spread as the style of gyaru, or gal(s). The ganguro within this girl culture appeared in 1998; their faces, heavily tanned in tanning salons, were so conspicuous that they were named ganguro.[1] One theory for the origin of the name is that they tanned their skin *gan gan* (onomatopoeia for "intensely"). The ganguro's hair was dyed brown, they wore clothes in primary colors, miniskirts, thick-soled footwear or sandals, and went about in a group. The media widely publicized them. Around 1999 ganguro with white or bleached hair appeared among brown-haired ganguro, and the appellation *yamanba* or *yamanba-gyaru* emerged (Shibuya Keizai Shinbun Henshūbu 2002). Indeed, Yoshie Mami, who has studied the yamanba-gyaru extensively, writes that the word *yamanba* first appeared in the July 31, 1999, issue of a magazine called *egg* (Yoshie 2010, 90).[2] It seems that the term arose when a ganguro adopted white or gray hair. According to Shibuya Keizai Shinbun Henshūbu, the heyday of the ganguro was from 1998 to 2000—they disappeared in spring of 2000 after just three years.

One of the reasons for appearing as ganguro was the popularity of youth fashion magazines such as *egg*, in which snapshots of young folks on the street—the readers of the magazines—adorned the covers. The idea that readers of the magazines instantly become the magazines' models—from passive viewers to active participants—accelerated the appearance of ganguro, who became progressively more distinctive (Hayami 2000; Yoshie 2010, 95; Shibuya Keizai Shinbun Henshūbu 2002). It was quite an incentive for teenage girls to look eccentric, because the more eye-catching their appearance, the better their chances of appearing in the magazines. *Egg* was considered the gyaru's Bible and exerted considerable influence on the girls who loitered in Shibuya (Yoshie 2010, 90). The exotic-looking gyaru had a strong desire to see and to be seen. Their youth combined with their unusual appearance certainly conveyed quaintness, and at the same time, a quantum of exotic sensuality.

Laura Miller discusses yamanba-gyaru in relation to the subcultures of young Japanese women:

> A method to discredit and contain the power of Girl culture is by calling *ganguro* types with very dark tans and white-rimmed eyes *yamamba* ("mountain ogress"), a figure from Japanese folklore who lives deep in

the mountains and is often described as having sparkling or flashing eyes. I suspect that the label as applied to Kogals is in reference to the way *yamamba* was depicted in noh plays, where she is very tall with disheveled hair and big round eyes.[3] The use of such negative labels and descriptors is meant to tarnish the cool allure of the Kogal . . . However, *ganguro* girls have cynically adopted the term *yamamba* and use it to refer to themselves, often in the cheeky form *mamba*. (Miller 2004, 240)

No one knows exactly who named them *yamanba*. The columnist Izumi Asato believes that it was probably some magazine's editorial staff (rather than the girls themselves) that first used the term. He writes that teenage girls could not possibly have known that the word originated in a noh play, let alone how to write it in Chinese characters (Izumi A. 1999, 5). Regardless of how use of the designation originated, common associations between the girls' looks in Shibuya and folkloric yamauba ensured that the word was accepted, disseminated, and established. These teenagers looked and behaved differently from established social and cultural norms. Yoshie Mami writes that the intimidating manners and appearance of the girls, who seemed to come from nowhere to gather at Shibuya, matched the image of folkloric yamauba, who came from the mountains down to the sato to eat children or kidnap people, then disappeared back into the mountains (Yoshie 2010, 90; 93).

Interestingly, Hayami Yukiko comments that the more outlandish the yamanba-gyaru's appearance, the more mundane the girl's household. The yamanba-gyaru does not want to stay at home: she thinks it boring to talk to her parents, and watching TV at home with a snack is equally depressing. So she seeks a public place of festivity (Hayami 2000, 54). In other words, a yamanba-gyaru wants to escape from the mundane, and yamanba-gyaru fashion is special clothing or dressing for festivity—a tool that transforms an ordinary girl into someone special. Aside from a chance to appear in teen fashion magazines, there are several reasons why these girls chose this type of makeup. Yoshie reports one yamanba-gyaru saying, "With this make-up, if someone bumps into me on a train, I can intimidate her/him with a glare. If I don't have this make-up—with a whitish complexion—in the Shibuya area, I can expect to be looked down upon because I'm coming from the countryside of Ibaraki (Prefecture)." The makeup has an aggressive or defiant impact on others; onlookers consider the yamanba-gyaru intimidating and are frightened by their stares (or glares). Yamanba-gyaru's threatening image was consistent from the start to the end of the fad. Simultaneously, it was a protective measure for the yamanba-gyaru to avoid being belittled by others (Yoshie 2010, 92–93).

Further, Yoshie observes the collective behavior or groupism of the yamanba-gyaru. Yamanba-gyaru gathering in Shibuya could bond with others. The voices of yamanba-gyaru include comments such as: "I have increased the number of my friends many times with this make-up"; "I hang out in group with my *gyaru* friends. When I walk in *yamanba* fashion, my comrades call out to me"; "The fashion is in, so I can make more friends. But if I quit being a *yamanba*, I won't be able to talk in the same language with my friends." Yoshie points out that it was important to the yamanba-gyaru that they existed within a category of a gyaru culture, and to live within that culture required collective behavior (Yoshie, 2010, 95). Hayami also considers yamanba-gyaru fashion a communal symbol (Hayami 2000, 54). Young yamanba-gyaru thrive collectively in a community of the same ilk.

Yamanba-gyaru Disappear from Shibuya

The yamanba-gyaru dominance in Shibuya was from August 1999 to April 2000 as far as magazines articles that mention yamanba-gyaru are concerned, and Yoshie Mami lists several reasons for the waning of yamanba-gyaru fashion: (1) the yamanba-gyaru fashions moved on to something else—what exactly that "something else" is, however, is not very clear; (2) the charismatic leader of yamanba-gyaru fashion, who was named Buriteri, chose to have natural makeup and whitish color skin; (3) yamanba-gyaru graduated from their high schools (and grew out of their fashion) (Yoshie 2010, 96–97).[4] As if to finish off the yamanba-gyaru trend, two seventeen-year-old yamanba-gyaru girls tortured their twenty-six-year-old female friend for six days in Ibaraki Prefecture, an incident that dominated the news in May 2000. The victim sustained an injury that took six months to heal completely ("Mimitabu-sogi yamanba-gyaru no gyōjō" 2000, 22). The news certainly capped the image of yamanba-gyaru as intimidating creatures, pushing the threatening image to the extreme.

Yoshie comments that when she conducted research on May 7, 2003, in Shibuya, a sixteen-year-old girl told her that she had two or three yamanba-gyaru friends; the number of yamanba-gyaru has drastically declined but they have not been completely extinguished (Yoshie 2010, 97). Indeed, when I went to Shibuya in 2007 I saw a yamanba-gyaru at Shibuya station. She was with a couple of her friends wearing similar fashion and did not appear threatening to me. She let me take her picture.

YAMAUBA AND YAMAUBAESQUE

So is a yamanba-gyaru a yamauba of contemporary Japan? The teenage girls who crowded the Shibuya 109 Building and Shibuya Central Street—a marketplace—with their yamanba-gyaru fashion were reminiscent of the protagonist of the noh play *Yamanba* and folkloric yamauba. These girls looked like yamauba and took the appellation *yamanba* in stride. Coming out of nowhere and disappearing into thin air does sound like yamauba.

Yamauba are, however, by and large, autonomous or independent. There is no yamauba who gathers with other yamauba for emotional support or wants to be seen by people. If one recalls from chapter 1, Yamanba, the protagonist of the noh play *Yamanba*, lives in nature and minds her own business. She appears in front of Hyakuma (the entertainer) only to request Yamanba's salvation with her dance. Although many helping yamauba in folklore try to be compassionate with a tale's main characters—good people—who need help, those good people usually encounter the yamauba in her place on a mountain. Basically, the yamauba lives independently and does not need human companionship, although she may enjoy human company now and then. The vicious yamauba who eat human flesh do not attack humans just for fun; they attack because they need something to eat or the humans have encroachd on their territories.

On the other hand, the yamanba-gyaru who hang out in Shibuya need human companionship. They put on their makeup to make friends—to seek out other teenagers. They are there to see and be seen. As Yoshie reports, some yamanba-gyaru adopt the appearance to fit in with a group or to not be ostracized. To be a yamanba-gyaru is to look and behave differently from—or even to defy the norms of—traditional adolescent femininity. While they have created their own culture with eye-catching fashion statements against conformity, by expressing their individuality in the same remarkable yamanba-gyaru fashion, collectively they become essentially identical—creating and staying in the comfort zone of the same ilk, as they want to connect with someone of the same age with a similar mindset. Although the yamanba-gyaru looks like a yamauba, the yamanba-gyaru's collective behavior does not fit the image of an independent-minded folkloric yamauba. Rather than a yamanba, perhaps, a yamanba-gyaru is yamaubaesque or, following Michael Dylan Foster's coinage, folkloresque.

Folkloresque is, according to Foster, "the hazily allusive quality that infuses certain popular creations" (Foster 2016, 3–4):

> Simply put, the folkloresque is popular culture's own (emic) perception and performance of folklore. That is, it refers to creative, often commercial

products or texts (e.g., films, graphic novels, video games) that give the
impression to the consumer (viewer, reader, listener, player) that they
derive directly from existing folklore traditions. In fact, however, a folkloresque product is rarely based on any single vernacular item or tradition;
usually it has been consciously cobbled together from a range of folkloric
elements, often mixed with newly created elements, to appear as if it
emerged organically from a specific source. (Foster 2016, 5)

I have borrowed the "-esque" part of *folkloresque* to create the appellation *yamaubaesque*: like a yamauba, yet not one. It certainly is a teen-age fashion—an
urban fashion. The yamanba-gyaru is not a commercial product for sure;
but someone, or the general public, certainly connected the yamauba-gyaru
with an existing folkloric tradition, and brought commercial success to
youth-culture fashion stores, magazines, and the media that covered the
phenomenon. Yamanba-gyaru fashion may have become extinct in Japan
but surprisingly, it still continues overseas, such as in Britain, among youth
culture (see, for example, Robinson 2009).

YUBABA IN THE FILM *SPIRITED AWAY*

Regarding yamaubaesque, there is another figure who fits this word. It is
Yubaba, a memorable character in a commercially and aesthetically successful animated film entitled *Sen to Chihiro no kamikakushi* (*Spirited Away*, 2001).
Directed by Hayao Miyazaki (1941–), *Spirited Away* became the highest-
grossing film of all time in Japan. It won a number of awards, including a
2003 Academy Award for Best Animated Feature Film and a Golden Bear
at the Berlin International Film Festival in 2002.

Spirited Away is an adventure and coming-of-age film in which the main
character, a young girl by the name of Chihiro, embarks on a quest to save
her family from a supernatural spell. The film opens with Chihiro's family
moving to a new town, making Chihiro uneasy and sulky. On their way to
their new house, the family unwittingly enters a supernatural realm, where
Chihiro's parents are turned into pigs. Chihiro is in a panic when a mysterious boy named Haku appears and offers his help. Chihiro learns that the
only way to break the spell and reenter the human world is to find work at a
bathhouse in the world of spirits owned by Yubaba. There, after experienc-
ing various challenges and pitfalls, Chihiro finds friendship, a way to help
her family and, most importantly, herself.

As I discuss elsewhere, Miyazaki portrays the film's spirit characters
as rich, multifaceted entities replete with cultural memories and histories

(Reider 2005, 11–14; 2010, 159–62). Among them is Yubaba, the old witch who owns the bathhouse. She is avaricious and quite strict with her workers. Yubaba, who is also seen excessively pampering her gigantic spoiled baby boy Bō, strikes me most as a descendant of a yamauba—not exactly a yamauba, but her descendant—hence, yamaubaesque. Yubaba is an old woman with white hair who controls her employees through the power of language and magic. She can freely transform humans into animals and eat them, which is entirely in accord with yamauba's cannibalism. As discussed in chapter 2, an example of the yamauba's motherhood appears in the legend of a mountain yamauba who gave birth to and raised a son, Kintarō, who possessed Herculean strength. The yamauba's motherly attitude toward her son is emphasized through a series of *yamauba-buyō*, or yamauba dances on the kabuki stage, which appeared in the late eighteenth to early nineteenth centuries and have continued to this day. In these dance pieces, the yamauba's doting motherhood is amplified as she speaks of her son: "Day and night, my pleasure is my only son, Kaidōmaru [i.e., Kintarō]" (Tsuruya 1975, 61). Kintarō is portrayed as full of energy and currently often identified with his red harakake (a large bib that covers one's chest and stomach), on which the character *kin* (from Kintarō) is printed.

In *Spirited Away*, Yubaba is the mother of a super-baby, Bō. Like Kintarō, Bō wears a red harakake; on his a big character *bō* is written. Again like Kintarō, Bō has prowess in accordance with his gigantic size—he can easily break Chihiro's arm if he wishes. In contrast to her strictness with her employees, Yubaba dotes on Bō, much as the yamauba dotes on hers in the kabuki dance pieces, protecting him to excess: she confines him in a germ-free playroom full of germ-free toys. The visual juxtaposition of a white-haired elderly mother and a baby boy has precedents, too. One notable example is a votive painting of Yamauba and Kintarō created by Nagasawa Rosetsu (1754–1799), a treasure of Itsukushima Shrine in Miyajima. In Rosetsu's painting, the yamauba looks like a distrustful old woman—what Robert Moes calls "a caricature of geriatric non-beauty." Moes, however, also comments, "There is a sympathetic humor in the way the mythical old hag stares out suspiciously at the beholder" (Moes 1973, 28).

Yubaba does, on occasion, have a humorous aspect embedded in her suspicious character. Indeed, Yubaba and Bō may be looked at as well-fed versions of Nagasawa Rosetsu's Yamauba and Kintarō. Further similarity is found in the absence of Yubaba's male partner. When a yamauba first appeared as the mother of Kintarō in a seventeenth-century text, her partner was never mentioned. Likewise, Yubaba's husband is nonexistent in the film.

Figure 6.3. *Yamauba, the Mountain Woman*, by Nagasawa Rosetsu (1754–1799). (Votive painting. Color on silk. 157.0 × 84.0 cm. About 1797. Itsukushima Jinja Shrine [Hiroshima]. Courtesy of Itsukushima Jinja Shrine.)

Moreover, while the avaricious Yubaba is strict toward her workforce, she also has the ability to acknowledge diligence in her workers. When Stink Spirit (Okusare-sama) visits the bathhouse, for example, Yubaba notes how hard Chihiro works, and decides to give her a helping hand. Similarly, as we saw in chapter 1, yamauba often help humans who are helpful to them. From the spatial point of view, too, there is a parallel between the yamauba and Yubaba. Komatsu Kazuhiko writes that "the concept of mountains, as a mountainous realm where oni and yōkai reside, is better understood as the 'spatial other world'" (Komatsu K. 1991, 58).[5] Indeed, the mountains are often the entry point to the realm where the oni and yōkai live, along with other mountain deities and deceased ancestors. Needless to say, yamauba is a resident of the mountains. Likewise, the environment where Yubaba's bathhouse is situated is a locus of the other world, where all the supernatural beings come to relax and unwind. Pertinent to the spatial aspect, a further parallel is seen in altitude—the mountain where yamauba and Yubaba live is higher than ordinary flatlands. Likewise, Yubaba lives on the top floor of the bathhouse—higher than anyone else, a command center from which she controls her operation and gives orders to her employees. Yubaba is the authority of the supernatural world, powerful and rich—similar to a mountain goddess. Yubaba is literally and figuratively bigheaded; she is independent-minded and does not conform to social norms. Yubaba has many yamauba qualities in her, and yet she is not yamauba. The yamauba is not known for avarice or a big head. She is Yubaba, a character created for the film *Spirited Away*. Yubaba is yamaubaesque.

YAMAUBA IN THE MANGA *HYAKKIYAKŌ SHŌ*

A yamauba—not a yamaubaesque entity—appears in an equally successful and beautifully narrated manga entitled *Hyakkiyakō shō* (Extracts of one hundred demons strolling at night, 1995–). The author, Ima Ichiko, a manga artist, received an Excellence Award in the Manga division of the tenth Japan Media Arts Festival (Bunkachō Media Geijutsusai) for *Hyakkiyakō shō* in 2006. *Hyakkiyakō shō* first appeared in a magazine entitled *Nemurenu yoru no kimyōna hanashi: Nemuki* in 1995 and still continues in the magazine *Nemuki+*. By and large, each episode of the ongoing story is a complete tale.

Hyakkiyakō shō revolves around the Iijima family and their strange encounter with things supernatural. The story starts with the death of a writer of the fantastic named Iijima Kagyū. Kagyū, sensitive to spiritual things since he was small, he researched the supernatural and trained his mysterious faculties to interact with (evil) supernatural creatures in order to control his uncanny power, to avoid bringing misfortune to his loved ones. Sometimes, however, his interactions with creatures in different realms had unintended consequences, and one of them resulted in the death of his son-in-law, Iijima Takahiro. The cause of Takahiro's death was considered a heart attack in the world of humans, but actually it was caused by Kagyū's magic going awry. Because Kagyū ordered Aoarashi, his dragon-shaped servant deity, or *shikigami*, to enter Takahiro's body soon after his death,

Takahiro was resurrected—or so it was believed by humans. On Kagyū's command, Aoarashi was supposed to protect Iijima Ritsu, the main character of the work and a grandson of Kagyū.

Iijima Ritsu also has a strong sixth sense and can see and hear things ordinary people cannot. He was sixteen years old when *Hyakkiyakō shō* started, but with the passage of time inside the story (and outside in real time—the series has been continuous for over twenty-six years), he is now a college student majoring in folklore studies. After his resurrection, Takahiro (in reality Aoarashi in Takahiro's body) is unable to work as a normal person, so his wife (Ritsu's mother) supports the family by teaching the tea ceremony and how to put on a kimono with her mother (Ritsu's grandmother). Probably because of their profession, Ritsu's mother and grandmother always wear kimonos in their traditional Japanese house, which fittingly evokes an atmosphere of Japanese life in the olden days. Fascinating characters such as Aoarashi, Tsukasa, and Akira—the latter two Ritsu's cousins, who also have a sixth sense to varying degrees—and Oshiro and Oguro—adorable yōkai birds who serve Ritsu—help Ritsu in his experiences with the strange and mysterious, and create a world of horror and fantasy for the audience.

An episode about yamauba, literally entitled "Yamauba," appears in the November 2003 issue of *Nemuki* (for the text, see Ima 1995–, 12:175–202). It starts with a description of the yamauba: "Yamauba is a female yōkai that lives in the mountains. It is said to be a fair-skinned beauty with long black hair or a white-haired crone" (Ima 1995–, 12:177). But most of the content has very little to do with the yamauba herself. When Ritsu's mother goes to a hospital to get her mother's prescription, she meets with two couples, both of whom claim to be the parents of a boy—a mysterious thirteen-year-old also named Ritsu (for the sake of clarity, I will call this boy Ritsu13). The couples are in the hospital for a DNA test to determine Ritsu13's parenthood. It is explained that previously Ritsu13 and his mother were living in an apartment, but the apartment caught fire. The boy was found alive but his mother's whereabouts were unknown. After a police search, Ritsu13 was considered to be one family's missing boy, but then another family claimed that Ritsu13 was their son, who had been missing since being kidnapped. Ritsu's mother takes pity on Ritsu13 and sends him to her house to spare him the unpleasantness of arguments in the hospital during the DNA test. At the Iijimas' home, Ritsu13 shows tremendously strong power—like Kintarō's.

On the following day, Ritsu13 is leaving the Iijimas' house, thinking that city life is too complicated and that he doesn't believe he can be of any use to people, when a mysterious woman in tattered clothes appears in the garden—her long hair is hiding her eyes, so her face is not clear. Ritsu13 calls this unknown, enigmatic woman his mother. An illustration shows the mother and son happily united and another picture portrays a sketch or copy of Utamaro's famous woodblock print "Yamauba to Kintarō kamisori" (Yamauba and Kintarō, shaving hair). The accompanying written text says, "Long ago, Minamoto no Yorimitsu (Raikō) passed by Mt. Ashigara on his way to the capital. There he saw a super-strong boy who was living with an extremely white-skinned woman with long black hair. Yorimitsu requested the woman to give him the boy and made him his vassal, naming him Sakata no Kintoki." From this description and illustrations, as well as the title of the episode, "Yamauba," the mysterious woman is believed to be a yamauba, and Ritsu13 corresponds to Kintarō. The narrator adds, "Legendary yamauba are said to be impregnated with red-haired babies, or kidnap children and raise them in the mountains" (Ima 1995–, 12:202). That yamauba kidnap children is known from tales such as the story type "Yamauba Go-Between," described in chapter 4 (see also Yanagita 1978–1979, 1:264). The story concludes with a note that the results of the DNA test reveal that Ritsu13 is not related to any of the claimants, and that Ritsu13's true identity remains unknown.

In one scene, Ritsu13 talks to himself: "Mom, I don't think I can be useful for people even if I stay here" (Ima 1995–, 12:199). I suppose that Ritsu13 was left alone in the city by the yamauba in the hope that he could be useful for people, like Kintarō—Kintarō certainly helped conquer evil creatures and was instrumental in keeping people safe. However, Kintarō was not left alone; Raikō begged him to become his retainer because of his strength and potential, and he is believed to have gone through rigorous training under the supervision of Raikō or some other expert. Ritsu13, on the other hand, was practically abandoned in a city with no one to serve or look after him. One could wish that the yamauba had at least advised him to go to the Japan Sumo Association—Kintarō was good at wrestling with animals in the mountains. The yamauba's action—abandoning her child in a burned-down apartment—looks more like parental neglect or child abandonment in present-day terms. The author may have meant to pay homage to the Kintarō setsuwa when Ritsu13 was left alone in the city to "help people." A little more explanation about the yamauba and Ritsu13 before the burning of the apartment would have given more depth and coherence to the story.

The yamauba episode is perhaps not Ima Ichiko's best work, but it is interesting how it gives critical information on the folkloric yamauba—some of her features and legends—and reveals how folkloric yamauba setsuwa continue to be handed down to new generations. While a yamauba being Kintarō's mother is still well known, the degree of familiarity is certainly not as great as it used to be. In much contemporary children's literature about Kintarō, a yamauba is not specifically mentioned as Kintarō's mother. Kintarō's mother is described simply as "mother." This is understandable as the focus of the story is Kintarō—and it could have been more accurate when the Kintarō legend was first created. Ima Ichiko's mysterious yamauba may represent someone who went to the mountains to live of her own volition. *Hyakkiyakō shō*, through its marvelous illustrations and narration, presents how this world of the living interacts with the world of the dead on a daily basis (see Ima 1995–, 9:211).

YAMAUBA IN FICTION
"HOLY MAN OF MT. KOYA"

Mysteriousness goes well with the yamauba. The yamauba in *Hyakkiyakō shō* is enigmatic—her face unrevealed and her upbringing and current whereabouts unknown. There is another modern work of fiction that, although not exactly contemporary, should not be missed. "Holy Man of Mt. Kōya" (*Kōya hijiri*, 1900) describes a mysterious, enchanting woman on an unknown mountain. The author, Izumi Kyōka (1873–1939), was a writer of the grotesque and fantastic. Living in an age of change and innovation characterized by the influx and adaptation of Western ideas, Kyōka is noted for his supernatural themes and adherence to the more traditional styles of Edo fiction, noh, and folklore. In "Holy Man of Mt. Kōya," a middle-aged itinerant monk named Shūchō, a holy man of Mt. Kōya in Wakayama Prefecture, tells a story of a strange experience in his youth to a young traveler he has met on a train. The backdrop is the beginning of the Meiji period (1868–1912), considered to be an era of rapid change and modernization, as the presence of the train attests.

Young monk Shūchō, the protagonist, was on a personal pilgrimage for enlightenment. Crossing the Hida Mountains in Gifu Prefecture, he saw a medicine peddler taking a wrong path. Shūchō decided to follow the peddler in order to direct him back onto the right path. The wooded road was dangerous, replete with snakes and huge mountain leeches that attached themselves all over his body, sucking his blood. When he finally passed a wooded area, he heard a horse neighing and, heading in the direction of the sound, found a lone house. In this secluded cottage Shūchō met a beautiful, bewitching woman and her handicapped husband, whom the monk described as an idiot. An old man standing nearby was preparing to take a horse to the village to sell. The woman helped Shūchō wash his wounded body in a nearby river. She also took off her clothes and entered the river, where monkeys and bats pestered her naked body. Those animals were formerly humans. The woman transformed them into beasts as they were lustful. During the night, the monk heard bird and animal noises around the house, so feeling ominous, he earnestly recited Dharani. On the following day, the monk left the lone house but the woman's raw sexuality seemed impossible to resist; he was seriously considering going back to the cottage to live with her, when he encountered the old man who had sold the horse. The old man related to the young monk the background of the woman, whom he described as a temptress. She was the daughter of a country doctor whose inept surgical skills had caused her husband's handicap. The daughter had possessed a special healing power since she was young, and "in the bloom of her youth, the people in the area came to believe that she was Yakushi, Healer of Souls" (Izumi K. 1996, 67). A huge flood thirteen years prior had swept away the doctor's village, but the daughter, the handicapped patient, and the old man, who were away from the village at the time, survived. The old man told Shūchō that the woman transformed those who succumbed to her sexual temptations into animals simply by breathing on them. The horse he had sold was the lecherous peddler; with the money he earned by the sale, he bought fish for the woman to eat. Hearing this, the monk quickly left the mountains (Izumi K. 2002, 315–400; 1996, 21–72).

Perhaps to many contemporary Japanese the alluring and dangerous woman in "Holy Man of Mt. Kōya" is not intuitively connected to yamauba because the yamauba image is generally of an old woman, as discussed in chapter 5. As explained in the introduction, however, the term *yamauba* is used to connote both young and old; young yamauba were considered *yama-hime*, whereas the old women were called *yamahaha* or *yamauba*. Indeed, Gerald Figal calls this mountain woman "Kyoka's *yama-hime*" (Figal 1999, 180).

As we have seen, there were a number of depictions of erotic, voluptuous mountain women in the Edo period, the most notable example being Kitagawa Utamaro's yamauba. The nameless, enigmatic woman of "Holy Man of Mt. Kōya" is perhaps slightly younger than Utamaro's yamauba—she is about thirty years old, and does not have a child. Figal describes her as "part innocent country woman, part erotic temptress, part beneficent healing goddess, and part vengeful sorceress," asserting that "the woman in this story is a classic example of the *chūkanteki* character, in between simple classifications of good and evil" (Figal 1999, 180), which is the duality of yamauba. The woman (indirectly) eats men—indirectly, because she first transforms them into animals and exchanges the animals for food. Yet she was considered by the villagers to be an incarnation of the medicine deity Yakushi for her healing powers. She was compassionate enough to take the poor boy whose surgery her father had terribly botched under her wing. As yamauba judge people's characters, the enchanting woman saw Shūchō's good character and let him go. Interestingly, Figal connects her with yamabushi, saying that she "is a powerful sorceress who has developed her supernatural powers over the years by practicing none other than *tengudō*, the occult mountain asceticism and sorcery associated with *yamabushi* and *tengu* that Yanagita writes about in 'Yūmeidan'" (Figal 1999, 182). But the mountain woman as a femme fatale is quite new. A femme fatale must have a dangerously bewitching appearance, and in the story, the river she and young Shūchō bathed in together rejuvenates her youth. She thus keeps her perpetually youthful appearance. She may represent Kyōka's—and, more broadly, men's—desired female figure.

As Charles Inoue notes, the young protagonist becomes a trespasser in the world of the sacred and the dead (Izumi K. 1996, 169); the mountainous area where young Shūchō travels is not on the map, indicating that it is an unknown area. Susan Napier explains that "the mountain valley cannot exist on any map, because a map signifies ordinary real space defined by modernity, and inscribed in the scientific and rational order. In other words, the snakes, leeches, and the woman have been banished by modernization and only a few remnants now lurk in the premodern darkness, nursing their hatred of modernity" (Napier 1996, 34–35). Napier further writes that an important critical dimension of "Holy Man of Mt. Kōya" is the implicit social criticism represented by the flood. She argues, "It would seem that the 'great flood' which swept away the woman's family some years before had occurred at about the time of the Meiji Restoration. The flood, therefore is evocative not only of the Restoration itself but of the sea change of modernization that occurred as a result of the Restoration, sweeping all before it except for a few remnants such as the woman and her households" (Napier 1996, 35–36). Kyōka was strongly opposed to modernization and longed for old Japan; Napier analyzes, "'Culturally repressed' values are actually the values of old Japan, hiding at the end of the dangerous 'old road' the monk is forced to travel. At the same time, the 'established order' is actually the new order of Meiji Japan," so that "ironically, what traditionally was considered Other, i.e., the grotesque, the alien, and the female, are now seen as linked to a yearned-for old Japan which in itself has become Other" (Napier 1996, 34–35). Kyōka's yamahine, with a newly acquired element of femme fatale, was left in the mountains. But the yamauba harks back in various forms, including simply as a human being—with or without any supernatural power.

"Yamanba"

The protagonist of a contemporary short work of fiction "Yamanba," authored by Setouchi Jakuchō (1922–), a well-known novelist who became a Buddhist nun in 1973, is also mysterious. Unlike the mountain woman in the "Holy Man of Mt. Koya" or in another modern work of fiction, Ōba Minako's "The Smile of a Mountain Witch," discussed in chapter 3, Setouchi's yamauba does not have any supernatural skill. Named Irie Tsuya, she is an old lady with completely white hair; her age is unknown. She lives alone in her house, which was formerly her husband's art studio, on a mountain in a rural area. Her artist husband had lived with his young model in the studio, and there the two had committed double suicide; after their deaths, Tsuya moved in. No one knows, or seems to care, exactly who she is, but the reader learns later that Tsuya lost her voice because of a surgery, that she is hard of hearing, and that she is headstrong, paying no attention to her doctor's orders.

Tsuya, a stubborn old lady, does not seem to be bothered by what people say about her and is adamant about staying in the art studio all alone—village people think that she will be found dead in the house some-day but, contrary to their expectations, at the end of the story, she leaves the house and disappears into the mountains on the first day of snow. This ending, as well as her penchant for solitude, somewhat reminds one of the noh play *Yamanba*. Indeed, Setouchi has one character sing lyrics from the noh play in the story: "In spring, waiting for the treetops to bloom, I seek out the blossoms, making my mountain rounds. In autumn, seeking the radiant light, I go to moon-viewing spots, making my mountain rounds . . . Around and around bound to fate, clouds of delusion, like bits of dust, mount up to become Yamanba, a demoness in form. 'Look, look!' she soars up peaks, resounds down valleys. Until now she was here, or so it seemed, mountain after mountain, making mountain rounds, her destination never to be known" (Setouchi 2009, 226; Bethe and Brazell 1998, 224–25; *SNKBZ* 1994–2002, 59:581–82). Interestingly, the male protagonist comments on the noh play: "Though Yamanba in the noh play portrayed the yamauba as a supernatural being with divinity, still she was a woman" (Setouchi 2009, 225–26). With all her enigmatic and contradictory powers and qualities, a yamauba is always female.

The image of Yamanba from the noh play is superimposed upon Tsuya. Tsuya is a female human being with the baggage of human desires. Her worldly desires are understood as her attachment to her house, in defiance of ordinary thinking that one would avoid living in a place where suicide had occurred. Unlike Yamanba in the noh play, Tsuya has a frail body, perhaps primarily because of her advanced age. The male protagonist, once a player of women, falls in love—platonic love—with this yamauba with pure white hair. Yanagita notes that there were women who went into the mountains of their own volition (Yanagita 1968, 378–80); fictional Tsuya definitely comes under this category as well—consistent with the traditional mysterious woman who was named yamauba by village people.

YAMAUBA IN POETRY: *WATASHI WA ANJUHIMEKO DE ARU* (I AM ANJUHIMEKO)

Vanishing from human sight on the first day of snow, Setouchi's yamauba is evocative, leaving a fragrance of romanticism behind. In comparison, the yamauba created by Itō Hiromi (1955–), poet and novelist, in her long narrative poem *Watashi wa Anjuhimeko de aru* (I Am Anjuhimeko, 1993) is dynamic, coarse, and fertile (or virile). She stands for contemporary feminist discourse.[6] Jeffrey Angles writes that *Watashi wa Anjuhimeko de aru* "explores the intersections of trauma, memory, language, and sexuality—all major preoccupations within contemporary feminist discourse" and that it could be called "a 'feminist' text because it reflects a central preoccupation of feminist art and writing—the use of creative processes to engage hegemonic forms of narrative to reexamine the experiences of women previously hidden from view" (Angles 2007, 51–52). Indeed, *Watashi wa Anjuhimeko de aru* is loaded with explicit memories and experiences of rape, raw sexuality, trauma, and survival. Importantly for this study, she displays various elements of the mystic yamauba—especially on the crude side.

The story of *Watashi wa Anjuhimeko de aru* is closely based upon, or an adaptation of, a little-known version of the famous *Sanshō Dayū* (Sanshō the Bailiff) legend.[7] Preserved among generations of *itako*, the blind shamans of southwestern Aomori Prefecture, this orally transmitted version was related by a thirty-five- or thirty-six-year-old itako named Sakuraba Sue to the anthropologist Takeuchi Nagao in August 1931 (Angles 2007, 55, 58). While the hardships of brother Zushiō and his supportive sister Anju or Anjuhime are the focus of the popular version of *Sanshō Dayū*, Anju is the main character in Sakuraba Sue's version (Angles 2007, 57). Itō's poem "dwells on the trauma—including the sexual molestation—that the character of Anju probably experienced. In her retelling of the story . . . Itō makes the abuse of the feminine body a central theme" (Angles 2007, 59). The main character Anjuhimeko in *Watashi wa Anjuhimeko de aru* is an abused and eventually murdered female infant "who rises from her grave, wanders through the countryside, searches for her lost parents, and undergoes various purgative hardships that force her to confront her own past" (Angles 2007, 53).

The yamauba appears in the fourth and final section of *Watashi wa Anjuhimeko de aru*. Itō's yamauba displays many of the typical yamauba characteristics. As Angles comments, the yamauba leads Anjuhimeko toward redemption.[8] Itō's yamauba is simultaneously Anjuhimeko's redemptory figure (helping yamauba) and her tormenter (evil yamauba)—she eats human flesh. Anjuhimeko says to the yamauba, "what is this? before today you've grabbed so many people and gobbled them up, what, now you have a request? come on!" In fact, the yamauba is presumed to have eaten Anjuhimeko as the yamauba scornfully responds, "what? when I've eaten you, haven't you always come back to life without any problem? . . . as long as I leave your navel or your clitoris, you'll come back to life, even if I grind you to dust in my teeth, even if I burn you black, even if I mash you to bits, or even if I pound you to smithereens" (Itō H. 2007, 89; 1993, 29).[9]

Phrases such as "even if I grind you to dust in my teeth, even if I burn you black, even if I mash you to bits, or even if I pound you to smithereens" remind one of an oni that torments sinners in hell, as depicted in *Jigoku sōshi* (Picture scrolls of Buddhist Hell, ca. twelfth century). This yamauba is the equivalent of a female oni that resides in hell. In fact, the power to bring Anjuhimeko back from death or to death is equivalent to the power of Datsueba, discussed in chapter 4. Datsueba is also in charge of death and life, possessing the duality of good and evil. Interestingly, the way Anjuhimeko comes back to life is through the yamauba's buttocks rather than her vagina. In response to Anjuhimeko's complaint that after the yamauba swallows her, she turns Anjuhimeko "into shit and squeeze[s her] out," the yamanba laughs and says, "you'll come back to life, it is precisely because I squeeze you from the hole in my backside that you come back to life" (Itō H. 2007, 89–90; 1993, 29). Fascinatingly, among "Sanmai no ofuda" ("Three Charms") folktales, a representative yamauba story type discussed in chapter 1, one tale from Akita Prefecture tells that an oni-baba (yamauba) is swallowed up by the bonze and comes out in his excrement the following morning; in some stories, the swallowed oni-baba comes out with his fart (*NMT* 1978–1980, 6:147). In these folktales, it is an oni/oni-baba/yamauba who goes through a "good" character's body. If this folktale-type pattern is applied to Itō's yamauba, the yamauba is a "good" figure and Anjuhimeko is an evil one. Or possibly in Itō's narrative, a good character and an evil character are one and the same—as described in the *Heart Sutra* and recounted by Yamanba in the noh play *Yamanba*.

Just as the Yamanba of the noh play appears in front of the entertainer's group to make a request, Itō's yamauba appears to Anjuhimeko with a request: that Anjuhimeko carry her into the mountains on her back. Here, she plays the nominal role of an old woman in the "Obasute-yama" tales discussed in chapter 5. The discourse of an abandoned woman in "Obasute-yama" is often sorrowful, giving the impression of frailty and sadness—after all, she is taken to a mountain to die alone, her fate at the mercy of her caregiver. On the other hand, Itō's yamauba is domineering and dynamic, exhibiting her burning desire for sexual intercourse. The yamauba says to Anjuhimeko, "this is my dying wish, please carry me on your back to that place, that place in the mountains . . . this is my dying wish, I want to have intercourse" (Itō H. 2007, 89; 1993, 29). Itō's yamauba is full of life and virility. She has an enormous sexual appetite and she continues to say, "I want to have intercourse, I want to have intercourse, I really want to, when you get to be my age you'll understand, at that time, who is going to carry you on their back into the mountains?" (Itō H. 2007, 90; 1993, 30).

Itō's yamauba is crude, shrewd, and cunning. As Anjuhimeko accedes to the yamauba's request and carries her on her back, the yamauba does disgusting things, such as rubbing her feces and urine into Anjuhimeko's back, and gouging out Anjuhimeko's moles with her fingernails and eating them. But when Anjuhimeko gives her a fierce look as though she is going to leave her, the yamauba shrewdly changes her shape or image. What Anjuhimeko sees on her back is "just a tiny, tiny, tiny, regular old woman, she says to me, please, please, please take pity on me, and she begins crying, she says in a heart-wrenching voice, because here are the breasts that once nursed you, the breasts she shows me are very, very, very shriveled" (Itō H. 2007, 90; 1993, 30). The yamauba invokes Anjuhimeko's sympathy and pity. Anjuhimeko's nightmarish experiences and memories seem to shift the shape of the yamauba into a mother figure. It is natural in the course of life that a child, dependent on its mother, grows up, and with the passage of time the mother becomes dependent on the child. The relationship between mother and daughter is fluid and the situation can be positive, negative, strong, weak, bright, dark, and so on, depending on one's perspective. Anjuhimeko and the yamauba may be paying tribute to the story of "Obasute-yama" and the circle of life.

Arriving at her destination on the mountain, the yamauba has intercourse with a large stone. Jeffrey Angles writes that the yamauba "clearly represents the voice of a powerful, liberated sexual desire ordinarily constrained under most regimes of power . . . When Anjuhimeko takes her to the mountains, the woman begins dancing around a gigantic stone phallus and copulating wildly with it" (Angles 2007, 66). The yamauba says to Anjuhimeko, "Just watch me! Listen to what kind of voices I make! Watch what kind of expressions I make! Anjuhimeko, your job is to bear witness!" The yamauba "shouts out in a loud voice, 'This is how you came out too!'" (Itō H. 2007, 90; 1993, 30). While the yamauba may want Anjuhimeko to be a witness to how Anjuhimeko was born, or to help Anjuhimeko overcome her traumatic experiences by seeing sexual activity, the yamauba could also be viewed as acting like a child who wants her parent to see what she is doing, or even considered an exhibitionist.

"As she speaks, she makes sure I [Anjuhimeko] can see her and gives her hips a strong shake, and with this, she gives birth to something I can't make heads or tails of" (Itō H. 2007, 90; 1993, 30). That amorphous something is named Hiruko (leech-child). And this is the yamauba's gift to Anjuhimeko, this present of a leech-child guides Anjuhimeko to Tennōji, her destination. It is the yamauba's gift to Anjuhimeko as she helped the yamauba. As Angles explains, Itō is refashioning the creation myth told in the *Kojiki* in these passages. According to the *Kojiki*, in the beginning of creating a country and family, Izanagi and Izanami built a palace at the center of which stood an august pillar; for their procreation they circled around the pillar, Izanami taking the initiative, and a leech-child was born. The proper procedure was that Izanagi had to take the initiative, speaking first. Angles explains,

> In Itō's reworking of the *Kojiki* creation myth, however, the *yamanba* takes her own sexual desire firmly in hand and copulates wildly with the stone pillar. Rather than subjugating her desire to the "proper order" of things, she celebrates it in a way that brings her ecstatic, orgiastic pleasure . . . Using the great stone phalluses, the *yamanba* disproves the lynchpin of phallocentrism: the fallacious (phallacious) assumption that feminine desire requires an active male partner. This kind of masturbatory, self-serving pleasure is a form of desire that is new to Anjuhimeko, whose sexual experiences have been either involuntary or carried out as a result of sexual subjugation or as unconscious reenactments of the traumas lingering in her sexual past. (Angles 2007, 67)

Further, Angles writes, "the leech-child and the formless, prelinguistic, deep-seated erotic desire that it represents guide Anjuhimeko forward

on her journey of psychological recovery from infantile sexual abuse"
(Angles 2007, 68).

Itō's yamauba is fertile; she gives birth to "slippery slimy things one
after another" (Itō H. 2007, 90; 1993, 31)—just like a fertile yamauba with
the qualities of a goddess. Unlike the helping yamauba of folktales, however, once she gives the leech-child to Anjuhimeko, she ignores her, completely wrapped up in having intercourse and producing many slimy things.
Itō's yamauba, who has given the main character a gift to help her out of
hardship, stands firmly on the mountain and on feminist discourse.

Adrienne Rich (1929–2012), poet and feminist, writes:

> Re-vision—the act of looking back, of seeing with fresh eyes, of entering
> an old text from a new critical direction—is for us more than a chapter
> in cultural history: it is an act of survival. Until we can understand the
> assumptions in which we are drenched we cannot know ourselves. And
> this drive to self-knowledge, for woman, is more than a search for identity:
> it is part of her refusal of the self-destructiveness of male-dominated soci-
> ety . . . We need to know the writing of the past, and know it differently
> than we have ever known it; not to pass on a tradition but to break its hold
> over us. (A. Rich 1972, 18–19)

Rich believes that prevailing patriarchal notions have to be readjusted to
fit the female perspective if equality between the sexes is to be achieved.
According to Kobayashi Fukuko (1943–), scholar of American literature
and gender studies, feminist methodologies such as Adrienne Rich's have
opened a passage to revisit past androcentric literatures and resurrect them
as gynocentric literatures. In Japan, likewise, using such a technique, a number of female writers like Ōba Minako and Tsushima Yūko (1947–2016)
have resurrected the legendary yamauba—known to eat a man lost in the
mountains—as the heroine of their works (Kobayashi Fukuko 2016, 2).[10]
While Itō's yamauba is not the heroine of *Watashi wa Anjuhimeko de aru*, the
poem is based on the gynocentric text of a little-known version of *Sanshō
Dayū* and, as Rebecca Copeland says, Itō describes the yamauba as a liberat-
ing being (Copeland 2016).

Contemporary yamauba—imaginary or real, frail or sturdy—live their
own lives. Yamaubaesque teenagers hailed as yamanba-gyaru are not visible on the streets of mega-cities anymore, but they have sown their seeds
overseas. The literally bigheaded Yubaba in *Spirited Away* may not strike the
audience as a yamauba with her avaricious nature, but she turns out to be a
yamaubaesque character, a helper to the studious heroine. Some yamauba
in manga are portrayed mysteriously in accordance with legends, and others

are erotically narrated, frequently from a feminist viewpoint. It is noteworthy that the image and diction of the noh play *Yamanba* continues to exert a strong influence on contemporary yamauba images. The yamauba character survives and continues to appear on the contemporary stage.

Conclusion

So THE YAMAUBA GOES, IN AND OUT OF the mountains, eating human flesh and drinking blood. She can transform herself into a spider, a beautiful woman, or bean paste. These characteristics are quite possibly adapted from her nascent origins in the oni. There are many similarities between yamauba and oni/oni-women; however, while the oni's gender is ambiguous and situational—an oni can be male, female, or it—a yamauba is always female. As far as I know, a yamauba does not change her appearance to lure her victims—usually men. Negative characteristics of yamauba such as anthropophagy may have led to the labeling of some senior citizens with severe dementia, who were deeply rooted in the life of the sato, as yamauba. Further, there were women living in the sato who chose a mountain home for themselves, but some were kidnapped and brought to the mountains. These yamauba remained in the mountains either because the mountains became their home, or because they lived in fear of reprisals from their kidnappers.

Duality is a major characteristic of the yamauba. She can be evil, nurturing, or divine. Yamaguchi Motoko explains that in ancient times yamauba was a goddess of Mother Nature, a mountain deity that hunters worshipped, and concurrently, a maiden serving a mountain god; yamauba was a holistic being encompassing good and evil sides. Yamaguchi continues, however, that in the ancient literary work the *Kojiki*, the yamauba's two dimensions were split into two pairs of goddesses: the positive bright side of the Sun Goddess Amaterasu and the negative dark side of Izanami—goddess of creation and death who was relegated to the dark realm of the other world—as well as Konohana sakuyahime, the beautiful wife of the god Ninigi (Amaterasu's grandson), and Iwanagahime, Konohana sakuyahime's ugly elder sister who was spurned by Ninigi (Yamaguchi 2009, 34–40). I believe it would be more accurate to say that in Japan's medieval period the good and evil aspects of an oni, an oni-like creature, and a goddess merged to create the yamauba. Retrospectively, yamauba's roots are found in mythological figures.

A yamauba can protect or harm the people she encounters. For example, when good people in need encounter a yamauba, and if those people

DOI: 10.7330/9781646420551.c007

accede to her requests, the yamauba gives them advice and/or a gift that leads to a happy ending. Sometimes the yamauba can divine a person's future or read his or her mind. The yamauba is often portrayed as spinning or weaving. The spinning wheel can be interpreted as a Buddhist motif representing the life of sentient beings as they travel through the six realms.

Kobayashi Fukuko notes that modern women writers of Japan have admired yamauba's liberty and freedom stemming from her position outside of conventional institutions, and her ability to resist the establishment—an ability nurtured by her strong and sturdy life force (Kobayashi Fukuko 2016, 3). Whether or not the yamauba of premodern texts expressed an attitude of resistance would depend on how the reader interprets these texts, but certainly modern authors of yamauba narratives emphasized such an attitude in yamauba. Yamauba are bodacious.

Mizuta asserts that an unfortunate event can trigger powerful suppressed emotions in a woman, including passion, jealousy, and rage, that allow her to transform herself into an oni in order to avenge herself, but that unlike oni, a yamauba does not avenge herself on people (see Mizuta 2002, 15). Probably that is why Yasaburō Basa is known as an oni-woman rather than a yamauba, although she is both oni and yamauba; Yasaburō Basa was terribly vengeful. She could also fly; flying is a lesser-known ability of yamauba. But when one recognizes yamauba's roots in oni and divinities, this flying power is quite understandable.

Many villagers recognized yamauba as a mountain goddess, the mother of divine or superhuman children. Yamauba are considered to be in tune with nature. The Mushikura Shrine located in Nakajō in Nagano City, Nagano Prefecture, enshrines Iwanagahime, but she is known as yamauba. The website Web Shūkan Nagano writes that this yamauba is a compassionate, child-rearing deity (Web Shūkan Nagano 2017). She protects children from drowning in ponds, kills a bug that was believed to cause convulsions in children, and is terribly fond of saké. Yamauba likes saké, as many Japanese do—and this trait, shared by Japanese deities and Shuten Dōji, makes her an approachable figure. Similar to the yamauba who appeared in Kiyomi village of Ōno district in Gifu Prefecture in chapter 6, the yamauba of Nagano Prefecture comes to a saké shop at the foot of Mt. Mushikura with a saké bottle that looks like it will hold only 360 milliliters, but in fact actually holds 3.6 liters. The yamauba was buying saké to celebrate the arrival of her new grandchild, and the saké shop prospered (Akutio-Nakajo Office 2011; Mushikurayama no Yamanba Henshū Iinkai 2007, 9–25). This yamauba is loved by people as a familiar deity. The images of yamauba, *koyasugami* (guardian deities of children and childbirth) and ubagami, as well as Datsueba, were all combined by the early modern period. Hagiwara Tatsuo writes that the activities of itinerant priestesses and priests were crucial for the dissemination of the present-day folklore telling of these figures and mixtures (Hagiwara 1985, 63). I believe that yamabushi were especially influential in the rise of yamauba's power, status, and roles. Yamauba, originally a product of the medieval zeitgeist, was encountered, imagined, or utilized by people in later generations who emphasized particular elements to fit their imagination and purposes. Komatsuzaki Susumu and Komatsuzaki Tatsuko write, "When yamauba was first created in the heads of the Japanese, there might have been a certain, unified image. But that image probably has been changed and changing little by little, depending upon the place the stories have been told, depending upon the relationship between the storyteller and the audience, and depending upon the content of the story" (Komatsuzaki and Komatsuzaki 1967, n.p.).

Itinerant priestesses and priests have been replaced by modern media as major carriers of the image of yamauba. The influence of the internet is significant; anime, manga, and fiction as well as guidebooks and research works are equally important. Again, each venue has its own perspective, adding, deleting, or emphasizing specific aspects of yamauba, passing on a reimagined yamauba image to the next generation.

Shiono Nanami, a historical fiction writer and the author of *Rōmajin no monogatari* (Tales of Romans), writes that the value of mythologies and legends lies more in how many and how long people have believed in them, rather than whether the narratives were factual or not (Shiono 1992, 33). Indeed, many Japanese have believed in the existence of yamauba—whether human or supernatural—in various guises.

So what is yamauba? A yamauba is an old woman living in the mountains. She is "an impossible bundle of contradictions" as Monica Bethe and Karen Brazell note (Bethe and Brazell 1998, 207). Since each creator or viewer of yamauba has a different take on and expectations of yamauba, the character produced is naturally multifaceted. A list of the yamauba's characteristics shows that she is truly full of contradictions—like human nature. I believe a holistic yamauba is is more than the sum of various yamauba attributes: she is a projection of human characteristics, with all their desires and fears. How people view such multidimensional yamauba depends on their own interpretation, and that is what makes yamauba interesting. Modern and ancient, powerful in their ability to express the human condition, yamauba can always be reimagined.

As yamauba's mythmaking and archetypes continue, how will Japanese embrace her as the twenty-first century progresses? Japan is changing, yet it is still a heavily patriarchal society. As described in the introduction, yamauba is always female. Yamauba's topos is the mountains, emitting the fragrance of nature, albeit secondary nature, that is, what a city dweller would consider as nature. Many women, especially elderly women, might aspire to be a yamauba—or perhaps are resigned to being one—someone outside of institutions, precisely because these women live in a society with many constraints. Japanese women's political and economic participation leave much to be desired. According to the World Economic Forum, Japan's ranking in the Global Gender Gap Index for 2019 is 121st among 153 countries (World Economic Forum 2019, 201). The Japanese government touts women's power. Former Prime Minister Abe Shinzō publicizes "Womenomics" to create a "Japan in which women can shine," with policies encouraging women to work and have a family at the same time; but public perceptions lag behind. "A 2016 poll found that 45 percent of men surveyed agreed with the idea that 'women should stay at home'" (Oda and Reynolds 2018).

No example is more conspicuous than some rules of the imperial institution: the only child of the current emperor and empress cannot ascend to the throne, simply because she is female. A female royal member becomes a commoner upon marriage. John Breen explains the situation in his insightful article, "Abdication, Succession and Japan's Imperial Future: An Emperor's Dilemma":

> Emperor Naruhito's younger brother, Crown Prince Akishino no Miya, is now next in line to the throne, and *his* son the 13-year-old Hisahito will succeed him. If Hisahito produces no male heirs, that is it. This dire situation has generated impassioned debate about the pros and cons of female succession to the throne. According to the latest polls, 76% of the population would be happy to see a woman enthroned. There is, after all, ample precedent for this: women have succeeded to the throne on ten previous occasions. What is striking is that 74% have no objection to the offspring of a woman emperor succeeding to the throne. If this were to happen, it would be an historical first. (Breen 2019, 8–9)[1]

The idea that succession is limited to males dates back only to the late nineteenth century; it is a modern invention. Indeed, there have been ten female emperors—eight female figures but two females among them were enthroned twice, making ten female emperors—in the 126 recorded emperors in Japan. On the day of succession to the throne, May 1, 2019, the new empress, Masako, was not allowed to attend the succession ceremony; Motoko Rich comments in her article in the *New York Times* that this was "another illustration of the diminished status of women in the imperial family, and of the challenges women face more broadly in Japanese society" (M. Rich 2019).[2] The message that a female is prohibited from occupying the throne or retaining royal status is strong—especially when the same government publicizes the advancement of women in various fields. In this environment, the yamauba, with her nonconformative lifestyle, will remain an appealing archetype for many Japanese for years to come.

Japanese and Chinese Names and Terms

A

Abe Masanobu	阿部正信
Abe no Seimei	安倍晴明
Abe no Yasuna	安倍保名
Adachigahara	安達原
Adachigahara no oni-baba	安達ヶ原の鬼婆
Ainōshō	壒嚢鈔
aka-gashira	赤頭
Akiha DaiGongen	秋葉大権現
Akiyoshi	秋好
Akiyoshikō	秋よしこう
akki	悪鬼
Amaterasu Ōmikami	天照大神
amatsukami	天つ神
Aoi no ue	葵上
Ashigara Heidayū	足柄兵太夫
Ashiya Dōman ōuchi kagami	葦屋道満大内鑑
Aya no tsuzumi	綾鼓
Azuma kagami	吾妻鏡

B

Baba-sugi	婆々杉
Bishamonten	毘沙門天
Bō	坊
boshin	母神
Buen	峯延
Bunkachō media geijutsusai	文化庁メディア芸術祭
buri no teriyaki	ブリの照り焼き
Buriteri	ブリテリ
Bussetsu enraō juki shishūgyakushu shichiōjō jōdokyō	仏説閻羅王授記四衆逆修七往生浄土経
Bussetsu Jizō bosatsu hosshin innen jūōkyō	仏説地蔵菩薩発心因縁十王経
Butokuden	武徳殿

C

chijoku	恥辱
Chikamatsu Monzaemon	近松門左衛門
Chi no ike jigoku	血の池地獄
chū-byō	注病

D

Daigo no sō Renshū kannon ni tsukōmatsurite yomigaeru o urukoto	醍醐僧蓮秀仕観音得活語
Daisenji engimaki	大山寺縁起巻
danna	檀那
Dao Shi	道世
Datsueba	奪衣婆
dōji	童子
Dōjōji	道成寺
Dōkō	道興

E

Ehon hyakumonogatari	絵本百物語
Eikai	叡海
eki-byō	疫病
Emperor GoDaigo	後醍醐天皇
Emperor Seiwa	清和天皇
Emperor Suinin	垂仁天皇
engi	縁起
"Enshū Akihayama honji Shōkanzeon Sanjakubō Daigongen ryaku engi"	遠州秋葉山本地聖観世音三尺坊大権現略縁起
Eryōju	衣領樹
etoki	絵解き

F

Fa yuan zhu lin (Jp. *Hōon jurin*)	法苑珠林
Fujiwara no Hōshō (or Yasumasa)	藤原保昌
Fukutomi Shinzō	福富新蔵
funshi	憤死
fūsō	風葬
Fusō Daiton	扶桑大暾
Fusō ryakki	扶桑略記
Fusō saigin	扶桑再吟
Fuyusame	冬雨
Fuyuyoshikō	冬よしこう

G

ganguro	ガングロ
Gaun nikkenroku	臥雲日件録
Gazu hyakki yagyō	画図百鬼夜行
Genji monogatari	源氏物語
Gen no naishi no suke	源典侍
genshitsu	原質
gentaiken	原体験
Gentō	玄棟
Getsuan suiseiki	月庵酔醒記
guishen	鬼神
gyaku-byō	瘧病

H

haikai	俳諧
Hanatare kozō	はなたれ小僧
Hanayo no hime	花世の姫
hannya	般若
Hannya shingyō	般若心経
harakake	腹かけ
haré	ハレ, 晴れ
harégi	晴れ着
haré no hi	晴れの日
haré no shokuji	晴の食事
Haruyoshi	春好
Hase temple	長谷寺
Hataori-i	機織井
Heike monogatari	平家物語
henge no mono	へんげのもの
hime	姫
Hime no minzokugaku	ヒメの民俗学
Hinaga-hime	肥長比売
hito o tasukuru waza o nomi	人を助くる業をのみ
Hōki no kuni Daisenji engi	伯耆国大山寺縁起
Hokke genki	法華験記
Homuchiwake no mikoto	本弁家和気王
Honchō shinsen-den	本朝神仙伝
hongaku shisō	本覚思想

honkaku	本格
hon'ne	本音
Hōon jurin (Ch. *Fa yuan zhu lin*)	法苑珠林
Hoori no mikoto	火遠理命
"Hotoke areba shujō ari, Shujō areba yamanba mo ari. Yanagi wa midori, hana wa kurenai no iroiro"	仏あれば衆生あり、衆生あれば山姥もあり。柳は緑、花は紅の色々。
Hyakkiyakō shō	百鬼夜行抄

I

Ibaraki (Kabuki play)	茨木
Ibaraki Dōji	茨木童子
Ibuki Dōji	伊吹童子
Ibukiyama	伊吹山
Ibukiyama Shuten Dōji	伊吹山酒典童子
Ichijō shūgyokushō	一乗拾玉抄
ikidōri	憤り
Ikkyū Sōjun	一休宗純
imo no chikara	妹の力
inasaku minzoku	稲作民族
Ise monogatari	伊勢物語
Ishimakura	石枕
iso onna	磯女
Isshiki Tadatomo (also Minamoto no Tadatomo)	一色直朝
Ito no dan	絲之段
ito-tsukushi	糸尽くし
Izanagi	伊弉諾, 伊邪那岐
Izanami	伊弉冉, 伊邪那美
Izumi Kyōka	泉鏡花

J

Jikidan innenshū	直談因縁集
jitō	地頭
jōruri	浄瑠璃
"Joshi o oshiyuru no hō"	女子を教ゆるの法

K

Kaikoku zakki	廻国雑記
"Kajiya no baba"	鍛冶屋の婆
kaku	玃

kamishibai	紙芝居
Kanawa	鐵輪
Kankyo no tomo	閑居の友
Kanryōjo	函量所
Kanze Kojirō Nobumitsu	観世小次郎信光
Kashiwabara Yasaburō	柏原弥三郎
ké	ケ, 褻
kégaré	ケガレ
kekkai	結界
Ken'eō	懸衣翁
Kenshō	顕昭
Ketsubonkyō	血盆経 (Ch. *Xuepen Jing*)
Ketsumimiko no Ōkami	家津美御子大神
kijin	鬼神
kijo	鬼女
kijo ga arisama	鬼女が有様
"Kiman, kendon no mono no ie ni hairite, hito o nayamasu. Kaerite jihi no mono"	きまん・けんどんの者の家に入て、人をなやます。還而慈悲の物
kin	金
Kinpira	金平
Kinpira nyūdō yamameguri	公平入道山めぐり
Kinpira tanjō-ki	金平たんじょうき
Kintarō	金太郎
Kishimojin	鬼子母神
Kōen	皇円
Koi no omoni	恋の重荷
Koike Yohachirō	小池与八郎
Kojiki	古事記
Kokin wakashū (or *Kokinshū*)	古今和歌集 (or 古今集)
Kokon hyakumonogatari hyōban	古今百 物語評判
"Komebuku Awabuku"	米福粟福
Komochi yamanba	嫗山姥
Konjaku monogatarishū	今昔物語集
Kōnoike	鴻池
Konparu Zenchiku	金春禅竹
Korobō Gaun	胡廬坊臥雲
kosodate rōbason	子育て老婆尊
kotobuki taisha	寿退社

kotodama	言霊
Koumitawa	子生嵶
"Kōya hijiri"	高野聖
koyasugami	子安神
Kumano *bikuni*	熊野比丘尼
Kumano kanshin jikkai mandara	熊野観心十界曼荼羅
Kumonosu-jō	蜘蛛巣城
kunitsukami	国つ神
"Kuramadera engi"	鞍馬寺縁起
Kurozuka	黒塚
kusemai	曲舞
"Kuwazu nyōbō"	食わず女房
Kuzunoha	葛の葉

M

mae-shite	前シテ
Majo to yōroppa	魔女とヨーロッパ
Majo wa naze hito o kūka	魔女はなぜ人を喰うか
mamin	魔民
Matsudaira Tadaaki	松平忠明
Matsutani Miyoko	松谷みよ子
miko	巫女、神子
mikudarihan	三行半
Minamoto no Raikō (or Yorimitsu)	源頼光
Minamoto no Shigeyuki	源重之
Minamoto no Tadatomo (also Isshiki Tadatomo)	源直朝
Modoribashi	戻り橋
mokko	もっこ
Momotarō	桃太郎
Motoori Norinaga	本居宣長
Mt. Akiha	秋葉山
Mt. Atago	愛宕山
Mt. Hongū	本宮山
Mt. Ibuki	伊吹山
Mt. Kuraki	久楽畿山、倉木山、くらき山
Mt. Nunohoshi	布干山
Mt. Togakushi	戸隠山

Mt. Yahiko	弥彦山
mukashibanashi	昔話
"Mushi mezuru himegimi"	虫めづる姫君
Myōkōji temple	明光寺
Myōtara Ten'nyo	妙多羅天女

N

Natsusame	夏雨
Natsuyoshikō	夏よしこう
Nemuki	ネムキ
Nemurenu yoru no kimyōna hanashi	眠れぬ夜の奇妙な話
Nihongi	日本紀
Nihon ryōiki	日本霊異記
Nihon sandai jitsuroku	日本三代実録
Nihon shoki	日本書紀
Nippo jisho	日葡辞書
Nippon Kaigi	日本会議
nochi-shite	後シテ
nyonin kinsei	女人禁制

O

oba	小母
Obasute (or Ubasute)	姨捨
Obasute-yama (or Ubasute-yama)	姨捨山
Ōe no Masafusa	大江匡房
Ōeyama	大江山
Ōeyama ekotoba	大江山絵詞
Ogino Yaegiri	荻野八重桐
Ogita Ansei	荻田安静
Ohase or Ohatsuse	オハセ、オハツセ
Ōkubi-e	大首絵
Ōmononushi no kami	大物主神
on	隠
ōna no oni	嫗鬼
oni	鬼
oni-baba, oni-banba, oni-basa	鬼婆
"Oni no ko Kozuna"	鬼の子小綱
onigo	鬼子
"Onna daigaku takarabako"	女大学宝箱

onna no oni	女の鬼
Ono no Komachi	小野小町
oshi	御師
otogizōshi	お伽草子
Ōyamatsumi no mikoto	大山祇命

R

Rashōmon (noh play)	羅生門
reiki	霊鬼
Reizei Meiyū (or Myōyū)	冷泉明融
Reizei-ke ryū Ise shō	冷泉家流伊勢抄
"Rōba oni no ude o mochisaru zu"	老婆鬼の腕を持去る図
rōjo	老女
rōni	老尼
ryōbosei	両墓制
"Ryōshi no haha oni to narite ko o kurawamu to suru koto"	猟師の母鬼と成りて子を噉はむとする語
Ryūgū kozō	竜宮小僧

S

Sadamoto, Prince	貞元親王
saisō	再創
sai-sōzō	再創造
saiwa	再話
Sakata no Kintoki	坂田金時 (or 公時)
Sanemori	実盛
Sangoku denki	三国伝記
sanjin	山人
"Sanmai no ofuda"	三枚のお札
Sanrōjo	三老女
"Sanseru onna minami Yamashina ni yuki oni ni aite niguru koto"	産女南山科 に行き鬼に値ひて逃ぐる語
Sanzugawa	三途川
Sanzu no kawa	三途の川
Sarashina nikki	更級日記
Sasaki Bicchū-no-kami Minamoto no Yoritsuna	佐々木備中守源頼綱
Sasaki Nobutsuna	佐々木信綱
Sasaki Sadatsuna	佐々木定綱
sato	里

satori	さとり, サトリ, 覚, 悟り
Sekidera Komachi	関寺小町
sendatsu	先達
setsuwa	説話
Setsuyōshū	節用集
Shibuya sentāgai	渋谷センター街
shikami	顰
shikisoku zekū, kūsoku zeshiki	色即是空、 空即是色
Shinodazuma	信太妻
Shinsen wakashū	新撰和歌集
shintai	神体
shite	シテ
Shōgoin	聖護院
Shōji	正治
Shōzuka	葬頭河, 正塚
Shōzuka no bāsan	正塚の婆さん
Shuchi Kongōbō	種智金剛房
Shugendō	修験道
shugenja	修験者
shugo	守護
shugyō no zensō	修行の禅僧
Shūi wakashū or *Shūishū*	拾遺和歌集、 拾遺集
shūmon aratamechō	宗門改帳
shuryō saishūmin	狩猟採集民
Shuten Dōji	酒呑童子, 酒顚童子
Shūyōji temple	秋葉寺
Sotoba Komachi	卒塔婆小町
Sōzuka	葬頭河
Sugawara no Takasue no musume	藤原孝標 女
Sukuyōkyō	宿曜経 (Ch. *Xiuyaojing*)
Sunkoku zasshi	駿國雜志
Susanoo	スサノオ

T

Taira no Kanemori	平兼盛
Taira no Sadamichi (or Sadamitsu) (or Usui no Sadamitsu)	平貞道 (光)
Taira no Suetake (or Urabe no Suetake)	季武 (or卜部季武)
Takehara Shunsensai	竹原春泉斎

tanroku-bon	丹緑本
Tatsutahime	竜田姫
tengu	天狗
Tenkai	典海 (Yasaburō Basa)
Tenkai	天海 (author of *Jikidan innenshū*)
Tenryū River	天竜川
Tentoku	天徳
"Tentōsan kin no kusari"	天道さん金の鎖
Terajima Ryōan	寺島良安
Tetsugaisho	鉄碍所
tobidashite	飛び出して
tobisari	飛び去り
Tōdaiki	当代記
Tōfuku-ji	東福寺
Tōji	東寺
Tokugawa Ieyasu	徳川家康
Tonoigusa	とのゐ草
Tōno monogatari	遠野物語
Toran-ni	都藍尼
Tōsanjin	桃山人
toshi no ichi	年(歳)の市
Tōshōji nezumi monogatari	東勝寺鼠物語
Tōtōmi no kuni fudokiden	遠江國風土記傳
Toyotama-bime	豊玉毘売
tsuchigumo	土蜘蛛
Tsukioka Yoshitoshi	月岡芳年
tsukumogami	九十九髪, 九十九神
Tsukumogami ki	付喪神記
tsukune	つくね
"Tsurugi no maki"	剣巻
Tsutsumi chūnagon monogatari	堤中納言物語

U

uba	姥
ubagami	姥神
ubai	優婆夷
"Ubakawa," *ubakawa*	姥皮
Ubasute (or Obasute)	姥捨

Ubasute-yama (or Obasute-yama)	姥捨山
uchide no kozuchi	打ち出の小槌
Uchiyama Matatsu	内山真龍
ukiyo-e	浮世絵
umi no kai	海の怪
Urabe Kanekata	卜部兼方
Urabe Suetake (or Taira no Suetake)	卜部季武 (or 平季武)
"Ushikata to yamauba"	牛方と山姥
Usui Sadamitsu (or Sadamichi) (or Taira no Sadamichi)	碓井貞光 (道)

W

"Waga kokoro/nagusamekanetsu/Sarashina ya/ Obastuteyama ni/ Teru tsuki o mite"	わが心なぐさめかねつ更科やをばすて山に照る月を見て
Wakan sansaizue	和漢三才図会
Wamyō ruijushō	倭名類聚抄
Watanabe no Tsuna	渡辺綱

X

Xiuyaojing	宿曜経 (Jp. *Sukuyōkyô*)
Xuepen Jing	血盆経 (Jp. *Ketsubonkyō*)

Y

Yaegiri	八重桐
yamabito	山人
yamabushi	山伏
yamagumo	山ぐも
yamahaha	山母
Yamahime	山姫
Yamanba (noh play)	山姥
yamanba-gyaru	ヤマンバギャル
Yamanba katabiraki	山姥帷子記
"Yamanba no bishō"	山姥の微笑
Yamanba no nishiki	やまんばのにしき
Yamaoka Genrin	山岡元隣
Yamato monogatari	大和物語
Yamatotohi momosobime no mikoto	倭迹迹日百襲姫命
yamauba (yamanba, yamamba)	山姥, 山優婆, 山祖母, 山婆, 山伯母
"Yamauba hōon"	山姥報恩
Yamauba monogatari	山姥物語
Yamauba monogatari jikki	山姥物語実記

"Yamauba no nakōdo"	山姥の仲人
"Yamauba to ishimochi"	山姥と石餅
"Yamauba to itoguruma"	山姥と糸車
Yamauba to Kintarō chibusa	山姥と金太郎 乳房
Yamauba to Kintarō ennenmai	山姥と金太郎 延年舞い
Yamauba to Kintarō genpuku	山姥と金太郎 元服
Yamauba to Kintarō kamisori	山姥と金太郎 剃刀
"Yamauba to okeya"	山姥と桶屋
Yasaburō Basa	弥三郎婆
yōkai	妖怪
Yomigatari	読みがたり
Yomotsu-shikome	予母都志許売, 泉津醜女
Yūkei	祐慶
"Yūmeidan"	幽冥談
yuki no sei	雪の精
yuki onna	雪女

Z

Zàng Chuān	蔵川 (Jp. Zōsen)
Zeami	世阿弥
Zenkōji	善光寺
Zōhōzōkyō	雑宝蔵経
Zoku zoku Kyūō dōwa	続々鳩翁道話
Zōsen	蔵川 (Ch. Zàng Chuān)
zōtan	雑譚
Zuikei Shūhō	瑞谿周鳳

Notes

INTRODUCTION

1. *Yōkai* is difficult to translate. Komatsu Kazuhiko writes that generally speaking, in its broadest definition, they are creatures, presences, or phenomena that could be described as mysterious or eerie. While such a thing in itself is seen in any society, "what is interesting about Japanese yōkai is that they were developed into a unique culture" (Komatsu K. 2016, 12). Foster explains that "a yōkai is a weird or mysterious creature, a monster or fantastic being, a spirit or a sprite," although it can also be a more complicated being (Foster 2015, 5).

2. See chapter 5 for a summary and discussion of the 156th episode of *Yamato monogatari* and "The Old Woman on the Mountain," and chapter 4 for the summary of "How the Hunters' Mother Became an Oni and Tried to Devour Her Children."

3. Likewise, Carmen Blacker notes, "Sacral power was believed to reside more easily and properly with women . . . in consequence women were recognized to be the natural intermediaries between the two worlds" (Blacker 1975, 28).

4. Of course, the growing number of female yōkai in narratives of the early modern period cannot be discussed without reference to the roles of the expanding transportation system, advanced printing technology, and commercialism in spreading stories of such yōkai at a rapid pace throughout Japan. But these subjects are beyond the scope of this book.

5. See for example, "yamauba" and "yamanba" in *Kōjien* (1978, 2230, 2237); "yamauba" and "yamanba" in *Nihon kokugo daijiten* (2004, 198, 245); "yamauba" in *Sekai daihyakka jiten* (Gōda and Yokomichi 1972, 475).

6. *Tōshōji nezumi monogatari* was perhaps written by a monk as a textbook to educate his disciples (Hayashi Y. 2002, 405).

7. Miyata Noboru follows Konno's classification, dividing female yōkai into three types: yamauba, *iso onna* (seashore women), and *yuki onna* (snow women) (Miyata 2000, 187).

8. Komatsuzaki Susumu is a member of the standing committee of the Federation of Japanese Literature Education, an elementary school teacher, and a juvenile literature writer. Komatsuzaki Tatsuko is a member of the standing committee of the Federation of Japanese Teacher Education and an elementary school teacher. Their survey was conducted at several elementary schools in Tokyo after the children read Matsutani Miyoko's *Yamanba no nishiki* (1967), a folktale of Akita Prefecture. This work has been translated into English, published as *The Witch's Magic Cloth* (1969).

9. Japan's medieval period is usually taken to mean 1185–1600. See Farris 2006, 114.

10. Setsuwa, a Japanese literary genre, broadly consists of myths, legends, folktales, and anecdotes. In the narrow sense of the term, these works are "short Japanese tales that depict extraordinary events, illustrate basic Buddhist principles or, less frequently, other Asian religious and philosophical teachings, and transmit cultural and historical knowledge. These narratives were compiled from roughly the ninth through mid-fourteenth centuries in collections such as *Konjaku monogatarishū* (*Tales of Times Now Past*, ca. 1120)" (Li 2009, 1). Setsuwa are now often considered secondhand stories that have an oral origin. They are presented as

true, or at least as possibly true. Also see Eubanks 2011, 8–11, especially for an explanation about Buddhist setsuwa literature.

11. This is the fifteenth story of chapter 27. For the Japanese text, see *SNKBZ* 1994–2002, 38:54–58. An English translation is found in Ury 1979, 161–63.

12. Similarly, "Amadomo yama ni irite take o kuite mau koto" ("About the Nuns Who Went into the Mountains, Ate Bamboo Shoots, and Danced"), the twenty-eighth story of chapter 28 of *Konjaku monogatarishū* (see *SNKBZ* 1994–2002, 38:226–28), tells of several woodcutters who go into the mountains and get lost. While they are sitting not knowing what to do, four or five nuns come out dancing from the deep mountains. The woodcutters think they must be oni or *tengu* (flying goblins) because they could not possibly be human beings. Again, if the term *yamauba* had been in existence at the time, surely they would have been thought to be yamauba.

13. According to the classification of folklorist Seki Keigo (1899–1990), "Yamauba to ishimochi" ("Yamauba and Stone Rice Cakes") is numbered 256 (also AT 953, AT1135, AT1137; see *NMT* 1978–1980, 10:112–17). Seki summarizes the story as follows: "Wood-cutter (or *oshō* [bonze]) is toasting and eating *mochi* [rice cakes]. *Bōzu* (old man or *yama-uba*) appears and asks for some mochi, but is given a burned stone or heated oil instead. He eats or drinks this and is killed" (Seki 1966, 56).

14. One such *engi* or origin/legend is "Kuramadera engi" ("Origin of Kurama Temple"), included in *Fusō ryakki* (A brief history of Japan), a twelfth-century history book written by a Buddhist monk named Kōen (ca. 1074–1169) ("Kuramadera engi" appears in the entry for the fifteenth year of the Enryaku period, which corresponds to 796. See Kōen 1897, 583). Mt. Kurama has been an important center for Shugendō since the olden days. A summary of the pertinent section of "Kuramadera engi" is as follows: a *shugyō no zensō* (Buddhist practitioner) visits a place called Dōu and makes a sacred fire to dispel the darkness. Late at night a demon/deity (*kijin*) that resembles a woman comes and warms herself at the fire. The practitioner is frightened; he stabs her in the chest with his burning-hot iron staff, then immediately flees and hides himself under a decayed tree at Nishitani. The (female-looking) oni chases after him and tries to eat him in one gulp. The practitioner recites the name of Bishamonten (Skt. Vaiśravaṇa) earnestly, whereupon rotten wood falls on the evil oni (*akki*, evil demon), killing it. The story ends with praises for Bishamonten's miraculous power (Gorai 1984, 29). It should be noted that the female-looking creature is first introduced as a deity/demon, then referred to as an oni, and finally called an evil oni. Incidentally, Gorai Shigeru explains that because this was before the introduction of Zen Buddhism, the shugyō no zensō was a practitioner in the mountains, i.e., he is a yamabushi (Gorai 1984, 29–30). However, as Komatsu Kazuhiko notes during the seminar held at International Research Center for Japanese Studies in 2019 (see Reider 2019), this practitioner is identified later as Buen (dates unknown) of Tōji temple; therefore, he is not considered to be a yamabushi.

15. Tokuda Kazuo surmises that this type of story, in which a religious person or travel-ing hero subjugates demons and yōkai, had long existed, and that these setsuwa were rooted in other miraculous mountains as well (Tokuda 2016c, 43–44).

16. The "gentle old woman in the mountains" expressed by these Chinese characters may have contributed to the image of a gentle, helping yamauba, which will be discussed in chapter 1.

17. The story appears in the seventy-fifth section of *Hōki no kuni Daisenji engi*.

18. Foster 2015, 59–61. Also see Yanagita 1968, 285–437. Karatani Kōjin (1941–), phi-losopher and literary critic, explains that Yanagita Kunio thought *yamabito* (mountain people)

were descendants of aboriginal people who had thrived on the islands of Japan long ago. These indigenous hunters and gatherers (*shuryō saishūmin*; Karatani adds the term *kunitsu-kami*) were either subjugated by the rice cultivators (*inasaku minzoku*; Karatani adds the term *amatsukami*) who arrived later, or they escaped to the mountains (Karatani 2014, 82–86).

19. Northrop Frye (1912–1991), literary critic and theorist, writes; "Archetypes are associative clusters, and differ from signs in being complex variables. Within the complex is often a large number of specific learned associations which are communicable because a large number of people in a given culture happen to be familiar with them" (Frye 2006, 95).

20. Marie-Louise von Franz (1915–1998), Jungian psychologist and scholar, interprets the witch in two of the Grimm fairy tales, "The Two Brothers" and "The Golden Children," as an archetypal figure of the Great Mother, and as an archetype of the unconscious (Franz 1974, 104). See also Jacoby, Kast, and Diedel 1992, 205–6.

21. Regarding the translation of Onmyōdō as "the Way of yin-yang" and the spelling of Onmyōdō without italics and with a capital O, I have followed Hayek and Hayashi 2013, 3. Onmyōdō is an eclectic practice whose roots are found in the theory of the cosmic duality of yin and yang and the five elements or phases (metal, wood, water, fire, and earth). With the theory of yin and yang and the five elements originally formed in ancient China, Onmyōdō adapted elements from the Buddhist astrology of the Xiuyaojing (Jp. Sukuyōkyō) and indigenous Japanese kami worship. The appellation Onmyōdō was formed in Japan between the tenth and eleventh centuries. See Hayek and Hayashi 2013, 1–18.

22. For the origins of the oni, see Reider 2010, 2–14.

23. Interestingly, the oni depicted in the scenes of Kanryōsho (Hell of fiery measuring containers) and Tetsugaisho (Hell of pulverized flesh in iron mortar) in *Jigoku sōshi* (Picture scrolls of Buddhist hell, ca. twelfth century), housed in Nara Kokuritsu Hakubutsukan, have drooping breasts, indicating that these are old female oni (Tokuda 2016b, 43). Indeed, Komatsu Shigemi calls them them just that—*baba-oni* (Komatsu and Akiyama 1977, 54, 56).

24. *Yomigatari*, published from 2004 to 2005, has forty-seven volumes altogether. Hayashi Shizuyo notes that *Yomigatari* were edited from collections of old tales in various regions that were first published around 1974 for the purpose of making the tales easy for children to understand. Various prefectural education-related organizations participated in the creation of *Yomigatari* for practical and educational use by children (Hayashi S. 2012, 69).

25. For a discussion of *tsukumogami*, see Rambelli 2007, 211–58; Reider 2016, chap. 7.

26. Barbara Leavy says of the swan maiden; "Woman *was* a symbolic outsider, was the *other*" (Leavy 1994, 2). I believe Leavy's statement about the swan maiden is applicable to yamauba as well.

CHAPTER 1: MAN-EATING, HELPING, SHAPE-SHIFTING YAMAUBA

1. See introduction, the section titled "The Term *Yamauba*." Interestingly, the word *yama-uba* is explained in *Shūeisha kokugojiten* as "female oni that is believed to live in the deep mountains. Also yamanba" (*Shūeisha kokugojiten* 1993, 1787).

2. Recent yamauba such as in Matsutani Miyoko's *kamishibai* "Three Charms," illustrated by Futamata Eigorō, are frequently portrayed with horns on their heads. I surmise that when yamauba's negative side is emphasized they tend to have horns.

3. For the Japanese texts, see Yanagita 1971, 113–17; *NMT* 1978–1980, 6:182–225. For an English translation, see Mayer 1986, 110–14; Seki 1966, 45.

4. Kawai writes it is important to note that the woman proposes to the man, and the man's attitude is passive (Kawai 1996, 29). This assertiveness of the woman has a commonality with the progressive attitude of animal wives, who also first approach the man. According to Kobayashi Fumihiko, in animal wife tales the Japanese "have preserved the ideal of the woman as an assertive gender" (Kobayashi Fumihiko 2015, 101). Kobayashi bases this interpretation on what he identifies as the tales' four pillar episodes: (1) the animal woman first approaches the man; (2) the animal woman ensconces herself in the man's house; (3) the man discovers the animal woman's nonhuman origin; and (4) the animal woman forsakes the man or simply vanishes. Contrary to the general misconception, Kobayashi argues that the tales reflect women's positive attitude toward their real lives.

5. For an insightful observation about human body parts, including the mouth as an entrance and exit for yōkai, see Yasui 2014, 205–55; 2019.

6. "Kokon hyakumonogatari hyōban" was compiled by either a student or the eldest son of Yamaoka Genrin and was printed fourteen years after Genrin's death. The work is in the form of a question-and-answer session between Genrin and his students. Yamaoka explains the yamauba as "an evil spirit of mountains and rivers," underscoring the yamauba's negative side.

7. The illustration is titled "Futakuchi onna" (Woman with two mouths), and is from the *Ehon hyakumonogatari* (One hundred strange and weird tales illustrated), published in 1841 (Takehara Shunsensai 1997). Takehara Shunsensai (dates unknown), a *ukiyo-e* artist in the late Edo period, illustrated the work and the written texts were done by Tōsanjin (dates unknown), a fiction writer. This illustration appears in a retribution tale: the sins of the stepmother visit her own daughter. More than 150 years later, Mizuki Shigeru (1922–2015) uses the same title, "Futakuchi onna," for an almost identical illustration in his *Yōkai gadan*, published in 2002. But Mizuki's illustration is about a yamauba—the yamauba from "The Wife Who Doesn't Eat." I have found the way that narratives and images are handed down fascinating. I adopt this illustration here because many contemporary observers consider that it depicts "The Wife Who Doesn't Eat," See chapter 4 for details about the creation and dissemination of narratives and images.

8. Snakes account for seventeen. See *NMT* 1978–1980, 6:158–81.

9. For other examples of a yamauba changing into a spider, see Konno 1981, 224–25.

10. Regarding transformation, Kawai Hayao points out the element of the Great Mother in relation to food the yamauba eats in "The Woman Who Eats Nothing": "Before one eats food, food exists outside of the body, but once it is consumed, the food becomes part of one's body," Kawai writes; "Eating archetypically contains the function of assimilation or identification . . . While she eats humans as her nourishment, she also appears as a Goddess of fertility who gives them food" (Kawai 1996, 32).

11. Donald Philippi notes, "The idea that partaking of the food of the dead magically disqualifies one from returning to his native land occurs also in the Greek myth of Persephone, in the *Kalevala*, among the Maoris, in China, and in the Ryukyus; the idea that one may not return home if he has eaten the food of any other world or society—such as the world of the spirits, fairies, or gods—was also widespread" (Philippi 1969, 401–2).

12. For the Japanese text, see *SNKBZ* 1994–2002, 1:45–47. For an English translation, see Philippi 1969, 61–64.

13. For the Japanese text, see *NMT* 1978–1980, 6:158–81; Yanagita 1971, 109–13. For an English translation, see Mayer 1986, 107–10; Seki 1966, 44.

14. Other main characters and the number of times they appear in this type are as follows: old woman, nine; tanuki, four; mountain man, three; one-eyed monster, two; spider, one; mountain mother, one; comb, one; and Sanshō Dayū, one. *NMT* 1978–1980, 6:158–81.

15. For the Japanese text, see *NMT* 1978–1980, 6:132–54. An English translation is found in Seki 1966, 43.

16. The rest are: mountain woman, one; mountain man, one; *mujina*, one; and monster, one.

17. For years, an elderly couple prays for a child. Eventually, the woman conceives, when she is long past the normal age for childbirth. The boy she gives birth to, however, never grows any larger than an inch (hence his name, Little One-Inch). One day, Little One-Inch decides to go to the capital in search of fortune and success. He gets a job as a servant to an aristocratic family and falls madly in love with the couple's beautiful daughter. He tricks her parents into believing she has stolen his rice and they disown her; she comes under his care, and together they leave the family's compound. On their journey, which has no destination, Little One-Inch and the daughter encounter a band of oni. One of the oni swallows Little One-Inch in one gulp but he fights back, plunging his little sword into the being from inside its body. Severely injured, the oni coughs up Little One-Inch and the demon band scampers away, leaving behind a magical wish-granting mallet. Little One-Inch picks up the mallet and, with the help of its supernatural power, he is transformed into a normal-sized human. He uses the mallet to produce food and treasures. Little One-Inch becomes rich, marries the aristocratic daughter, and they live happily ever after. For the Japanese text, see Ichiko 1958, 319–26. For an English translation, see McCullough 1990, 495–98.

18. The oni can be a bringer of fortune through prized tools such as a wish-granting mallet that can produce any materials (see Antoni 1991; Reider 2010), but voluntarily helping humans and bringing wealth are not foregrounded features of oni.

19. This action of the yamauba resembles that of the giant's wife in the English fairytale "Jack and the Beanstalk."

20. Other helpers are: ghost of the biological mother, ten; bird, seven; Kōbō daishi, two; Jizō Boddhisattva, two; beggar, two; deity, one; biological living mother, one; small woman, one; and cow, one.

21. Other helpers are: wet nurse, one; young priest, one; and person, one.

22. It should be noted that an oni is a mirror image of a human being. When humans hide in an oni's house, the oni says, "I smell something fishy," referring to the smell of humans. The same phrase describing a "fishy smell" is usually used when oni appear before humans.

23. "It was widely believed during the medieval period that song and dance, as well as other arts, could function as a means to salvation" (Bethe and Brazell 1998, 213).

24. Yamaoka Genrin considers the yamauba "an evil spirit of deep mountains and valleys. When the world exists, people exist. Water entails the birth of fish. When *chi* accumulates, evil spirits are born" (Yamaoka 1993, 46).

25. In noh, there are five types of plays, categorized according to the role of the shite (lead actor): works that focus on gods, warriors, women, mad persons, or demons. The plays *Yamanba* and *Kurozuka* are fittingly categorized as demon plays.

26. Daisetz Suzuki writes that *Yamanba* "was probably written by a Buddhist priest to propagate the teaching of Zen" (Suzuki 1959, 419).

27. In *Atsumori*, the ghost of Atsumori, a young aristocrat, appears as a grass cutter, and the ghosts of Matsukaze and Murasame, female divers, scoop brine in *Matsukaze*.

28. For the Japanese text, see *SNKBZ* 1994–2002, 59:459–73; *SNKBT* 1989–2005, 57:502–3. For an English translation, see Shimazaki C. and Comee 2012, 307–35. Shimazaki and Comee's translation is preceded by a wonderful introduction to this play (299–306).

29. This story is handed down in Kanze temple in Adachigahara, Nihonmatsu of Fukushima Prefecture.

30. The Ishimakura setsuwa was written down by Dōkō (1430–1527), head priest of Shōgoin temple, in his travel journal, *Kaikoku zakki* (completed in 1487). Ishimakura is the name of a stone in Asakusa in Musashi province. The story goes as follows: a lower-ranking samurai had a daughter. He and his wife made her a prostitute. The daughter-prostitute invited travelers to make love beside Ishimakura, and after the travelers fell asleep, her parents crushed their heads and took their belongings. The daughter disapproved of her parents' conduct. One day she took the position of a traveler and her parents, unknowingly, bashed in her head. Realizing it was their own daughter they had killed, they repented and held a memorial service for their daughter (Matsuoka S. 1998, 89). Kishimo, or Hārītī in Sanskrit, had ten thousand children whom she loved. But she was violent in disposition and killed and ate human children. The bereaved humans begged Gautama Buddha to save them, whereupon he hid Kishimo's youngest child. After a desperate but unsuccessful search for her missing son, Kishimo learned of the Buddha's omniscience and appealed to him for help. Buddha remonstrated with her, pointing out the great suffering she caused parents by eating their. After he returned her youngest child, Kishimo became the protector of children and women in childbirth as the deity Kishimojin or Kishimo (Motai 1972, 127).

31. See the section titled "Mother of Divine Children and Anthropophagy" in chapter 2 for a summary and texts of Shuten Dōji's story.

32. For the Japanese text, see *SNKBZ* 1994–2002, 12:290–91. For an English translation, see Tahara 1980, 31–33.

33. For the Japanese text, see *SNKBT* 1989–2005, 7:160. For an English translation, see Fujiwara A. 1995, 1:136.

34. Li describes a female oni that appears in the tale "Deeply Jealous Woman Becomes an Oni While Still Living" in a Buddhist setsuwa collection called *Kankyo no tomo* (A companion in solitude, complied 1222) as a lonely and pitiful being. The main character is a woman who, after being abandoned by her lover, makes herself look like an oni, using starch syrup to fashion her hair into five horns. She kills her former lover and eventually eats other innocent people (see Keisei 1993, 422).

35. Oda Sachiko notes that the shite in *Kurozuka* reveals not only the demonic spirit but also the woman's karma, through the text and by the mask and costumes the shite wears (Oda 1986, 82).

36. An example of being pursued by the one who is seen is the episode of Homuchiwake no mikoto, the son of Emperor Suinin, who wedded Hinaga-hime for one night. When he stole a glance at her, she was a snake. The prince was afraid and ran away. Grieving for him, Hinaga-hime pursued him in a boat, lighting up the ocean. He, more and more afraid, fled up the mountain and escaped (Philippi 1969, 222–23; *SNKBZ* 1994–2002, 1:209–10).

37. It is interesting to note Kawai's opinion: "It seems to me that the essence of Japanese fairy tales can be seen better through 'female eyes' rather than 'male eyes' . . . To look at things with female eyes means, in other words, that the ego of a Japanese is properly symbolized by a female and not by a male. The patriarchal social system that prevailed in Japan until the end of World War II obscured our eyes to this fact. In fairy tales, however, 'female *heroes*' could freely take an active part. The investigation of those female figures will cast light on the psyche of the Japanese" (Kawai 1996, 26).

CHAPTER 2: MOTHER YAMAUBA AND WEAVING

1. Yamaoka Genrin states that the *kusemai* was written by Ikkyū Sōjun (1394–1481), monk of the Rinzai sect of Zen Buddhism (Yamaoka 1993, 46).

2. For the study of midwifery skills and roles, see Yasui 2013. Some women who died during pregnancy or while giving birth were believed to become a female yōkai called *ubume*. See Shimazaki 2016, 194–227 for a study of ubume.

3. For an English translation of the Shibukawa version of *Shuten Dōji* published in the eighteenth century, see Reider 2010, 185–203. For an English translation of *Ōeyama ekotoba* (*Illustrations and Writing of Mt. Ōe*, ca. fourteenth century), the oldest extant Shuten Dōji text, see Reider 2016, 37–56.

4. See Akihasan Hongū Akiha Jinja n.d. According Tamura Sadao, currently 800 Akiha shrines are registered at Jinja Honchō (Association of Shinto Shrines), and when one includes shrines within Akiha shrine compounds, the number goes up to about 4,000 shrines all over Japan. Also, 1,500 temples of the Sōdō sect of Buddhism enshrine Akiha Gongen (the manifestation of a buddha or boddhisattva in the form of an Akiha deity). Many Tendai and Shingon sects of Buddhism also enshrine Akiha Gongen (Tamura 2014, 20–21).

5. Sakamoto Tarō explains that "it is a *miko*'s job to weave the Gods' garments. Hence, the description reveals that Sun Goddess Amaterasu was a *miko*" (*SNKBT* 1989–2005, 67:560; also see Okamoto 2012, 35). For the celestial weaver maiden in Chinese and Japanese myth, see Como 2009. In regard to the importance of spinning, Sasaki Takahiro, during the seminar held at International Research Center for Japanese Studies in 2019 (see Reider 2019), references the three sisters of fate in Greek mythology—Clotho spins the thread of life, representing birth; Lachesis measures the length of the thread; and Atropos cuts the thread, deciding one's death. Also, it is interesting to note, Sasaki has reminded me (see Reider 2019) that the legend of Mt. Miwa described in *Nihon shoki* (see the section titled "Yamanba in *Kurozuka*" in chapter 1) narrates the death of Yamatotohi momosobime no mikoto after her shrieking when she sees the real form of her husband, Ōmononushi no kami. In *Kojiki*, the legend is narrated differently; a beautiful daughter becomes pregnant by a mysterious young handsome man who comes to her chamber nightly. Instructed by her parents, she threads hemp yarn to a needle and sews it onto the hem of his garment. On the following morning, she and her parents follow the yarn; the path leads to Mt. Miwa and leaves off at the shrine of the deity, so they learn that the man is the god of Mt. Miwa (Philippi 1969, 203–4; *SNKBZ* 1994–2002, 1:185–88). The pregnant wife of the god in *Kojiki* narrates the (future) birth of their child and her story includes string. Together with Yamatotohi momosobime no mikoto, the wives of Mt. Miwa's deities represent death, birth, and string.

6. "Hataori gozen" are legends about a supernatural maiden weaving on a loom on a mountain or deep in the water. Many stories recount that the sound of weaving on a loom is heard coming from the water. See Yanagita, 1970a, 186–95. "Daishi ido" are tales about Kūkai (or Kōbō Daishi, 774–835), the founder of the Shingon sect of Buddhism, who traveled to various places in Japan and smote the ground to bring forth water. See Yanagita 1970a, 152–68.

7. Also in *Nihon ryōiki*, it is the husband who writes a poem for his wife.

8. For a study of the fox wife and shape-shifting, see Bathgate 2004.

9. Seki Keigo classifies these stories as 253C; AT304 (Ikeda-AaTh 121Y; see Ikeda Hiroko 1971, 32).

10. This type of story is also found in *Tonoigusa* (another name for this work is *Otogi monogatari* [Nursery tales]), written by the *haikai* poet Ogita Ansei (d. 1699) and published

in 1677. The form the tale takes is that the narrator has heard the story from a masterless samurai, who in turn heard it from a hunter when the samurai visited a mountain village in present-day Okayama Prefecture. When the hunter went into the deep mountains, he came across an incomparably beautiful woman of age twenty or so. He felt so weird that he shot the woman, but the woman caught the bullet with her right hand and smiled. He shot a second time and the woman caught the bullet with her left hand and smiled. Frightened, he fled, but the woman did not chase him. Later the hunter told the story to an elderly man, who said that she was a mountain princess. If she was pleased, she would give one treasure (Ogita 1989, 91–92). Apparently, by the early Edo period, the story of a huntsman shooting a mysterious yamahime or yamauba on a mountain was a popular one to tell.

11. A possible original form of the legend was that a dragon woman more than 1,000 years old lived in Ogase Pond. Sometimes transforming into a beautiful woman, and other times into an old woman, she troubled villagers by eating humans and animals. See Taki 1986, 45.

12. For the historical figures of Minamoto no Raikō and Sakata no Kintoki, see Reider 2016, chap. 1.

13. Jizōdō is the name of the area as well as of the temple hall.

14. The play was first performed for jōruri in 1712. The first recorded kabuki performance was in 1714. For the text of *Komochi yamauba*, see Chikamatsu 1959, 177–226.

15. For a discussion of *Komochi yamauba*, see Reider 2010, 76–84.

16. Takagi Tadashi asserts that the legal treatment of divorce among commoners clearly argues against the idea that women's status was vastly inferior to men's (Takagi 2006, 97–115). Still, women's status was far from equal to men's.

17. However, upon divorce, money and land related to the dowry had to be returned to the woman, except in cases where the divorce was initiated by the wife or her family. See Nakada 1956, 99–110, 140.

18. Ihara Saikaku (1642–1693), one century before Utamaro's time, calls an unsightly old woman a yamauba in a short tale included in *Saikaku shokoku banashi*. When the main character was young, she was exceptionally beautiful and was called a flower in a mountain village, but her eleven lovers died one after another before she was eighteen years of age. After that, she remained single, supporting herself by spinning. As she grew old, she became less attractive and more frightening in appearance. This is probably why Saikaku called her "yamauba." She was shot to death by an arrow while stealing oil from a shrine. When the arrow cut off her head, the head flew in the air and breathed fire. After that, anyone who saw the fire-breathing head passed out, and some even died (Ihara 1996, 142–44). The fire-breathing head is new to yamauba lore, although the character's evil side was known to cause men to pass out or die. By this time yamauba were avidly discussed with much curiosity.

19. Regarding *Hyakkiyakō shō*, see the section titled "Yamauba in the Manga *Hyakkiyakō shō*" in chapter 6. The episode is entitled "Shiroi ago" (A white chin, Ima 1995–, 12:3–44). The story first appeared in the March 2003 issue.

20. Seki Keigo writes, "Demon (or stepmother) is killed and the fragments of his flesh turn to fleas, lice, and mosquitoes; mucus turns into frogs; blood into fleas; and the ashes into flies" (Seki 1966, 23).

21. See the section titled "Female Cohabitant in Oni's House" in chapter 1 for summary.

22. The *Yabatai* poem is a text of *mirai-ki* (writings on the future), foretelling Japan's demise—stating that after the one hundredth emperor, self-proclaimed warlords would vie for hegemony and Japan would eventually perish. The text comprises 120 characters altogether, but the characters are placed at random so that the reader has to decipher in what

order they should be read. When the characters are properly ordered, the text becomes a poem consisting of twenty-four lines, each of five characters. During the medieval period, the poem had great authority as the textual source for naming Japan "Yamato." As an authoritative text that directly concerns Japan, the poem spawned many annotations and quotes. Throughout the medieval period, it was firmly believed that Dhyana Master Bao Zhi (418–514), a mysterious monk during the time of Emperor Wu of Liang (464–549, reigned 502–549), was the composer of this poem. During the Edo period, however, a Confucian scholar, Hayashi Gahō (1618–1680) suspected that this prediction poem was written by a Japanese during the Heian period (see Komine 2003).

23. See Reider 2016, chap. 2 for detailed discussion. During the early modern period, the earth spider was notorious in literature and theatrical performance as a shape-shifting killer, appearing in *Kanhasshū tsunagiuma* (Tethered steed and the eight provinces of Kantō, a kabuki piece and puppet theater play), written by Chikamatsu Monzaemon (1653–1725); *Tsuchigumo* (Earth spider, 1881, a kabuki dance piece), by Kawatake Mokuami (1816–1893); and *Shiranui monogatari* (The tale of Shiranui; a *gesaku*, popular literature of the late Edo period), written by Ryūkatei Tanekazu (1807–1858), to name a few. The female spider-woman character uses her whitish threads to catch her prey to kill. The maiden with a deep-seated grudge named Kochō in *Kanhasshū tsunagiuma* turns into the evil spirit of an earth spider after her death and attempts to murder her living rival with the spider's web. The kabuki dance piece *Tsuchigumo* follows the story of the noh play *Tsuchigumo*. In *Shiranui monogatari*, Princess Wakana, the heroine and child of the late Ōtomo Sōrin, a feudal lord in the Warring States period, receives magical skills from an ancient earth spider and fights against her enemies with her main weapon, spider threads. The source for the deadly female spider can be mainly attributed to the noh play *Tsuchigumo* (ca. beginning of fifteenth century; date given by Baba Kazuo 1990, 80), and the play's widely recognized sources, the *Nihon shoki* or *Nihongi* and "Tsurugi no maki" from the *Tale of the Heike*. I believe that *Tsuchigumo zōshi* should be included among the sources for the noh play *Tsuchigumo*.

24. Mark Hudson considers the tsuchigumo "an example of the Yamato language of political allegiance, whereby people who opposed the state were assigned the status of barbarian" (Hudson 1999, 201).

CHAPTER 3: READING MINDS AND TELLING FUTURES

1. "Komekko nukakko" is "Komebuku Awabuku." See chapter 1 for plot.

2. Other times, the mind reader is a tengu, tanuki (raccoon-dog), mountain father, yama-otoko (mountain man), mountain deity, or a one-legged, one-eyed yōkai.

3. Gorai notes that when a mountain deity is worshipped by a high priest of Buddhism or yamabushi, it becomes a dōji (Gorai 1984, 34).

4. This is the sixty-fifth story of volume 1.

5. *Fusō saigin* is Fusō Daiton's work, which was compiled by his disciples.

6. Roger K. Thomas cogently states that kotodama is "a concept of ancient vintage that was resuscitated and variously interpreted during the early modern period" (Thomas 2012, 6).

7. A very old cat is believed to transform into a monster cat and to eat human beings. One famous folktale titled "Kajiya no baba" ("The Blacksmith's Old Mother"): Seki's type 252; AT121 (Ikeda-AaTh 121, see Ikeda Hiroko 1971, 29–31) is a good example. See *NMT* 1978–19807:10–11; Seki 1966, 49–50.

8. The translation of "The Smile of a Mountain Witch" quoted here is by Noriko Mizuta Lippit. See Ōba M. 1991, 194–206. For the Japanese text, see Ōba M. 2009, 461–77.

9. Matsutani Miyoko writes that depending on the situation, saiwa can even start from the story collector's sorting out of what a storyteller has narrated: the reteller can repeat certain aspects, insert an explanation, or omit important sections. Sometimes a saiwa writer may correct the end of sentences to accommodate readers unfamiliar with difficult dialect and the storyteller's unique narration rhythm. Other times, the plot summary is the same but the saiwa writer expresses it in his or her own writing style (Matsutani 1979, 247–48).

10. Kinoshita Junji (1914–2004) lists his play *Yūzuru* (Twilight crane, 1949), as an example of sai-sōzō (Kinoshita 1958, 259–60).

11. The narrator says, "Now, the woman about whom I am going to speak was a genuine mountain witch" (Ōba M. 1991, 196; Ōba M. 2009, 463).

12. The book was published in 1946 by Sankyūsha, and has been published by Iwanami Shoten since 1953 as part of the *Iwanami Library for Young Children* series. An English translation of this book is titled *Canute Whistlewinks and Other Stories*, translated from the Swedish by C. W. Foss.

13. Star Eye, a child who brings wealth to the family who takes care of her, reminds one of "Hanatare kozō" ("Snot-Nosed Boy") or "Ryūgū kozō" ("The Boy from Ryūgū [dragon palace]"). It is classified by Seki Keigo as number 223. The plot goes as follows: "A poor man (or a woman) (a) throws fire-wood or New Year's pine branches into the sea; or (b) saves a fish (or frog). He is taken by a turtle (or a woman) to Ryūgū to be entertained by the princess of Ryūgū, who thanks him for the pine branches or for his kindness to the fish. On parting from the princess the man asks her, as he was told to by the turtle, for a supernatural boy (white dog, black cat, turtle, hen, horse, or magic object) which produces various things. The supernatural boy or animal produces or buys as much gold as the quantity of food which he is fed every day. Then (a) The man's wife (brother, or a neighbor) borrows the supernatural animal to try to make it produce more gold, but fails; or (b) the man becomes immodest and lets the supernatural boy go away. Then he loses wealth" (Seki 1966, 87–88).

14. See, for example, Mizuta and Ōba 1995, 142.

15. The survey was conducted at several elementary schools in Tokyo after the children readg Kanzawa Toshiko's version of "Naranashi-tori," titled *Nashi-tori kyōdai*.

16. In Fujita Hiroko's work *Folktales from the Japanese Countryside*, translated by Fran Stallings, the character is called "an old woman," but the story is placed under the heading of "Stories of Yamanbas" (see Fujita 2008).

17. Unless noted otherwise, I use Linda Hoaglund's translation.

18. "Noh drama develops ideas such as the impermanence of human existence, man's sinfulness, and the likelihood of retribution," McDonald writes. "This is doubly appropriate, since Kurosawa's thematic concern throughout is with questions of man's moral nature. These themes shared with noh drama are reinforced, too, both visually and aurally in a circular pattern" (McDonald 1994, 129).

19. The Noble Eightfold Path is Right View, Right Resolve, Right Speech, Right Conduct, Right Livelihood, Right Effort, Right Mindfulness, and Right Concentration.

20. The Wheel of Suffering occupies the largest part of the Wheel of Life, portraying the Buddhist cosmology. See Robinson and Johnson 1997, 20–27.

21. "The witch in the wood was represented by the mask named Yamanba" (Manvell 1971, 103).

22. This is obviously an effect based on Shakespeare's play. The witches always appear with an accompaniment of thunder and/or lightning. See Shakespeare 1978, 419, 446.

23. Most likely, Kurosawa used Tsubouchi Shōyō's translation, which is widely available. In Tsubouchi's work, published in 1932, the stage direction "dance" is also translated (see Shakespeare 2004). *Macbeth* was also translated by Fukuda Tsuneari. But Fukuda's translation was published in 1969, much later than Kurosawa's film.

CHAPTER 4: YAMAUBA, YASABURŌ BASA, DATSUEBA

1. Miyata compares and contrasts European witches and Japanese oni-women in the chapter "Majo to kijo," which first appeared as an article in the journal *Yū* in 1982.

2. The play *Ibaraki* was created by Kawatake Mokuami (1816–1893). The plot starts from where the noh play *Rashōmon* ended. This kabuki play is a *matsubamemono*, a noh-based kabuki dance drama performed in front of a panel of a picture of pine trees, adopting the art of noh.

3. Also, in explaining the legendary oni-woman of Mt. Togakushi who is the source for the noh play *Momijigari* (Hunting Momiji), Takahashi calls the main character both oni-woman and yamauba (Takahashi 1995, 51).

4. See the section titled "Mother of Divine Children and Anthropophagy" in chapter 2 for summary and texts of the Shuten Dōji story.

5. For various accounts of Yasaburō Basa, see *NDT* 1982–1990, 3:111–28.

6. Miyata does not provide his source.

7. The hole in the gable allows smoke to escape.

8. Also see "Yahiko no mukashibanashi."

9. For the story of Kishimo, see note 30 of chapter 1.

10. Yanagita Kunio writes that although it is written as Sōzuka with difficult kanji in an apocryphal scripture, *Bussetsu Jizō bosatsu hosshin innen jūōkyō*, there was no such place as Sōzuka in Buddhist cosmology. *Sōzuka* originally meant "a border" in Japanese, but someone later applied complicated kanji to the word (Yanagita 1970a, 143).

11. Niigata Prefectural Government writes on its website that there are three statues of Myōtara Ten'nyo enshrined at Hōkōin and that they look frightening, reminding people of Datsueba. One of the three statues is unveiled on October 15 every year. When the statue is unveiled, cotton is put on its head, and it is widely believed that a child's whooping cough will be healed if the child wears this cotton around his or her neck (Niigata Prefectural Government n.d.). The posture of one knee raised and the other leg crossed under the body was a formal sitting posture for women of high status in the medieval period.

12. The sutra was compiled in Japan at the end of the twelfth century based on the Chinese *Bussetsu enraō juki shishūgyakushu shichiōjō jōdokyō* (Sutra of Jizō Bodhisattva and Ten Kings) by Zàng Chuān (in Japanese, Zōsen, Tang Dynasty [618–907]).

13. In *Hokke genki* it is written that "there is an old female oni on the north side of the [Sanzu] river. Her appearance is ugly and she lives under a large tree. She hangs thousands of pieces of clothing on the tree branches. The oni said . . . 'I'm an old woman of the Sanzu River. Take off your clothes before crossing the river'" (*Dai Nihonkoku Hokke genki* 1995, 138–39).

14. As in *Hokke genki*, the phrase *ōna no oni* is used in *Konjaku monogatarishū*. The story is titled "Daigo no sō Renshū kannon ni tsukōmatsurite yomigaeru o urukoto." See *SNKBZ* 1994–2002, 16:284–86. Also see Ogurisu 2014, 22.

15. For stories about Datsueba in English, see Hirasawa 2013, 159–81; Saka 2017.

16. Unlike other mountainous religious headquarters, which prohibited women from entering designated areas of the sacred grounds (*kekkai*), Kumano allowed women to enter freely. On Kumano and Kumano bikuni, see Moeman 2000; Ruch 2002. For the influence of Kumano bikuni on national literature, see Ruch 1991, 143–84.

17. No boulder or cavern is mentioned in *Jizō jūōkyō*, *Hokke genki*, or *Konjaku monogatarishū* (see *Bussetsu Jizō bosatsu hosshin innen jūōkyō* 1998, 300; *Dai Nihonkoku Hokke genki* 1995, 138–39; and *SNKBZ* 1994–2002, 16:284–86).

18. One folding screen housed in the Freer Gallery of Art in Washington, DC, depicts a scene of a bikuni explaining a mandala picture to the public. This bikuni is also portrayed with one knee up. Hagiwara 1983, 57–58; also see Ruch 2002, 561.

19. See also Yanagita 1970a, 140–41. An example of this type of ubagami is a story included in *Sunkoku zasshi* (Topography of Shizuoka Prefecture, 1843) written by Abe Masanobu (dates unknown). A nurse holding the child of her lord in her arms was passing by a pond when the child had a severe coughing attack. She put the child down on the ground to get some water from the pond to alleviate its pain, and while she was distracted, the child rolled, fell into the pond, and died. The nurse felt so guilty that she drowned herself (Yanagita 1970a, 141).

20. One example concerns Toran-ni (Nun Toran), a legendary person who appeared in narratives about the ban on women entering sacred mountains (*nyonin kinsei*). According to the *Honchō shinsen-den* (Biography of Japanese immortals; late eleventh century) by Ōe no Masafusa (1041–1111), Toran-ni was a native of Yamato province and lived for several hundred years thanks to her mystical ascetic training. "Regrettably, however, her overconfidence led her to penetrate the sacred Mt. Kinpusen, only to have Kongō Zaō [the tutelary deity of Mt. Kinpusen], who never permits women to cross its boundary, strike her with lightning. Toran's staff changed into a tree, the earth caved in to create a lake. She left traces of her nail marks on the mountain rock" (translation by Ikumi Kaminishi). Ikumi Kaminishi writes: "Toran, a fearless nun who dared to enter Kinpusen, becomes a symbol that supports the male institution of the *nyonin kinsei* system, a policy of cordoning off women. The system prohibited all women from penetrating designated areas of sacred ground (*kekkai*) such as Mt. Kinpusen . . . In these mountains, Toran's obstinate spirit is often represented by rocks on the roadside on the way to the top of the mountain or wooden statues of a seated old hag (variably called *Onba-sama* or Datsueba)" (Kaminishi 2016, 331).

21. As mentioned in note 11 above, the cotton put on the head of the unveiled statue of Myōtara Ten'nyo also has healing powers to heal whooping cough.

22. Hagiwara Tatsuo claims that the wide dissemination of folklore relating to *koyasugami* (guardian deities of children and childbirth), ubagami, and yamauba in modern times owes much to the active support of itinerant priestesses. Hagiwara 1985, 63; 1983, 284–87.

23. There are many families with the surname Ibaraki who claim to be descendants of Ibaraki Dōji (Tokuda 2001, 86–87). Tanigawa notes that Ibaraki Dōji's attack on Tsuna is very similar to that of Yasaburō Basa (Tanigawa 2005, 317). Further, Sasaki Raita comments that legends of the Mt. Yahiko area as the birthplace of Shuten Dōji have been spread in the Mt. Yahiko area since the beginning of the early modern period, and this belief was widely adapted into various mukashibanashi (Sasaki R. 2008, 204).

24. Satake explains that the reason Yasaburō's conqueror in *Azuma kagami*, Sasaki Nobutsuna, became Sasaki Bicchū-no-kami Minamoto no Yoritsuna (Raikō in the sino-reading) (1244–1310) in *Sangoku denki* is because Raikō is a homophone of Minamoto no

Raikō (948–1021), Shuten Dōji's conqueror. Hence, Yoritsuna (Raikō), as the conqueror of legendary, villainous Yasaburō with supernatural power, was more acceptable than Nobutsuna. It also reveals that the Ibukiyama version of Shuten Dōji already existed before the compilation of *Sangoku denki* in 1407 (Satake 1977, 39).

25. As Yasaburō Basa stories do not describe how Yasaburō Basa kidnapped and ate children after she fled to the mountains, one can only imagine how she comes down from her mountain residence and eats them. It could well be like the opening section of a famous yamauba mukashibanashi story type titled "Tentōsan kin no kusari" ("Golden Chain from Heaven"). A mother and three children live in a house in the mountains. While the mother is away, the yamauba comes to the house disguised as her. The yamauba eats the baby, but the older siblings narrowly escape by climbing up a golden chain sent from heaven. She pursues them, climbing another rope sent from heaven, but slips and plummets into a field of buckwheat. Her blood turns the buckwheat red (Seki 1957, 113–15; 1963, 54–57; *NMT* 1978–1980, 6:226–50). While the yamauba in "Tentōsan kin no kusari" meets her demise in the end like her fellow anthropophagous yamauba, Yasaburō Basa is connected to a proselytizing setsuwa intended to propagate the efficacy of Buddhism, and is deified in the end.

26. Incidentally, during the Edo period the authorship of *Yamanba* (or the added verse "willows are green, blossoms crimson") was sometimes attributed to Ikkyū Sōjun (1394–1481), a monk of the Rinzai sect of Zen Buddhism. This view was already germinating at the end of the medieval period (Sasaki R. 2008, 208–9). Yamaoka Genrin also follows this view (Yamaoka 1993, 46).

27. Another good example of the re-creation of new setsuwa are the variations of *Momotarō* (Peach boy). The pattern, which includes (1) an oni having his arm or part of his body severed by a man; (2) the oni, disguised as an old woman, retrieving his arm or part of his body; and (3) the oni disappearing soon after that, has been very popular in Japan. In fact, Ikeda Hiroko classifies this pattern as "Retrieving of Severed Hand" (Ikeda-AaTh 971; there is no equivalent classification by Keigo Seki). Ikeda notes that this classification is based on the plot of the kabuki play *Ibaraki* (Ikeda Hiroko 1971, 216). The "Retrieving of Severed Hand" pattern has been adapted in a number of tales, including a variation of *Momotarō*, one of the most well-known oni-conquering folktales. For a discussion of *Momotarō*, see Namekawa 1981; Antoni 1991; Dower 1986, 250–58; Reider 2010, 141–45. Here, too, one sees a mixture of an oni and yamauba. Momotarō is so named because he was born from a peach that floated down a stream. As the boy grew older, he began to demonstrate miraculous strength. At that time, oni from a distant island were frequenting the capital, looting treasures and abducting people. The young Momotarō decided to confront and subjugate the oni. His elderly parents provided him with dumplings for food. En route, Momotarō met a dog, a monkey, and a pheasant, which all became his vassals in exchange for his remarkably delicious dumplings. Momotarō and his three vassals went to the oni's island, defeated the oni, and took back all the island treasures with them. The folktale *Momotarō* originated sometime between 1550 and 1630, but Momotarō's image—as good, affectionate, and a filial son, the perfect model of good conduct for young Japanese—is more recent, dating to the eighteenth century (Namekawa 1981, 2–3, 206). A variation of *Momotarō* found in the southern Kaga region of Ishikawa Prefecture is a little different. First discussed by Yamashita Hisao in 1935, in this version what Momotarō acquired from the oni was not treasure, but the oni's fangs. Just like the mainstream Momotarō, the variant Momotarō (hereafter called Yamashita's *Momotarō*) was smart and defeated the oni on their island. But after Momotarō took the oni's fangs as spoils, the oni retrieved his fangs in a way very similar to the actions

of the oni in Tsuna's Modoribashi episode. The oni in Yamashita's *Momotarō*, disguising himself as a yamauba who had taken care of Momotarō, asked Momotarō for a glimpse of the fangs—because she had nursed him since he was small. As soon as Momotarō placed the oni's fangs in the yamauba's hand, she disappeared with a gust of wind coming from a mill-stone (Yamashita 1975, 93–94). It is noteworthy that the storyteller describes the oni shape-shifting into a yamauba, not an old woman or Momotarō's mother. In the same region, an almost identical Momotarō story was told by Nakajima Sugi (b. 1897) in 1972 (Matsumoto K. 2007, 93–97). According to Nakajima's version, however, Momotarō was mischievous. Importantly for this study, when retrieving the oni's fangs, in this version the oni trans-formed into the old woman who raised Momotarō, not a yamauba. This is closer to Tsuna's Modoribashi episode. As she disappears with the wind, the yamauba does fly. These stories indicate that it does not make much difference whether the old woman transforms herself into a yamauba, an oni-baba, or an oni. Again, when the beings are perceived as harmful or destructive to humans, they can be described as any one of these three. In the case of the *Momotarō* variations, a description of oni eating humans is absent.

28. Seki Keigo notes that only a handful of this story type exists in Shizuoka and Niigata Prefectures (*NMT* 1978–1980, 10:314).

29. Tengu, famous mountain-resident yōkai that exerted great influence during the medi-eval period, are known for flying. For a study of tengu, see Wakabayashi 2012.

30. This painting is installed in the Myōkōji temple in Sakuma, Tenryū-ku, Shizuoka Prefecture.

CHAPTER 5: AGING, DEMENTIA, AND ABANDONED WOMEN

1. Usually, when Chinese characters are applied to the syllabic *tsukumogami*, the char-acters, which literally mean "hair of ninety-nine [years of age]," are employed. Written this way, the term signifies the hair of a ninety-nine-year-old person. Komatsu Kazuhiko explains that the syllabic can also mean "ninety-nine deities" (*kami*, hair, and *kami*, deity, are homonyms), signifying spirits that are impregnated in extraordinarily long-lived persons or objects. When the spirit does something mysterious, it becomes a specter of an old person or object (Komatsu K. 1994, 330). Tanaka Takako, on the other hand, writes that according to the *Reizei-ke ryū Ise shō* (Reizei school annotations to *The Tales of Ise*; ca. thirteenth century; *Ise* episode 63), wolves, foxes, and tanuki (racoon-dogs) that live for more than one hundred years will have both the power to change their shapes and the will to harm humans. Those transformed animals are called tsukumogami. Tanaka notes that calling an aging, shape-shifting animal a tsukumogami is just one step away from calling the shape-shifting specters of nonsentient beings tsukumogami (Tanaka T. 1992, 206–8).

2. The literal translation of the comment's beginning is actually "Their mother had become terribly old and turned into an oni" rather than "Senile and demented, their mother had become an oni." But Ury has aptly translated this sentence using "Senile and demented."

3. Komatsu Kazuhiko cites Matsumoto Minoru's comments that when a yamauba pos-sesses a house, not an individual, that possession is generally considered positive because the yamauba brings wealth to the house (Komatsu K. 1979, 347), as the following example story tells. The Nakao household in the village was poor. One cold night at the end of the year, an old woman whom the Nakao family had never seen before visited their house and asked

the family to feed her husband rice cakes to fill his stomach once a year in exchange for her making the family rich. The family agreed to feed the old man on December 28, and the old woman left with them an ear of an enormous millet plant. On the promised day, the old man visited the Nakao household and heartily ate the rice cakes the family had prepared for him. The following year the Nakao family planted the millet grains, which resulted in an abundant harvest. Copious harvests followed year after year, and the Nakao family became rich. The old man continued to visit once a year to eat the rice cakes, but the family started to consider him a nuisance. One year they put a burning stone among the rice cakes they gave to the old man, who begged for tea to help wash it down his throat. The family then gave him lamp oil instead of tea. As he left the house, he melted because of the effect of the burning oil. After that, the Nakao family became poor again, and no longer made rice cakes on December 28. According to Monobe villagers, the old man and woman are yamauba and *yamajii* (old man in the mountains), and it is believed that this really happened. Because the Nakao family was kind-hearted, the yamauba made them wealthy, but as the family became arrogant and treated the yamauba and yamajii poorly, the yamauba left or de-possessed the house. Komatsu Kazuhiko finds a relationship between the yamauba's possession of the household and villagers' observance of social morality and order (Komatsu K. 1979, 347–48). This goes along well with the yamauba's selective rewards discussed in chapter 1.

4. Susan Hanley reports that life expectancy at birth was 42.1 years for males and 43.2 years for females, according to the first reliable life expectancy table compiled for Japan from the first modern census conducted between 1920 and 1925, and that this was "a life expectancy similar to that in western Europe prior to 1859" (Hanley 1974, 141).

5. The symptoms of FTD "progressively worsen with time, almost always over years, eventually requiring 24-hour care" (Mayo Clinic n.d.).

6. The Association for Frontotemporal Degeneration posts on their website that FTD is "the most common dementia for people under age 60" (Association for Frontotemporal Degeneration n.d.).

7. Yanagita Kunio first made this division of four types in his article "Oyasute-yama" (Abandoned parents in the mountains) published in 1945. He notes that the first two types have foreign origins, whereas the third and fourth types are native Japanese stories. In Yanagita's *Nihon mukashibanashi meii*, published in 1971, however, he divides the stories into two categories: the first is about "a land of abandoned old people. The wisdom of an old person, hidden and cared for, helps solve problems and they became happy . . . The second type is where children who take their parents to the mountains to abandon them are moved by the love of their parents and try to live with them again" (Mayer 1986, 168). Many scholars follow the division into four types. Ōshima Tatehiko calls them four types that are independent of each other (Ōshima 1979, 513), and Mihara Yukihisa calls the four categories subtypes (Mihara 1977, 110). See also Inada et al. 1977, 110–11; Yanagita 1971, 173–75.

8. The five categories of noh are works that focus on gods, warriors, women, mad persons, or demons.

9. The translation of the poem is mine.

10. On the other hand, the total fertility rate (TFR) of Japanese women in 2016 was 1.44 (Kōsei Rōdōshō 2018b). The demographic imbalance brought about by Japan's declining birth rate and the rise in numbers of elderly people is a major national issue.

11. The definition of healthy life expectancy is, according to the World Health Organization, the "average number of years that a person can expect to live in 'full health'

by taking into account years lived in less than full health due to disease and/or injury" (World Health Organization 2017).

12. The average life expectancy of Japanese women in 2017 was 87.26 years, and for Japanese men it was 81.09 years. See Kōsei Rōdōshō 2018c, 2.

CHAPTER 6: YAMAMBA MUMBO JUMBO

1. Yoshie notes that the first appearance of the term *ganguro* in a magazine was in May 1998 (Yoshie 2010, 87).

2. The magazine *egg* was launched in 1995 and lasted until 2014.

3. Miller explains Kogals (*kogyaru*) as "the mainstream media label used to describe young women between the ages of 14 and 22 who project new types of fashion, behavior, and language," and says that "during the 1990s the mainstream media incited a moral panic over Kogals, amplifying their perceived deviant behaviors and language." See Miller 2004, 225–26.

4. The name Buriteri originated from the Japanese dish *buri no teriyaki* (grilled or broiled teriyaki-flavored yellowtail) because her skin was tanned so heavily it had a similar color.

5. According to Komatsu Kazuhiko, an anthropologist, "the other world" can be understood from two levels: one is to look at the world from a temporal point of view—a time axis—and the other is a spatial viewpoint—a space axis. The temporal view considers the time from birth until death as "this world," and the time prior to birth and after death as "the other world." From the spatial viewpoint, the space where everyday life exists is regarded as "this world" and the space outside of everyday life—the meta-everyday-life realm—is regarded as "the other world." Heaven, oceans, rivers, underground, and strange lands are understood as "the other world" from the spatial point of view. The "spatial other world" cannot be visited easily, but unlike the "temporal other world," if certain conditions are met, one can go without dying (Komatsu K. 1991, 57–58).

6. I am indebted to Angles 2007 in writing this section, especially about feminist discourse.

7. The widely known version of *Sanshō Dayū* performed as a *sekkyō-bushi* was printed in the seventeenth century. The popular version of *Sanshō Dayū* relates "the tribulations of the family of a young aristocrat who has been exiled from his post in far northeastern Honshu to a location far from his family. As his wife travels with her two children to join him in exile, bandits capture and separate the family. The wife ends up working on the island of Sado, while her daughter Anju (sometimes also known as Anjunohime) and son Zushiō (sometimes also known as Tsushiōmaru) are sold as menial laborers into the household of the cruel landowner Sanshō Dayū in Tango province. When Zushiō escapes, Sanshō Dayū and one of his particularly cruel sons torture his sister Anju to learn his whereabouts, but rather than tell them, she silently endures the pain. In the end, their cruelty proves too much for her frail body and she dies rather than confess her brother's destination. Much of the rest of the story focuses on Zushiō's quest to collect the scattered remnants of his family. Thanks to a protective amulet of the bodhisattva Jizō, he makes it to the capital, where he is recognized to be of a noble family. Eventually he is promoted to a high rank, which he uses to free the slaves of Tango province, although his sister is already dead. After much searching, Zushiō eventually locates his parents. His mother, who has gone blind from weeping, is making her living as a human scarecrow, chasing sparrows from a field of millet. With the amulet of Jizō, Zushiō miraculously heals her

sight—a miracle no doubt included to inspire listeners to believe in the great benevolence and power of the bodhisattva" (Angles 2007, 54).

8. Jeffrey Angles notes that this final section diverges radically from the itako's Sanshō Dayū text, and that "Itō draws on Japanese mythology in order to explore the issue of psychological recovery and the important role that sexuality, which has so far been the principal means of Anjuhimeko's subjugation, might play in her recuperation" (Angles 2007, 64).

9. All translations of this work are by Angles.

10. Similarly, Rebecca Copeland said that writers of the recent generation such as Kurahashi Yumiko (1935–2005), Ōba Minako, and Tsushima Yūko have availed themselves of the female demonic, drawing a new and positive power from the formerly abject image of the yamamba (Copeland 2016).

CONCLUSION

1. In his article, John Breen introduces the strong influence of "ultra-conservative groups, the self-appointed guardians of Japan's imperial legacy. The most vociferous among them today is Nippon Kaigi (Japan Conference; hereafter NK). This is a powerful group, whose board features many Shinto religious leaders. The chief priests of the Ise Shrines, the Yasukuni Shrine, and the Meiji Shrine are among them. But NK matters because Prime Minister Shinzō Abe and the majority of his cabinet are members" (Breen 2019, 3).

2. Rich reports: "Under the Imperial Household Law, which governs the line of succession as well as most matters of protocol related to Japan's monarchy, women in the royal family are not permitted to be in the room when the new emperor receives the sacred regalia signifying his rightful succession to the world's oldest monarchy" (M. Rich 2019). Still, one woman, Katayama Satsuki, minister of state for the Promotion of Overcoming Population Decline and Vitalizing Local Economy in Japan, was present in the room.

References

Akihasan Hongū Akiha Jinja. n.d. "Homepage." Accessed July 17, 2016. http://www
.akihasanhongu.jp/index.html.

Akutio-Nakajo Office. 2011. "Michi no eki Nakajō 'Yamauba densetsu.'" http://nakajyo
-actio.jp/yamanba/index.html.

Angles, Jeffrey. 2007. "Reclaiming the Unwritten: The Work of Memory in Itō Hiromi's
Watashi wa Anjuhimeko de aru (I Am Anjuhimeko)." *U.S.–Japan Women's Journal*
32:51–75.

Antoni, Klaus. 1991. "Momotarō (The Peach Boy) and the Spirit of Japan: Concerning the
Function of a Fairy Tale in Japanese Nationalism of the Early Shōwa Age." *Asian
Folklore Studies* 50 (1): 155–88.

Asahi shinbun degitaru. 2019. "Ninchishō fumei, saita 16,929-nin itai de mitsukatta hito,
508-nin sakunen." *Asahi shinbun degitaru*, June 21. https://www.asahi.com/articles
/DA3S14064203.html?iref=pc_ss_date.

Association for Frontotemporal Degeneration. n.d. "AFTD." Accessed December 27,
2016. http://www.theaftd.org/.

Aston, W. G., trans. 1956. *Nihongi: Chronicles of Japan from the Earliest Times to A.D. 697.*
London: George Allen & Unwin. First published 1896.

Baba Akiko. 1988. *Oni no kenkyū.* Tokyo: Chikuma Shobō. First published 1971.

Baba Kazuo. 1990. "'Tsuchigumo' no kenkyū (ge)." *Kikan hōgaku* 62 (3): 78–81.

Backus, Robert L., trans. 1985. *The Riverside Counselor's Stories: Vernacular Fiction of Late
Heian Japan.* Introduction and notes by Robert L. Backus. Stanford, CA: Stanford
University Press.

Bathgate, Michael. 2004. *The Fox's Craft in Japanese Religion and Folklore: Shapeshifters,
Transformations, and Duplicities.* New York: Routledge.

Bethe, Monica, and Karen Brazell. 1978. *Nō as Performance: An Analysis of the Kuse Scene of
Yamamba.* Ithaca, NY: Cornell University Press.

Bethe, Monica, and Karen Brazell, trans. 1998. "Yamamba." In *Traditional Japanese Theater:
An Anthology of Plays*, edited by Karen Brazell, 207–25. New York: Columbia
University Press.

Blacker, Carmen. 1975. *The Catalpa Bow: A Study of Shamanistic Practices in Japan.* London:
George Allen & Unwin.

Blumenthal, J. 1965. "*Macbeth* into *Throne of Blood.*" *Sight and Sound* 34 (Autumn): 191–95.

Breen, John. 2019. "Abdication, Succession and Japan's Imperial Future: An Emperor's
Dilemma." *Japan Focus: The Asia-Pacific Journal* 17 9 (3): 1–14.

Bussetsu Jizō bosatsu hosshin innen jūōkyō. 1998. Translated by Yabuki Keiki. In vol. 5 of
Kokuyaku issaikyō: Indo senjutsubu daishūbu, ed. Gotō Osamu, 299–312. Tokyo: Daitō
Shuppansha.

Chikamatsu Monzaemon. 1959. *Chikamatsu jōrurishū.* Vol. 50 of *Nihon koten bungaku taikei*,
edited by Shuzui Kenji and Ōkubo Tadakuni. Tokyo: Iwanami Shoten.

Como, Michael. 2009. *Weaving and Binding: Immigrant Gods and Female Immortals in Ancient
Japan.* Honolulu: University of Hawai'i Press.

DOI: 10.7330/9781646420551.c008

Copeland, Rebecca L. 2005. "Mythical Bad Girls: The Corpse, the Crone, and the Snake."
  In *Bad Girls of Japan*, edited by Laura Miller and Jan Bardsley, 15–31. New York:
  Palgrave.

Copeland, Rebecca L. 2016. "Demonizing the City: Saegusa Kazuko and the Passage to
  Hell." Paper presented at the 75th Annual Conference of the Association for Asian
  Studies, Seattle, Washington. April 1.

Cornell, Laurel L. 1991. "The Deaths of Old Women: Folklore and Differential Mortality
  in Nineteenth-Century Japan." In *Recreating Japanese Women, 1600–1945*, edited by
  Gail Lee Bernstein, 71–88. Berkeley: University of California Press.

Cornyetz, Nina. 1999. *Dangerous Women, Deadly Words: Phallic Fantasy and Modernity in Three
  Japanese Writers.* Stanford, CA: Stanford University Press.

Dai Nihonkoku Hokke genki. 1995. In *Ōjōden, Hokke genki*, annotated by Inoue Mitsusada
  and Ōsone Shōsuke, 43–219. Tokyo: Iwanami Shoten.

Dickerson, Bradford C. 2014. "Frontotemporal Dementia." In *Dementia: Comprehensive
  Principles and Practice*, edited by Bradford C. Dickerson and Alireza Atri, 176–97.
  Oxford: Oxford University Press.

Doi Tadao, Morita Takeshi, and Chōnan Minoru, eds. 1980. *Hōyaku Nippo jisho.* Tokyo:
  Iwanami Shoten.

Dower, John D. 1986. *War without Mercy: Race and Power in the Pacific War.* New York:
  Pantheon Books.

Drott, Edward R. 2016. *Buddhism and the Transformation of Old Age in Medieval Japan.*
  Honolulu: University of Hawaiʻi Press.

Eberhard, Wolfram. 1965. *Folktales of China.* Chicago: University of Chicago Press.

Ema Tsutomu. 1923. *Nihon yōkai henge-shi.* Kyoto: Chūgai Shuppan.

Eubanks, Charlotte. 2011. *Miracles of Book and Body: Buddhist Textual Culture and Medieval
  Japan.* Berkeley: University of California Press.

Fairchild, William P. 1962. "Shamanism in Japan." *Folklore Studies* 21:1–122.

Farrer, Claire R. 1975. *Women and Folklore.* Austin: University of Texas Press.

Farris, William Wayne. 2006. *Japan's Medieval Population: Famine, Fertility, and Warfare in a
  Transformative Age.* Honolulu: University of Hawaiʻi Press.

Figal, Gerald. 1999. *Civilization and Monsters: Spirits of Modernity in Meiji Japan.* Durham, NC:
  Duke University Press.

Fisher, Robert E. 1993. *Buddhist Art and Architecture.* New York: Thames & Hudson.

Foster, Michael Dylan. 2015. *The Book of Yōkai: Mysterious Creatures of Japanese Folklore.*
  Oakland: University of California Press.

Foster, Michael Dylan. 2016. "Introduction: The Challenge of the Folkloresque." In *The
  Folkloresque: Reframing Folklore in a Popular Culture World*, edited by Michael Dylan
  Foster and Jeffrey A. Tolbert, 3–33. Logan: Utah State University Press.

Franz, Marie-Louise von. 1974. *Shadow and Evil in Fairy Tales.* Zurich: Spring.

Frye, Northrop. 2006. *Anatomy of Criticism: Four Essays.* Vol. 22 of *Collected Works of
  Northrop Frye*, edited by Robert D. Denham. Toronto: University of Toronto Press.

Fujishiro Yumiko. 2015. "'Kuwazu nyōbō' to sesshoku no yamai." *Nihon bunka kenkyū*,
  edited by Komazawa Joshi Daigaku Nihon Bunka Kenkyūjo, 11 (3): 52–65.

Fujita Hiroko. 2008. *Folktales from the Japanese Countryside.* Edited by Fran Stallings with
  Harold Wright and Miki Sakurai. Westport, CT: Libraries Unlimited.

Fujiwara Akisuke. 1995. *A Collection of Verbal Blooms in Japanese Verse.* 2 vols. Translated by
  Donald M. Richardson. Winchester, VA: D. M. Richardson.

Fujiwara Tokihira, Sugawara Michizane, Ōkura Yoshiyuki, and Mimune Masahira,
  eds. 1941. *Nihon sandai jitsuroku.* Vol. 10 of *Rikkokushi*, edited by Saeki Ariyoshi.
  Tokyo: Asahi Shinbunsha.

Fukada Masatsugu. 1999. *Owari-shi: Niwa-gun, Haguri-gun hen.* Vol. 4 of *Owari-shi.* Edited by Uematsu Shigeoka, Nakao Yoshine, and Okada Kei. Nagoya: Bukkushoppu MyTown. First published 1892.

Fukazawa Shichirō. 1981. "Narayama bushikō." In *Narayama bushikō, Fuefukigawa,* 245–77. Tokyo: Shinchōsha. First published 1956.

Fukuda Akira. 1984. "Mukashibanashi no keitai." In vol. 4 of *Nihon mukashibanashi kenkyū shūsei,* edited by Fukuda Akira, 2–18. Tokyo: Meicho Shuppan.

Fukuda Mitsuko. 1995. "Ie to kon'in no kisō o saguru—dai nibu no hajime ni." In *Ranjukusuru onna to otoko: Kinsei,* edited by Fukuda Mitsuko, 255–75. Vol. 4 of *Onna to otoko no jikū: Nihon josei-shi saikō.* Tokyo: Fujiwara Shoten.

Fusō Daiton. 1976. *Fusō saigin.* Edited by Komazawa Daigaku Bungakubu Kokubungaku Kenkyūshitsu. Tokyo: Kyūko Shoin.

Glassman, Hank. 2008. "At the Crossroads of Birth and Death: The Blood Pool Hell and Postmortem Fetal Extraction." In *Death and the Afterlife in Japanese Buddhism,* edited by Jacqueline I. Stone and Mariko Namba Walter, 175–206. Honolulu: University of Hawai'i Press.

Gōda Hirofumi and Yokomichi Mario. 1972. "Yamauba." In vol. 30 of *Sekai daihyakka jiten,* edited by Shimonaka Kunihiko, 475. Tokyo: Heibonsha.

Goodwin, James. 1994. *Akira Kurosawa and Intertextual Cinema.* Baltimore, MD: Johns Hopkins University Press.

Gorai Shigeru. 1984. *Oni mukashi: Mukashibanashi no sekai.* Tokyo: Kadokawa Shoten.

Gorai Shigeru. 2000. "Yoshino Shugendō no seiritsu." In *Yoshino Kumano shinkō no kenkyū,* edited by Gorai Shigeru, 47–75. Tokyo: Meicho Shuppan.

Hagiwara Tatsuo. 1983. *Miko to bukkyō-shi: Kumano bikuni no shimei to tenkai.* Tokyo: Yoshikawa Kōbunkan.

Hagiwara Tatsuo. 1985. "Kumano bikuni to etoki." In vol. 3 of *Nihon no koten,* edited by Issatsu no Kōza Henshūbu, 57–67. Tokyo: Yūseidō Shuppan.

Hamaguchi Kazuo. 1959. "Nomi ni baketa Yamanba." In *Sado no minwa,* edited by Hamaguchi Kazuo, 175–82. Tokyo: Miraisha.

Hanawa Hokinoichi, ed. 1959. *Hōki no kuni Daisenji engi.* In *Zoku gunsho ruijū,* part 1 of vol. 28, 197–216. Tokyo: Zoku Gunsho Ruijū Kanseikai.

Hanley, Susan. 1974. "Fertility, Mortality, and Life Expectancy in Pre-modern Japan." *Population Studies* 28 (1): 127–42.

Hansen, Kelly. 2014. "Deviance and Decay in the Body of a Modern Mountain Witch: Ōba Minako's 'Yamanba no bishō.'" *Japanese Language and Literature* 48 (1): 151–72.

Hara Yukie. 1997. "Heianchō ni okeru 'obasute' no denshō to tenkai." *Nihon bungaku fūdo gakkai kiji* 22:18–28.

Hara Yukie. 2004. "'Obasute' kō—yōkyoku to kago no aida." *Geinō* 10:23–34.

Hashimoto Shūji. 2016. "Kenkō jumyō no shihyōka ni kansuru kenkyū: Kenkō Nihon 21 (dai 2 ji) nado no kenkō jumyō no kentō." *Kenkyō jumyō no pēji.* http://toukei.umin .jp/kenkoujyumyou/.

Hayami Yukiko. 2000. "Yamanba-gyaru ga dekiru made." *Queer Japan* 3:52–56.

Hayashi Reiko. 1982. *Henshū kōki to Kinsei.* In vol. 3 of *Nihon joseishi,* edited by Joseishi Sōgō Kenkyūkai, 325–34. Tokyo: Tokyo Daigaku Shuppankai.

Hayashi Shizuyo. 2012. "'Oni' no seibetsu ni tsuite no ichikōsatsu: Yomigatari ni tōjōsuru 'oni' no hanashi kara." *Kyōiku sōgō kenkyū sōsho* 5 (3): 69–88.

Hayashi Yasuhiro. 2002. "'Tōshōji nezumi monogatari' kaidai." In *Tamamo no mae, Tenjin goengi, Tōshōji nezumi monogatari,* vol. 5 of *Kyōto Daigaku zō Muromachi monogatari,* edited by Kyōto Daigaku Bungakubu Kokugogaku Kokubungaku Kenkyūshitsu, 399–417. Kyoto: Rinsen Shoten.

Hayek, Matthias, and Hayashi Makoto, eds. 2013. "Editors' Introduction: Onmyōdō in Japanese History." *Japanese Journal of Religious Studies* 40 (1): 1–18.

Hirakawa Akira. 1972. "Ubai." In vol. 3 of *Sekai daihyakka jiten*, edited by Shimonaka Kunihiko, 244. Tokyo: Heibonsha.

Hirasawa, Caroline. 2013. *Hell-Bent for Heaven in Tateyama Mandara: Painting and Religious Practice at a Japanese Mountain*. Boston: Brill.

Honma Saori. 2018. "Heisei kazoku: 'Sengyō-shufu mo kagayakeru' josei katsuyaku e no gimon 'kazoku o sasaeteiru no wa watashi.'" *Yahoo! Japan News*, January 5. https://news.yahoo.co.jp/story/856.

Hori Ichirō. 1968. *Folk Religion in Japan: Continuity and Change*. Chicago: University of Chicago Press.

Hori Takehiko. 2018. "Kyokuana kara kigyōka e, kosodate no kurō o bijinesu ni: Popinzu Nakamura Noriko kaichō." *Nikkei Style*, April 7. https://style.nikkei.com/article/DGXMZO28886590S8A400C1000000?channel=DF180320167075&n_cid=LMNST011.

Hudson, Mark J. 1999. *Ruins of Identity: Ethnogenesis in the Japanese Islands*. Honolulu: University of Hawai'i Press.

Hulvey, Yumiko S. 2000. "Myths and Monsters: The Female Body as the Site for Political Agendas." In *Body Politics and the Fictional Double*, edited by Debra Walker King, 71–88. Bloomington: Indiana University Press.

Ichiko Teiji, ed. 1958. *Otogizōshi*. Vol. 38 of *Nihon koten bungaku taikei*. Tokyo: Iwanami Shoten.

Ihara Saikaku. 1996. *Saikaku shokokubanashi*. In vol. 67 of *Shinpen Nihon koten bungaku zenshū*, edited by Munemasa Isoo, Teruoka Yasutaka, and Matsuda Osamu, 15–147. Tokyo: Shōgakukan.

Ikeda Hiroko. 1971. *A Type and Motif Index of Japanese Folk-Literature*. Helsinki: Suomalainen Tiedeakatemia.

Ima Ichiko. 1995–. *Hyakkiyakō shō*. 28 vols. Tokyo: Asahi Sonorama.

Inada Kōji, Ōshima Tatehiko, Kawabata Toyohiko, Fukuda Akira, and Miyara Yukihisa, eds. 1977. *Nihon mukashibanashi jiten*. Tokyo: Kōbundō.

Inoue Yasushi. 1974. "Obasute." In vol. 11 of *Inoue Yasushi shōsetsu zenshū*, 7–20. Tokyo: Shinchōsha. First published 1955.

Inoue Yasushi. 2000. "Obasute." In *The Counterfeiter and Other Stories*, translated by Leon Picon, 73–96. North Clarendon, VT: Tuttle.

Isao Toshihiko. 2001. *Kaisetsu to Yoshitoshi yōkai hyakkei*. Edited by Toshihiko Isao. Tokyo: Tosho Kankōkai.

Ishibashi Gaha. 1998. "Oni." In vol. 1 of *Shomin shūkyō minzokugaku sōsho*, edited by Shimura Kunihiro, 1–160. Tokyo: Bensei Shuppan. First published 1909.

Ishikawa Matsutarō, ed. 1977. *Onna daigaku-shū*. Tokyo: Heibonsha.

Ishinabe Hitomi. 2014. "Josei to ryūkōgo no 45 nen-shi: An'non zoku kara rikejo made." *Nikkei Style*, December 27. Accessed October 13, 2018. https://style.nikkei.com/article/DGXMZO81317950V21C14A2TY5000.

Isshiki Tadatomo. 2008. *Getsuan suiseiki*, vol. 2. Edited by Hattori Kōzō, Minobe Shigekatsu, and Yuge Shigeru. Tokyo: Miyai Shoten.

Itagaki Shunichi, ed. 1988. *Zen-Taiheiki*, vol. 1. Tokyo: Tosho Kankōkai.

Itō Hiromi. 1993. *Watashi wa Anjuhime-ko de aru: Itō Hiromi shishū*. Tokyo: Shichōsha.

Itō Hiromi. 2007. "I Am Anjuhimeko." Translated by Jeffrey Angles. *U.S.–Japan Women's Journal* 32:76–91.

Iwatagun Kyōikukai, ed. 1971. *Shizuoka-ken Iwatagun-shi*, vol. 2. Tokyo: Meicho Shuppan. First published 1921.

Izumi Asato. 1999. "Yamanba." *Asahi shinbun*, November 27. Evening edition.

Izumi Kyōka. 1996. *Japanese Gothic Tales*. Translated by Charles Shirō Inoue. Honolulu: University of Hawai'i Press.

Izumi Kyōka. 2002. *Izumi Kyōka shū*. Vol. 2 of *Shin Nihon koten bungaku taikei Meiji hen*, edited by Tōgō Katsumi and Yoshida Masashi. Tokyo: Iwanami Shoten.

Jacoby, Mario, Verena Kast, and Ingrid Diedel. 1992. *Witches, Ogres, and the Devil's Daughter: Encounters with Evil in Fairy Tales*. Translated by Michael H. Kohn. Boston: Shambhala.

Jones, Stanleigh H., Jr. 1963. "The Nō Plays: Obasute and Kanehira." *Monumenta Nipponica* 18 (1–4): 261–85.

Kamata Teruo. 2002. "Adachigahara no kijo densetsu: Yōkyoku 'Kurozuka' no shitezō o motomete." *Sōgō geijutsu to shite no nō* 8:18–32.

Kaminishi, Ikumi. 2006. *Explaining Pictures: Buddhist Propaganda and Etoki Storytelling in Japan*. Honolulu: University of Hawai'i Press.

Kaminishi, Ikumi. 2016. "Women Who Cross the Cordon." In *Women, Gender and Art in Asia, c. 1500–1900*, edited by Melia Belli Bose, 321–42. London: Routledge.

Kanzawa Toshiko. 1967. *Nashitori kyōdai*. Illustrations by Endō Teruyo. Tokyo: Popurasha.

Karatani Kōjin. 2014. *Yūdōmin: Yanagita Kunio to yamabito*. Tokyo: Bungei Shunjū.

Kawai Hayao. 1975. "Jiga, shūchi, kyōfu—taijin kyōfu-shō no sekai kara." *Shisō* 611 (May): 76–91.

Kawai Hayao. 1996. *The Japanese Psyche: Major Motifs in the Fairy Tales of Japan*. Thompson, CT: Spring.

Kawamura Kunimitsu. 1994. "Datsueba/Ubagami kō." In *Nihon shūkyō e no shikaku*, edited by Okada Shigekiyo, 367–85. Tokyo: Tōhō Shuppan.

Kawamura Kunimitsu. 1996. "Onna no jigoku to sukui." In vol. 3 of *Onna to otoko no jikū: Nihon joseishi saikō*, edited by Okano Haruko, 31–80. Tokyo: Fujiwara Shoten.

Keene, Donald. 1955. *Anthology of Japanese Literature: From the Earliest Era to the Mid-Nineteenth Century*. New York: Grove.

Keene, Donald. 1961. *The Old Woman, the Wife and the Archer: Three Modern Japanese Short Novels*. New York: Viking.

Keisei. 1993. *Kankyo no tomo*. In *Hōbutsu shū; Kankyo no tomo; Hirasan kojin reitaku*, vol. 40 of *Shin Nihon koten bungaku taikei*, edited by Hiroshi Koizumi, 355–453. Tokyo: Iwanami Shoten.

Kenshō. 1990. *Shūchūshō*. Vol. 5 of *Karon kagaku shūsei*, edited by Kawamura Teruo. Tokyo: Miyai Shoten.

Kinoshita Junji. 1958. *Nihon minwa sen*. Tokyo: Iwanami Shoten.

Kitayama Osamu. 1993. *Miruna no kinshi*. Vol. 1 of *Kitayama Osamu chosakushū, Nihongo rinshō no shinsō*. Tokyo: Iwasaki Gakujutsu Shuppansha.

Knecht, Peter. 2010. Foreword to *Japanese Demon Lore: Oni, from Ancient Times to the Present*, by Noriko Reider, xi–xxvi. Logan: Utah State University Press.

Knecht, Peter, Hasegawa Masao, Minobe Shigekatsu, and Tsujimoto Hiroshige. 2012. *"Hara no mushi" no kenkyū: Nihon no shinshinkan o saguru*. Nagoya: Nagoya Daigaku Shuppankai.

Knecht, Peter, Hasegawa Masao, and Tsujimoto Hiroshige. 2018. "'Oni' no motarasu yamai Chūgoku oyobi Nihon no koigaku ni okeru byōinkan to sono igi (jō): Diseases Caused by '鬼' (Chin. 'gui,', Jap. 'ki'/ 'oni')." *Academia: Humanities and Natural Science* 16 (June): 1–28. Offprint.

Kobayashi Fukuko. 2016. "Nichibei josei sakka ni okeru 'yamaubateki sōzōryoku' to ekorojī—Tsushima Yūko, Shirukō, Ozeki, Itō Hiromi nado o chūshin ni." *Ecocriticism Review* 9:1–14.

Kobayashi Fumihiko. 2015. *Japanese Animal-Wife Tales: Narrating Gender Reality in Japanese Folktale Tradition*. New York: Peter Lang.

Kodama Kōta. 2006. *Kinsei nōmin seikatsushi*. Tokyo: Yoshikawa Kōbunkan. First published 1957.

Kōen. 1897. *Fusō ryakki*. Edited by Keizai Zasshisha. Vol. 6 of *Kokushi taikei*. Tokyo: Keizai Zasshisha.

Kōjien. 1978. 5th ed. Edited by Shinmura Izuru. Tokyo: Iwanami Shoten.

Kokonoe Sakon. 1998. *Edo kinsei buyō-shi*. Vol. 32 of *Kinsei bungei kenkyū-sho: Dai ni ki geinō-hen*, edited by Kinsei Bungei Kenkyūsho Kankōkai. Tokyo: Kuresu Shuppan. First published 1919.

Komatsu Kazuhiko. 1979. "Yōkai." In *Kami kannen to minzoku*, vol. 3 of *Kōza Nihon no minzoku shūkyō*, edited by Gorai Shigeru, Sakurai Tokutarō, Ōshima Tatehiko, and Miyata Noboru, 330–55. Tokyo: Kōbundō.

Komatsu Kazuhiko. 1991. *Shinpen oni no tamatebako*. Tokyo: Fukutake Shoten.

Komatsu Kazuhiko. 1994. *Hyōrei shinkō ron*. Tokyo: Kōdansha.

Komatsu Kazuhiko. 1995. "Ijinron—'ijin' kara 'tasha' e." In *Tasha, Kankei, Komyunikēshon*, vol. 3 of *Iwanami kōza gendai shakaigaku*, edited by Inoue Shun, 175–200. Tokyo: Iwanami Shoten.

Komatsu Kazuhiko. 1999. "Supernatural Apparitions and Domestic Life in Japan." *Japan Foundation Newsletter* 27 (1): 3.

Komatsu Kazuhiko. 2000. "Kaisetsu: *Tengu to yamauba*." In *Kaii no minzokugaku*, vol. 5, edited by Komatsu Kazuhiko, 417–34. Tokyo: Kawade Shobō Shinsha.

Komatsu Kazuhiko. 2004. "Nō no naka no ikai (15) Adachigahara no kurozuka: Adachigahara." *Kanze* 71 (10): 46–51.

Komatsu Kazuhiko. 2016. *An Introduction to Yōkai Culture: Monsters, Ghosts, and Outsiders in Japanese History*. Translated by Hiroko Yoda and Matt Alt. Tokyo: Japan Publishing Industry Foundation for Culture.

Komatsu Kazuhiko and Naitō Masatoshi. 1990. *Oni ga tsukutta kuni Nihon*. Tokyo: Kōbunsha.

Komatsu Sakyō. 2015. *Uenakatta otoko; Ore no shitai o sagase; Nemuri to tabi to yume: Tanpen shōsetsushū*. Chiba: Jōsai Kokusai Daigaku Shuppankai.

Komatsu Shigemi and Akiyama Ken, eds. 1977. *Gaki sōshi; Jigoku sōshi; Yamai no sōshi; Kusōshi emaki*. Vol. 7 of *Nihon emaki taisei*. Tokyo: Chūō Kōronsha.

Komatsuzaki Susumu and Komatsuzaki Tatsuko. 1967. "Kodomo to minwa: *Yamanba no nishiki*." In *Yamanba no nishiki*, by Matsutani Miyoko. Tokyo: Popurasha.

Komatsuzaki Susumu, Komatsuzaki Tatsuko, and Sakamoto Hideo. 1967. "Kodomo to minwa: *Nashitori kyōdai*." In *Nashitori kyōdai*, by Kanzawa Toshiko. Tokyo: Popurasha.

Komine Kazuaki. 2003. *"Yaba taishi" no nazo: Rekishi jojutsu to shite no miraiki*. Tokyo: Iwanami Shoten.

Kondō Yoshihiro and Miyachi Takakuni, eds. 1971. *Daisenji engimaki*. In *Chūsei shinbutsu setsuwa zoku zoku*, 129–229. Tokyo: Koten Bunko.

Konno Ensuke. 1981. *Nihon kaidanshū: Yōkai hen*. Tokyo: Shakai Shisōsha.

Kōsei Kagaku Shingikai Chiiki Hoken Kenkō Zōshin Eiyōbukai and Jiki Kokumin Kenkōzukuri Undō Puran Sakusei Senmon Iinkai. 2012. *Kenkō Nihon 21 (dai 2 ji) no suishin ni kansuru sankō shiryō*. Tokyo: Kōsei Rōdōshō.

Kōsei Rōdōshō. 2018a. "Dai jūikkai kenkō Nihon 21 (dai niji) suishin senmon iinkai shiryō: Shirō 1–2." *Kenkō jumyō no enshin・kenkōkakusa no shukushō*, 6. March 9. https://www.mhlw.go.jp/file/05-Shingikai-10601000-Daijinkanboukouseikagakuka -Kouseikagakuka/0000166297_5.pdf.

Kōsei Rōdōshō. 2018b. "Kekka no gaiyō." *Heisei 28 nen jinkō dōtai tōkei geppō nenkei (gaisū) no gaikyō*, 6. June 1. https://www.mhlw.go.jp/toukei/saikin/hw/jinkou/geppo /nengai16/index.html.

Kōsei Rōdōshō. 2018c. "Omona nenrei no heikin yomei." *Heisei 29 nen kan'eki seimeihyō no gaikyō*, 2. July 20. https://www.mhlw.go.jp/toukei/saikin/hw/life/life17/dl/life 17-15.pdf.

Kosugi Kazuo. 1986. *Chūgoku bijutsushi: Nihon bijutsu no genryū*. Tokyo: Nan'undō.

Koyama Naotsugu, ed. 1996. *Niigata-ken densetsu shūsei: Kaetsu*. Tokyo: Kōbunsha.

Kubota Osamu. 1975. "Ryōbu shintō seiritsu no ichi kōsatsu." *Geirin* 26 (1): 2–20.

Kumasegawa Kyōko. 1989. "Oni no imi to sono hensen." *Kikan jinruigaku* 20 (4): 182–219.

Kuraishi Tadahiko. 2002. "Toshi minzokugaku: Toshi seikatsu kara minkan denshō o miidasu kokoromi." *Risen* 71:54–65.

Kurosawa Akira, dir. 2003. *Throne of Blood*. DVD. Criterion Collection.

Kyōgoku Natsuhiko and Tada Katsumi, eds. 2008. *Yōkai gahon · Kyōka hyakumonogatari*. Tokyo: Kokusho Kankōkai.

Leavy, Barbara Fass. 1994. *In Search of the Swan Maiden: A Narrative on Folklore and Gender*. New York: New York University Press.

Li, Michelle Osterfeld. 2009. *Ambiguous Bodies: Reading the Grotesque in Japanese Setsuwa Tales*. Stanford, CA: Stanford University Press.

Li, Michelle Osterfeld. 2012. "Human of the Heart: Pitiful Oni in Medieval Japan." In *Ashgate Research Companion to Monsters and the Monstrous*, edited by Asa Simon Mittman and Peter Dendle, 173–96. Surrey, UK: Ashgate.

Makita Shigeru. 1972. "Toshi no ichi." In vol. 22 of *Sekai daihyakka jiten*, edited by Shimonaka Kunihiko, 443. Tokyo: Heibonsha.

Manvell, Roger. 1971. *Shakespeare and the Film*. New York: Praeger.

Matsumoto Kōzō. 2007. *Minkan setsuwa "denshō" no kenkyū*. Tokyo: Miyai Shoten.

Matsumoto Ryūshin. 1963. "Otogizōshi no honbun ni tsuite." *Shidō bunko ronshū* 2 (March): 171–242.

Matsuoka Shinpei. 1998. "Adachigahara no kijo." *Kokubungaku kaishaku to kyōzai no kenkyū* 43 (5): 83–89.

Matsutani Miyoko. 1967. *Yamanba no nishiki*. Tokyo: Popurasha.

Matsutani Miyoko. 1969. *The Witch's Magic Cloth*. New York: Parents' Magazine.

Matsutani Miyoko. 1979. "Saiwa no hōhō." In vol. 12 of *Nihon mukashibanashi taisei*, edited by Seki Keigo, 247–61. Tokyo: Kadokawa Shoten.

Mayer, Fanny Hagin, ed. and trans. 1986. *The Yanagita Kunio Guide to Japanese Folk Tales*. Bloomington: University of Indiana Press.

Mayo Clinic. n.d. "Frontotemporal Dementia." Accessed September 17, 2018. https://www.mayoclinic.org/diseases-conditions/frontotemporal-dementia/symptoms-causes/syc-20354737.

McCullough, Helen Craig, trans. 1968. *Tales of Ise*. Stanford, CA: Stanford University Press.

McCullough, Helen Craig. 1990. *Classical Japanese Prose: An Anthology*. Stanford, CA: Stanford University Press.

McCurry, Justin. 2016. "Japan's Dementia Crisis Hits Record Levels as Thousands Go Missing." *Guardian*, June 16. https://www.theguardian.com/world/2016/jun/16/record-12208-people-with-dementia-reported-missing-in-japan.

McDonald, Keiko I. 1994. *Japanese Classical Theater in Films*. Cranbury, NJ: Associated University Presses.

Mihara Yukihisa. 1977. "Ubasute-yama." In *Nihon mukashibanashi jiten*, edited by Inada Kōji, Ōshima Tatehiko, Kawabata Toyohiko, Fukuda Akira, and Miyara Yukihisa, 110–11. Tokyo: Kōbundō.

Miller, Laura. 2004. "Those Naughty Teenage Girls: Japanese Kogals, Slang, and Media Assessments." *Journal of Linguistic Anthropology* 14 (2): 225–47.

"Mimitabu-sogi yamanba-gyaru no gyōjō: Ibaragi, 17 sai futarigumi rinchi no zenbō." 2000. *Shūkan asahi* (June): 22.

Minamiashigara City. 2014. "Kintarō densetsu." https://www.city.minamiashigara.kanagawa
   .jp/kankou/kintaro/kintarodensetu.html.

Mitani Eiichi. 1952. *Monogatari bungakushiron.* Tokyo: Yūseidō Shuppan.

Miyake Hitoshi. 1978. *Shugendō: Yamabushi no rekishi to shisō.* Tokyo: Hanbai Kyōikusha
   Shuppan Sābisu.

Miyake Hitoshi. 2001. *Shugendō: Essays on the Structure of Japanese Folk Religion.* Ann Arbor:
   Center for Japanese Studies, University of Michigan.

Miyata Noboru. 1997. "Nihonjin no rōjinkan: Ubasute, happyaku bikuni densetsu." *Rekishi
   hyōron* 565 (June): 17–26.

Miyata Noboru. 2000. *Hime no minzokugaku.* Tokyo: Chikuma Shobō. First published 1987.

Miyazaki Kazue, ed. 1969. *Kunisaki hantō no mukashibanashi.* Tokyo: Miyai Shoten.

Mizuki Shigeru. 2002. *Yōkai gadan.* Tokyo: Iwanami Shoten.

Mizuta Noriko. 2002. "Yamauba no yume: Joron to shite." In *Yamaubatachi no monogatari:
   Josei no genkei to katarinaoshi,* edited by Mizuta Noriko and Kitada Sachie, 7–37.
   Tokyo: Gakugei Shorin.

Mizuta Noriko and Ōba Minako. 1995. *Taidan "yamauba" no iru fūkei.* Tokyo: Tabata
   Shoten.

MJMT (Muromachi jidai monogatari taisei). 1987–1988. 13 vols., plus 2 supp. vols. Edited
   by Yokoyama Shigeru and Matsumoto Ryūshin; supp. vols. edited by Matsumoto
   Ryūshin. Tokyo: Kadokawa Shoten.

Moeman, David Leo. 2000. *Localizing Paradise: Kumano Pilgrimage in Medieval Japan.* Ann
   Arbor, MI: ProQuest.

Moes, Robert. 1973. *Rosetsu.* Denver, CO: Denver Museum of Art.

Morson, Gary Saul, and Caryl Emerson. 1990. *Mikhail Bakhtin: Creation of a Prosaics.*
   Stanford, CA: Stanford University Press.

Motai Kyōko. 1972. "Kishimojin." In vol. 7 of *Sekai daihyakka jiten,* edited by Shimonaka
   Kunihiko, 127. Tokyo: Heibonsha.

Murakami Kenji. 2000. *Yōkai jiten.* Tokyo: Mainichi Shinbunsha.

Murasaki Shikibu. 2001. *The Tale of Genji.* Translated by Royall Tyler. New York: Penguin
   Books.

Murayama Shūichi. 1970. *Yamabushi no rekishi.* Tokyo: Hanawa Shobō.

Muroki Yatarō, ed. 1966. *Kinpira tanjō-ki.* In vol. 1 of *Kinpira jōruri shōhon shū,* 192–211.
   Tokyo: Kadokawa Shoten.

Muroki Yatarō, ed. 1969. *Kinpira nyūdō yamameguri.* In vol. 3 of *Kinpira jōruri shōhon shū,*
   144–62. Tokyo: Kadokawa Shoten.

Mushikurayama no Yamanba Henshū Iinkai, ed. 2007. *Mushikurayama no yamanba.* Nagano:
   Saijō Insatsujo.

Nagoya Sangoku Denki Kenkyūkai, ed. 1983. *Sangoku denki,* vol. 2. Tokyo: Koten Bunko.

Naikaku-fu. 2017. "Kōreisha no kenkō to fukushi." In *Heisei 29 nenban kōrei shakai hakusho
   (gaiyōban) (PDF ban).* http://www8.cao.go.jp/kourei/whitepaper/w-2017/gaiyou
   /29pdf_indexg.html.

Nakada Kaoru. 1956. *Tokugawa jidai no bungaku ni mietaru shihō.* Tokyo: Sōbunsha.

Nakamura, Kyoko Motomochi. 1997. *Miraculous Stories from the Japanese Buddhist Tradition:
   The "Nihon ryōiki" of the Monk Kyōkai.* Surrey, UK: Curzon. First published 1973.

Namekawa Michio. 1981. *Momotarō-zō no hen'yō.* Tokyo: Tokyo Shoseki.

Napier, Susan. 1996. *The Fantastic in Modern Japanese Literature: The Subversion of Modernity.*
   New York: Routledge.

National Eating Disorders Association. 2017. "Bulimia: Overview and Statistics." https://
   www.nationaleatingdisorders.org/bulimia-nervosa.

NDT (Nihon densetsu taikei). 1982–1990. 17 vols. Edited by Araki Hiroyuki, Nomura Jun'ichi,
   Fukuda Akira, Miyata Noboru, and Watanabe Shōgo. Tokyo: Mizūmi Shobō.

Nihon kokugo daijiten. 2004. Edited by Nihon Kokugo Daijiten Dainihan Henshū Iinkai. 2nd ed. Tokyo: Shōgakukan.

Niigata Prefectural Government. n.d. "Niigata no fūdo no naka de hagukumareta yōkaitachi." *Niigata bunka monogatari.* Accessed July 5, 2019. https://n-story.jp/topic/41/page1.php.

Nishizawa Shigejirō. 1973. *Obasuteyama: Kojitsu to bungaku.* Nagano: Shinanoji.

NKBT (Nihon koten bungaku taikei). 1957–1967. 102 vols. Tokyo: Iwanami Shoten.

NMT (Nihon mukashibanashi taisei). 1978–1980. 12 vols. Edited by Seki Keigo. Tokyo: Kadokawa Shoten.

The-Noh.com. n.d. "Kurozuka." Accessed May 23, 2016. http://www.the-noh.com/jp/plays/data/program_035.html.

Nose Asaji. 1938. *Nōgaku genryū kō.* Tokyo: Iwanami Shoten.

Ōba Minako. 1991. "The Smile of a Mountain Witch." Translated by Noriko Mizuta Lippit. In *Japanese Women Writers: Twentieth Century Short Fiction,* edited by Noriko Mizuta Lippit and Kyoko Iriye Selden, 194–206. New York: M. E. Sharpe.

Ōba Minako. 2009. "Yamanba no bishō." In vol. 5 of *Ōba Minako zenshū,* 461–77. Tokyo: Nihon Keizai Shinbun Shuppansha.

Ōba Minako. 2010a. "Majo ni atta yamanba." In vol. 14 of *Ōba Minako zenshū,* 434–39. Tokyo: Nihon Keizai Shinbun Shuppansha.

Ōba Minako. 2010b. "Zoku onna no danseiron." In vol. 18 of *Ōba Minako zenshū,* 305–45. Tokyo: Nihon Keizai Shinbun Shuppansha.

Oda Sachiko. 1986. "Nō no kata, nō no shōzoku—kijo idetachi no hensen." *Kokubungaku kaishaku to kyōzai no kenkyū* 31 (10): 76–82.

Oda Shoko and Isabel Reynolds. 2018. "What Is Womenomics, and Is It Working for Japan?" *Bloomberg,* September 20. https://www.bloomberg.com/news/articles/2018-09-19/what-is-womenomics-and-is-it-working-for-japan-quicktake.

Ogita Ansei. 1989. *Tonoigusa.* In vol. 1 of *Edo kaidanshū,* edited by Takada Mamoru, 13–176. Tokyo: Iwanami Shoten.

Ogurisu Kenji. 2014. *Jigokuezu Kumano kanshin jikkai mandara etoki daihon.* Kyoto: Hōjōdō Shuppan.

Okada Keisuke. 1976. "Otogizōshi no bukkyō shisō to minkan denshō—'Hachi kazuki,' 'Hanayo no hime,' 'Ubakawa' ni tsuite." *Kokugo kokubungaku ronkyū* 8:145–64.

Okada Keisuke. 1977. "'Hanayo no hime' to minkan denshō." *Nihon bungaku* 26 (2): 63–71.

Okamoto Makiko. 2012. *Ragyō to chakusō no ningyō-shi.* Kyoto: Tankōsha.

Orikuchi Shinobu. 1995. *Orikuchi Shinobu zenshū,* vol. 2. Edited by Orikuchi Shinobu Zenshū Kankōkai. Tokyo: Chūō Kōronsha.

Orikuchi Shinobu. 2000. "Usokae shinji to yamauba." In *Tengu to yamauba,* vol. 5 of *Kaii no minzokugaku,* edited by Komatsu Kazuhiko, 295–304. Tokyo: Kawade Shobō. First published 1929.

Ōshima Tatehiko. 1979. "Ubasute-yama no mukashibanashi to densetsu." In *Ronsan setsuwa to setsuwa bungaku,* edited by Mitani Eiichi, Kunisaki Fumimaro, and Kubota Jun, 479–522. Tokyo: Kazama Shoin.

Ōshima Tatehiko. 2001a. "Obasute no denshō." *Nihon bungaku bunka* 1:2–18.

Ōshima Tatehiko. 2001b. "Ubagami." In *Nihon no shinbutsu no jiten,* edited by Ōshima Tatehiko, Sonoda Minoru, Tamamuro Fumio, and Yamamoto Takashi, 179. Tokyo: Taishūkan.

Ōwa Iwao. 1996. *Majo wa naze hito o kūka.* Tokyo: Daiwa Shobō.

Ozawa Toshio. 1979. *Sekai no minwa: Hito to dōbutsu to no kon'in-tan.* Tokyo: Chūō Kōronsha.

Philippi, Donald D., trans. 1969. *Kojiki.* Princeton, NJ: Princeton University Press.

Rambelli, Fabio. 2007. *Buddhist Materiality: A Cultural History of Objects in Japanese Buddhism.* Stanford, CA: Stanford University Press.

Reider, Noriko T. 2005. "*Spirited Away*: Film of the Fantastic and Evolving Japanese Folk Symbols." *Film Criticism* 29 (3): 4–27.

Reider, Noriko T. 2010. *Japanese Demon Lore: Oni, from Ancient Times to the Present*. Logan: Utah State University Press.

Reider, Noriko T. 2016. *Seven Demon Stories from Medieval Japan*. Logan: Utah State University Press.

Reider, Noriko T. 2019. "Yamauba(zō) ni tsuite no ichikōsatsu." Paper delivered at Kokusai Nihon Bunka Kenkyū Sentā Kikan Kyotengata Kikan Kenkyū Purojekuto: Taishū Bunka no Tsūjiteki, Kokusaiteki Kenkyū ni yoru Atarashii Nihonzō no Sōshutsu. Kyoto: International Research Center for Japanese Studies, July 13.

Rich, Adrienne. 1972. "When We Dead Awaken: Writing as Re-Vision." *College English* 34:18–30.

Rich, Motoko. 2019. "As a New Emperor Is Enthroned in Japan, His Wife Won't Be Allowed to Watch." *New York Times*, April 29. https://www.nytimes.com/2019/04/29/world/asia/japan-emperor-women.html.

Robinson, Nina. 2009. "Japan's Fashion Rebellion Goes West." *BBC World Service*, July 3. http://news.bbc.co.uk/2/hi/asia-pacific/8132726.stm.

Robinson, Richard H., and Willard L. Johnson. 1997. *The Buddhist Religion*. 4th ed. Belmont, CA: Wadsworth.

Rodd, Laurel Rasplica, trans. 1984. *Kokinshū: A Collection of Poems Ancient and Modern*. Princeton, NJ: Princeton University Press.

Ruch, Barbara. 1991. *Mō hitotsu no chūseizō: Bikuni, otogizōshi, raisei*. Kyoto: Shibunkaku.

Ruch, Barbara. 2002. "Woman to Woman: Kumano Bikuni Proselytizers in Medieval and Early Modern Japan." In *Engendering Faith: Women and Buddhism in Premodern Japan*, edited by Barbara Ruch, 537–80. Ann Arbor: University of Michigan Press.

Saitō Shunsuke. 2010. "Nihon bunka to yamamba—minzoku shakai ni okeru yōkai no yakuwari." *Teikyō Nihon bunka ronshū* 17 (10): 273–90.

Saka Chihiko. 2017. "Bridging the Realms of Underworld and Pure Land: An Examination of Datsueba's Roles in the Zenkōji Pilgrimage Mandala." *Japanese Journal of Religious Studies* 44 (2): 191–223.

Sasaki Kizen. 1964. *Kikimimi no sōshi*. Tokyo: Chikuma Shobō.

Sasaki Raita. 2008. "Hochū." In vol. 2 of *Getsuan suiseiki*, by Isshiki Tadatomo, edited by Hattori Kōzō, Minobe Shigekatsu, and Yuge Shigeru, 203–10. Tokyo: Miyai Shoten.

Satake Akihiro. 1977. *Shuten Dōji ibun*. Tokyo: Heibonsha.

Seki Keigo. 1957. *Nihon no mukashibanashi*, vol. 3. Tokyo: Iwanami Shoten.

Seki Keigo. 1962. *Folk Legends of Japan*. Rutland, VT: Tuttle.

Seki Keigo. 1963. *Folktales of Japan*. Chicago: University of Chicago Press.

Seki Keigo. 1966. "Types of Japanese Folktales." *Asian Folklore Studies* 25 (2): 1–220.

Setouchi Jakuchō. 2009. "Yamanba." *Shinchō* 106 (1): 220–31.

Shakespeare, William. 1978. "Macbeth." In *The Annotated Shakespeare III: The Tragedies and Romances*, edited by A. L. Rowse, 412–65. New York: Clarkson N. Potter.

Shakespeare, William. 2004. *Makubesu*. Translated by Tsubouchi Shōyō. Vol. 24 of *Sekai meisaku hon'yaku zenshū*. Tokyo: Shun'yōdō Shoten. First published 1932.

Shibuya Keizai Shinbun Henshūbu. 2002. "Kenshō! 'Yamanba' no tōjō to suitai: Kokugakuin Daigaku kōza 'Shibuyagaku' rendō kikaku." *Shibuya Keizai shinbun*, November 15. http://www.shibukei.com/special/118/.

Shikama Hiroji. 2013. *Datsueba: Yamagata no ubagami*. Tsuruoka: Tōhoku Shuppan Kikaku.

Shimazaki Chifumi and Stephen Comee, trans. 2012. *Supernatural Beings: From Japanese Noh Plays of the Fifth Group*. Ithaca, NY: East Asia Program, Cornell University.

Shimazaki Satoko. 2016. *Edo Kabuki in Transition: From the Worlds of the Samurai to the Vengeful Female Ghost*. New York: Columbia University Press.

Shimizu, Christine. 1990. "Kintaro to Yamauba." In vol. 7 of *Ukiyo-e Masterpieces in European Collections*, edited by Narazaki Muneshige and Musée Guiment, 231. Tokyo: Kodansha.

Shinjuku-ku Kyōiku Iinkai. 1997. "Shōjuin no *Datsueba zō*." Tokyo: Shinjuku-ku Kyōiku Iinkai.

Shiono Nanami. 1992. *Rōmajin no monogatari I: Rōma wa ichinichi ni shite narazu*. Tokyo: Shinchōsha.

Shirane, Haruo. 2012. *Japan and the Culture of the Four Seasons: Nature, Literature, and the Arts*. New York: Columbia University Press.

Shizuoka-ken Joshi Shihan Gakkō Kyōdo Kenkyūkai, ed. 1934. *Shizuoka-ken densetsu mukashibanashishū*. Shizuoka: Shizuoka Yashimaya Shoten.

Shūeisha kokugojiten. 1993. Edited by Morioka Kenji, Tokugawa Munemasa, Kawabata Yoshiaki, Nakamura Akira, and Hoshino Kōichi. Tokyo: Shūeisha.

SNKBT (Shin Nihon koten bungaku taikei). 1989–2005. 100 vols., plus 5 separate volumes and index. Tokyo: Iwanami Shoten.

SNKBZ (Shinpen Nihon koten bungaku zenshū). 1994–2002. 88 vols. Tokyo: Shōgakukan.

Snowden, Julie S., David Neary, and David M. A. Mann. 2002. "Frontotemporal Dementia."*British Journal of Psychiatry* 180:140–43.

Spiegel, David R. 2012. "Protection for Abused Seniors: Cause or Afterthought?" *Family Law Quarterly* 46 (1): 169–75.

Sudō Maki. 2002. " 'Tsuchigumo sōshi' seiritsu no haikei o megutte." *Setsuwa bungaku kenkyū* 37 (June): 62–80.

Sugawara no Takasue no musume. 1971. *As I Crossed a Bridge of Dreams: Recollections of a Woman in Eleventh-Century Japan*. Translated by Ivan Morris. New York: Dial.

Sugimoto Yoshio. 2014. *An Introduction to Japanese Society*. 4th ed. Port Melbourne, AU: Cambridge University Press.

Suzuki, Daisetz T. 1959. *Zen and Japanese Culture*. Princeton, NJ: Princeton University Press.

Tahara, Mildred M., trans. 1980. *Tales of Yamato: A Tenth-Century Poem-Tale*. Honolulu: University of Hawai'i Press.

Takagi Tadashi. 2006. "Kekkon, rikon." In *Edo e no shinshiten*, edited by Takahashi Shūji and Tanaka Yūko, 97–115. Tokyo: Shin Shokan.

Takahashi Mariko. 1975. "Otogizōshi 'Hanayo no hime' to minkan shinkō—ubakawa, hachi, yamauba o chūshin ni." *Kokubun* 42 (March): 22–32.

Takahashi Masaaki. 1992. *Shuten Dōji no tanjō: Mō hitotsu no Nihon bunka*. Tokyo: Chūō Kōronsha.

Takahashi Yoshito. 2011. *Majo to yōroppa*. Tokyo: Iwanami Shoten. First published 1995.

Takashima Yōko. 2014. "Minkan setsuwa, denshō ni okeru yamanba, yōsei, majo." *Jinbun kenkyū* 65:115–35.

Takehara Shunsensai. 1997. *Ehon hyakumonogatari: Tōsanjin yawa*. Edited by Tada Katsumi. Tokyo: Kokusho Kankōkai.

Takei Masahiro. 1983. "Enshū Akihayama honji Shōkanzeon Sanjakubō Daigongen ryaku engi." In *Shugendō shiryōshū higashi Nihon hen*, vol. 17 of *Sangaku shūkyōshi kenkyū sōsho*, edited by Gorai Shigeru, 423–25, 698–99. Tokyo: Meicho Shuppan.

Takemoto Mikio. 2000. *Adachigahara Kurozuka: Taiyaku de tanoshimu*. Tokyo: Hinoki Shoten.

Taki Kiyoshi. 1986. *Yamanba monogatari to sono shiteki haikei*. Nagoya: Bukku Shoppu Mai Taun.

Tamura Sadao. 2014. *Akiha shinkō no shinkenkyū*. Tokyo: Iwata Shoin.

Tanaka Takako. 1992. *Akujo-ron*. Tokyo: Kinokuniya Shoten.

Tanigawa Ken'ichi. 2005. *Kajiya no haha*. Tokyo: Kawade Shobō Shinsha.

Taniguchi Kōkyō. 1919. *Ikō gashū*. Edited by Taniguchi Ikō Iboku Tenrankai. Tokyo: Geijutsudō.

Tenkai. 1998. *Nikkō Tenkaizō: Jikidan innenshū, honkoku to sakuin.* Edited by Hirota Tetsumichi, Abe Yasuo, Tanaka Takako, Kobayashi Naoki, and Chikamoto Kensuke. Osaka: Izumi Shoin.

Thomas, Roger K. 2012. "A Land Blessed by Word Spirit: Kamochi Masazumi and Early Modern Constructs of *Kotodama.*" *Early Modern Japan: An Interdisciplinary Journal* 29:6–32.

Toida Michizō. 1964. *Nō: Kami to kojiki no geijutsu.* Tokyo: Mainichi Shinbunsha.

Tokieda Tsutomu. 1986. "Chūsei Tōgoku ni okeru *Ketsubonkyō* shinkō no yōsō: Kusatsu Shiraneyama o chūshin to shite." *Shinano* 36 (8): 586–603.

Tokuda Kazuo. 2001. "Echigo no Shuten Dōji." *Denshōbungaku kenkyū* 51:84–90.

Tokuda Kazuo. 2016a. "Nō to setsuwa • denshō *Yamanba* o megutte: Zeami jidai no yamauba denshō (1)." *Kanze* 83 (6): 36–41.

Tokuda Kazuo. 2016b. "Nō to setsuwa • denshō *Yamanba* o megutte: Zeami jidai no yamauba denshō (2)." *Kanze* 83 (8): 42–48.

Tokuda Kazuo. 2016c. "Nō to setsuwa • denshō *Yamanba* o megutte: Zeami jidai no yamauba denshō (3)." *Kanze* 83 (10): 42–47.

Tokudome Shinkan, Hashimoto Shuji, and Igata Akihiro. 2016. "Life Expectancy and Healthy Life Expectancy of Japan: The Fastest Graying Society in the World." *BMC Research Notes*, October 28. https://www.ncbi.nlm.nih.gov/pmc/articles/PMC 5084424/.

Tokunaga Seiko. 2015. "Shugendō no seiritsu." In *Shugendōshi nyūmon*, edited by Okieda Susumu, Hasegawa Kenji, and Hayashi Makoto, 77–92. Tokyo: Iwata Shoin.

Tokyo Daigaku Shiryō Hensanjo, ed. 1961. *Dainihon kokiroku: Gaun nikkenroku batsuyū.* Tokyo: Iwanami Shoten.

Topelius, Zacharias. 1927. "Star Eye." In *Canute Whistlewinks and Other Stories*, translated by William C. Foss, edited by Frances Jenkins Olcott, and illustrations by Frank McIntosh, 144–63. New York: Longmans, Green.

Torii Fumiko. 1993. *Dentō to geinō: Kojōruri sekai no tenkai.* Tokyo: Musashino Shoin.

Torii Fumiko. 2002. *Kintarō no tanjō.* Tokyo: Bensei Shuppan.

Toriyama Sekien. 1992. "Konjaku gazu zoku hyakki." In *Toriyama Sekien gazu hyakki yagyō*, edited by Inada Atsunobu, 97–173. Tokyo: Kokusho Kankōkai.

Tsuda Sōkichi. 1963. *Nihon koten no kenkyū.* Vol. 1 of *Tsuda Sōkichi zenshū.* Tokyo: Iwanami Shoten.

Tsuruya Nanboku. 1975. "Hakone Ashigarayama no ba." *Modoribashi sena ni go-hiiki.* Kokuritsu gekijō kabuki kōen jōen daihon, edited by Toshikura Kōichi, 59–75. Tokyo: Kokuritsu Gekijō.

Tyler, Royall. 1987. *Japanese Tales.* New York: Pantheon Books.

Tyler, Royall. 1992. *Japanese Nō Dramas.* London: Penguin Books.

Uchiyama Matatsu. 1969. *Tōtōmi no kuni fudokiden.* Translated by Katō Sugane and Minagawa Gōroku. Tokyo: Rekishi Toshosha.

Ueno Kenji. 1984. "'Tsuchigumo zōshi' ni tsuite." In *Tsuchigumo zōshi; Tengu zōshi; Ōeyama ekotoba*, vol. 19 of *Zoku Nihon emaki taisei*, edited by Komatsu Shigemi et al., 106–13. Tokyo: Chūō Kōronsha.

Urabe Kanekata. 1965. *Shaku Nihongi.* Vol. 8 of *Shintei zōho kokushi taikei*, edited by Kuroita Katsumi. Tokyo: Yoshikawa Kōbunkan.

Ury Marian. 1979. *Tales of Times Now Past: Sixty-Two Stories from a Medieval Japanese Collection.* Berkeley: University of California Press.

Viswanathan, Meera. 1996. "In Pursuit of the Yamamba: The Question of Female Resistance." In *The Woman's Hand: Gender and Theory in Japanese Women's Writing*, edited by Paul G. Schalow and Janet A. Walker, 239–61. Stanford, CA: Stanford University Press.

Wakabayashi Haruko. 2012. *The Seven Tengu Scrolls: Evil and the Rhetoric of Legitimacy in Medieval Japanese Buddhism*. Honolulu: University of Hawai'i Press.

Wakamori Tarō. 1958. "Rekishigaku to no kankei kara." In vol. 2 of *Nihon minzokugaku taikei*, edited by Ōmachi Tokuzō, Oka Masao, Sakurada Katsunori, Seki Keigo, and Mogami Takayoshi, 213–32. Tokyo: Heibonsha.

Wakita Haruko. 2002. "Yamauba no mai: Nōgaku 'Yamanba' ni miru onnatachi no geinō no dentō." In *Yamauba tachi no monogatari: Josei no genkei to katarinaoshi*, edited by Mizuta Noriko and Kitada Sachie, 41–54. Tokyo: Gakugei Shorin.

Walthall, Anne. 1998. *The Weak Body of a Useless Woman: Matsuo Taseko and the Meiji Restoration*. Chicago: University of Chicago Press.

Watanabe Kazuko. 2012. *Okareta basho de sakinasai*. Tokyo: Gentōsha.

Web Shūkan Nagano. 2017. "Seichō mimamoru yamauba 'kosodate no kami' Mushikura jinja." http://weekly-nagano.main.jp/2010/06/02-6.html.

Wilson, Michiko N. 2013. "Ōba Minako the Raconteur: Refashioning a Yamauba Tale." *Marvels & Tales* 27 (2): 218–33.

World Economic Forum. 2019. *The Global Gender Gap Report 2020*. Geneva: World Economic Forum. http://www3.weforum.org/docs/WEF_GGGR_2020.pdf.

World Health Organization. 2017. "Healthy Status Statistics: Mortality." http://www.who.int/healthinfo/statistics/indhale/en/.

Yahikoson Kyōiku Iinkai, ed. 2009. "Myōtara Ten'nyo to Baba-sugi." In *Yahikoson-shi jiten*, 384. Niigata-ken: Yahikoson Kyōiku Iinkai.

Yamada Shōji. 2002. *Nihon bunka no mohō to sōzō: Orijinaritī to wa nani ka*. Tokyo: Kadokawa Shoten.

Yamagami Izumo. 2000. "Reizan no kirō to yōrō." In *Tengu to yamauba*, vol. 5 of *Kaii no minzokugaku*, edited by Komatsu Kazuhiko, 367–87. Tokyo: Kawade Shobō. First published 1990.

Yamaguchi Motoko. 2009. *Yamauba, yama o oriru: Gendai ni sumau mukashibanashi*. Tokyo: Shin'yōsha.

Yamamoto Naoyuki, ed. 2003. *Akiha jinja*. Vol. 48 of *Shūkan jinja kikō*, edited by Kurakami Minoru. Tokyo: Gakushū Kenkyūsha.

Yamaoka Genrin. 1993. *Kokon hyakumonogatari hyōban*. In *Zoku hyakumonogatari kaidan shūsei*, vol. 27 of *Sōsho Edo bunko*, edited by Tachikawa Kiyoshi, 5–77. Tokyo: Tosho Kankōkai.

Yamashita Hisao. 1975. *Zenkoku mukashibanashi shiryō shūsei 19: Kaga mukashibanashi-shū*. Tokyo: Iwasaki Bijutsusha.

"Yamauba katabiraki." 2001. In vol. 16 of *Shokoku sōsho*, edited by Matsuzaki Kenzō, 119–21. Tokyo: Seijō Daigaku Minzokugaku Kenkyūjo.

Yanagita Kunio. 1933. *Mukashibanashi saishū no shiori*. Tokyo: Azusa Shobō.

Yanagita Kunio. 1960. *Nippon no mukashibanashi kaiteiban*. Tokyo: Kadokawa Shoten.

Yanagita Kunio. 1966. *Japanese Folk Tales: A Revised Selection*. Translated by Fanny Hagin Mayer. Tokyo: Tokyo News Service.

Yanagita Kunio. 1968. *Teihon Yanagita Kunio shū*, vol. 4. Tokyo: Chikuma Shobō.

Yanagita Kunio. 1969. *Teihon Yanagita Kunio shū*, vol. 8. Tokyo: Chikuma Shobō.

Yanagita Kunio. 1970a. *Nihon no densetsu*. In vol. 26 of *Teihon Yanagita Kunio shū*, 131–261. Tokyo: Chikuma Shobō.

Yanagita Kunio. 1970b. "Oyasute-yama." In vol. 21 of *Teihon Yanagita Kunio shū*, 294–305. Tokyo: Chikuma Shobō.

Yanagita Kunio. 1971. *Nihon mukashibanashi meii*. Tokyo: Nihon Hōsōkyōkai Shuppan.

Yanagita Kunio. 1978–1979. *Shinpen Yanagita Kunio shū*. 12 vols. Tokyo: Chikuma Shobō.

Yanagita Kunio. 1988. *About Our Ancestors: The Japanese Family System*. Translated by Fanny Hagin Mayer and Ishikawa Yasuyo. New York: Greenwood.

Yanagita Kunio. 2008. *The Legends of Tono*. Translated by Ronald A. Morse. Lanham, MD: Lexington Books.

Yanagita Kunio. 2014. *Nihon no mukashibanashi to densetsu: Minkan denshō no minzokugaku*. Tokyo: Kawade Shobō Shinsha.

Yanagita Kunio. 2015. "Miko kō." In *Miko*, edited by Tanigawa Ken'ichi and Ōwa Iwao, 207–91. Tokyo: Daiwa Shobō.

Yanagita Kunio and Suzuki Tōzō. 2004. *Tōno monogatari shūi*. In *Tōno monogatari: Fu Tōno monogatari shūi*, 75–212. Tokyo: Kadokawa Shoten.

Yasui Manami. 2013. *Shussan kankyō no minzokugaku: "Dai san ji osan kakumei" ni mukete*. Kyoto: Shōwadō.

Yasui Manami. 2014. *Kaii to shintai no minzokugaku: Ikai kara shussan to kosodate o toinaosu*. Tokyo: Serika Shobō.

Yasui Manami. 2019. "Where *Yōkai* Enter and Exit the Human Body: From Medieval Picture Scrolls to Modern Folktales in Japan." Translated by Kristopher Reeves. *Studies in Japanese Literature and Culture* 2 (March): 61–72.

Yoshida Atsuhiko. 1992. *Mukashibanashi no kōkogaku: Yamauba to Jōmon no megami*. Tokyo: Chūō Kōronsha.

Yoshie Mami. 2010. "Shibuya no yamanba—sono tanjō to tenkai." In *Shibuya o kurasu: Shibuya minzokushi no kokoromi*, edited by Kuraishi Tadahiko, 63–99. Tokyo: Yūzankaku.

Yoshikawa Yūko. 1998. "Umare kiyomari no minkan setsuwa—kirō tan no shūkyō minzoku." *Setsuwa denshōgaku* 6 (April): 117–36.

Zoku Gunsho Ruijū Kanseikai, ed. 1995. *Tōdaiki sunpuki*. Tokyo: Zoku Gunsho Ruiju Kanseikai.

About the Author

NORIKO TSUNODA REIDER is professor of Japanese at Miami University of Ohio in the Department of German, Russian, Asian, and Middle Eastern Languages and Cultures. Her research interest is the supernatural in Japanese literature, folklore, and art. She is the author of *Seven Demon Stories from Medieval Japan* (Utah State University Press, 2016), *Japanese Demon Lore: Oni, from Ancient Times to the Present* (Utah State University Press, 2010), *Tales of the Supernatural in Early Modern Japan* (Edwin Mellen Press, 2002), and many articles. She was a visiting research scholar at the International Research Center for Japanese Studies (Nichibunken) from January 2019 through July 2019.

Index

214 *Index*

brides, kidnapped, 118
Buddha's Law, 99
"Buddha's subjugating evils," 85
Buddhism, 48, 127, 163, 181(n21), 188(nn19, 20); misogyny in, 111, 130; and Mt. Akiha shrines, 57, 185(n4); and noh plays, 40, 46
bulimia nervosa, 29
burial sites, 8, 132
Bussetsu Jizō bosatsu hosshin innen jūōkyō (The sutra on the Bodhisattva Jizō's aspiration . . .), 108, 167, 189(n10)
Butokuden, 24, 167

cannibalism. *See* anthropophagy
caves, on Mt. Kintoki, 64
cedar trees, sacred, 107
cerebral microemboli (mini-strokes), 123
charms, 30, 43
Chihiro, 146, 147
Chikamatsu Monzaemon, 52, 168, 187(n23); *Komochi yamanba*, 66, 119
Chikuzen province, year-end market in, 139
childbirth, 20, 49, 73, 79, 159, 183(n17), 190(n22); help in, 53, 55, 56; multiple, 14, 15, 54
children, 14, 15, 54, 60, 109, 184(n30), 190(n19); abandonment of, 90, 151; eating of, 10, 55, 107, 118, 191(n25); of oni, 34, 74; supernatural, 19, 20–21, 53, 56, 64, 67, 115–16, 147, 163, 191–92(n27)
Children's Day (Boy's Day), 64
China, 6, 78, 127, 138
Chōfuku, Mt., 53
Chūbu region, 82
civil war, and yamabushi, 12
cloth, 59, 74
clothes, 139; of dead people, 107, 109, 119, 189(n13)
collective behavior, of yamanba-gyaru, 143–44
Confucianism, 125, 130
containers, magic, 138
coopers, in Yamauba stories, 21, 81, 82–84
corpses, 107; eating, 105, 113; in *Throne of Blood*, 99–100, 101
creation myth, Izanagi and Izanami in, 28
crocodile, Toyotama-bime as, 49

Dai Nihonkoku Hokke genki (Miraculous stories of the Lotus Sutra in Japan), 108, 189(n13)
Daisen, Mt., 13, 14

Daisenji engimaki (Legends of Daisenji temple), 13, 111, 168
"Daishi ido" ("Kūkai's Well"), 59, 60, 185(n6)
dances, 69, 100–101, 120, 130, 147
danna, 12, 168
Dao Shi, 168; *Hōon jurin,* 127
Datsueba, 21, 107, 112, 119, 120, 157, 164, 168; depictions and characteristics of, 108–10
daughter-in-law–mother-in-law relationships, 3, 133
daughters, kidnapping of, 34
dead, 8, 14; souls of, 36–37, 40; stripping clothes from 21, 107, 119
death, and rebirth, 15
deities. *See* kami
dementia, 3, 122, 134–35, 162, 192(n2), 193(nn5, 6); and missing persons, 123–24
demons, 25, 30, 45, 84, 111, 186(n20); Yamanba as, *38, 39*
Densetsu shūsei (*Niigata ken densetsu shūsei*), 105, 107
Denshi-byō (chū-byō), 78
desire, and suffering, 99
diseases, 189(n11); causes of, 78–79
divorce, 5, 68, 186(nn16, 17)
dōji, 84, 168, 187(n3)
Dōjōji (Dōjōji temple), 46, 168
double-grave system (ryōbosei), 8, 132
dragons, 15, 64
dragon woman, in Ogase Pond, 62, 63, 186(n11)
duality, 20, 25, 41, 54, 109, 162; fear and worship, 79–80; good and evil, 19, 23, 40, 89, 134, 157–58; of Great Mother, 16–17; of yamaubas, 10, 29, 34–35, 52, 153–54; Yasaburō Basa/Myōtara Ten'nyo, 106–7, 108, 117–18, 120

eating, 182(n10); nothing, 28, 182(n11), oni-baba, 157–58
eating disorders, 29, 124
Echigo province, 114
Edo period, 61, 64, 71, 84, 85, 109, 191(n26), 253; women's social status in, 67–69, 120
egg (magazine), on yamanba-gyaru, 142–43
Ehon Raikō ichidai ki, 65
Eight-Headed Serpent, 115
Eikai, 168; *Ichijō shūgyokushō,* 84
Ekoin, 56
elders, 3; demographic of, 134–35; treatment of, 125–27, 131–32

47–48; in *Throne of Blood*, 96–*97*; use of term, 51–52; Yasaburō Basa as, 106–7, 163
Onmyōdō, 17, 181(n21)
"Onna daigaku takarabako" (Treasure box for women's great learning), 67–68, 173
Ono no Komachi, 129, 174
"Origin of Fleas and Mosquitos, The," 73
Orikuchi Shinobu, 15, 59
Orpheus, and Eurydice, 28
oshi, 12, 174
Other, 181(n26); tsuchigumo as, 77–78
other world, 194(n5); mountains as, 148–49
otogībanashi, 89, 174
otogizōshi, 35, 51, 89
Owari province, 60
Owari-shi (History of Owari), 60, 61
Ōymatsumi no mikoto, 80, 174
Ōymatsumi Shrine, 79–80
Ōyamazu no mikoto, 14

passion, 4, 163
patriarchy, 35, 92, 160, 165, 184(n37)
personality changes, 123
pilgrimages, 12, 57, 62, 152
poems, poetry, 134, 185–86(n10); on Adichigahara oni-hag, 43–44; left by yamauba, 60–61, 63; "Obasute-yama," 133; prophetic, 186–87(n22); spiders as omens in, 75–76; *Watashi wa Anjuhimeko de aru*, 156–60
population growth, 10–11
possession, by yamauba, 122–23
post-traumatic stress disorder, 123
prayer, Buddhist, 46, 48
pregnancy, 185(n2); supernatural, 64, 67, 115
prophecy, 81, 186–87(n22); in *Hanayo no Hime*, 94–95; in "Naranashi tori," 93–94; in *Throne of Blood*, 100, 101
puppet theater. *See* jōruri

racoon-dogs, 62, 187(n2)
rage, 121, 163
Rashōmon, 113, 174, 189(n2)
rebirth, 15
reiki, 40
relatives, abandonment by, 129–30
religious practitioners, traveling, 58–59
religious services, for departed souls, 36–37
resentment, 46, 48, 106
respect, for elders, 125
resurrection, 157
rewards, for helping yamauba, 53–54, 192–93(n3)

"Rōba oni no ude o mochisaru zu" (Old woman leaving with the oni's arm), 103, 104(fig.), 113–14, 174
Rokujō Haven, 48
Rōmajin no monogatari (Tales of Romans), 164
royalty, Japanese, 165–66, 195(n2)
ryōbosei, 8, 132
"Ryōshi no haha oni to narite ko o kurawamu to suru koto" ("Hunters' Mother"), 112, 117, 174
Ryūchikubō, 54, 55, 56

Sadamato, Prince, 44, 174
Sado Island, 74, 194(n7)
Sai-sozō, 88, 174, 188(n10)
Saiwa, 88, 174, 188(n9)
Sakata clan, 65
Sakata no Kintoki, 56, 64–65, 66, 67, 151, 174. *See also* Kintarō
Sakata no Tokiyuki, 66
saké, 73, 115, 116, 138–39, 163
samurai, 55, 56, 58, 60, 66, 185–86(n10)
Sanemori, 129, 174
Sangoku denki (Stories from three countries), 115, 190–91(n24)
"Sanmai no ofuda" ("Three Charms") stories, 20, 30–31, 35, 42, 45, 74, 86, 157, 174
Sanrōjo plays, 131, 174
"Sanseru onna minami Yamashina ni yuki oni ni aite niguru koto," ("How a Woman with Child went to South Yamashina . . ."), 10, 174
Sanshō Dayū (Sanshō the Bailiff), 156–57, 160, 194–95(nn7, 8)
Sanzu River, 21, 107, 109, 119, 189(n13)
Sarashina, Lady, 9, 10, 128, 130–31
Sarashina nikki (As I Cross a Bridge of Dreams), 9, 10, 174
Sasaki Bicchūō-no-kami Minamoto no Yoritsuna (Raikō), 115, 174, 190–91(n24)
Sasaki Nobutsuna, 115, 174, 190–91(n24)
Sasaki Sadatsuna, 114–15, 174
satori, 102, 174
satori no wappa (satori boy), 82, 84, 85
satori setsuwa, 85–86
satoyama, 11
secondary nature, 40
Segawa Jokō, 69
Segawa Kikunojō III, 69
Sekidera Komachi (Komachi at Seki-dera), 129, 131, 175
Sendatsu, 12, 13, 175